Crocheting For Dummies®

International Crochet Symbols

Check out the following quick reference guide to the International Crochet Symbols and the abbreviations (in parentheses) for common crochet stitches. **Note:** The info in brackets describes the version of the stitch that the symbol represents.

chain stitch (**ch**)	⌒		V-stitch (**V-st**)	
slip stitch (**sl st**)	• OR ➤		crossed double crochet (**crossed dc**)	⨉ OR ⨉
single crochet (**sc**)	✕ OR +		shell [of 4 dc]	
half double crochet (**hdc**)	T		picot [of ch 3, sl st]	
double crochet (**dc**)	T̶		cluster [of 4 dc]	
triple crochet (**tr**)	T̶̶		reverse [sc]	X̃
double triple crochet (**dtr**)	T̶̶̶		puff st [of 3 dc]	
triple triple crochet (**trtr**)	T̶̶̶̶		popcorn (**pop** or **pc**) [of 5 dc]	
single crochet in front loop only (**flp**)	X̲		bobble [composed of 5 loops]	
single crochet in back loop only (**blp**)	✕		loop stitch (**loop st**)	
front post double crochet (**FP dc**)	⌐		long stitch (**long st**) or spike	
back post double crochet (**BP dc**)	⌐			

More Crochet Abbreviations

alternate (**alt**)	contrast color (**CC**)	loop (**lp**)	repeat (**rep**)
approximately (**approx**)	decrease(s), (d), or (ing) (**dec**)	main color (**MC**)	ribbing (**rib**)
back loop only (**blp**)		meter(s) (**m**)	right side (**RS**)
back post (**BP**)	follow or following (**foll**)	ounce(s) (**oz**)	round(s) (**rnd** or **rnds**)
beaded chain (**Bch**)	foot or feet (**ft**)	pattern (**pat**)	space (**sp**)
beaded single crochet (**Bsc**)	front loop only (**flp**)	popcorn (**pop** or **pc**)	stitch(es) (**st** or **sts**)
begin(ning) (**beg**)	front post (**FP**)	quadruple triple crochet (**quad tr**)	together (**tog**)
between (**bet**)	gram or grams (**gm**)		turning ch (**tch**)
centimeter(s) (**cm**)	group (**gr**)	quintuple triple crochet (**quin tr**)	wrong side (**WS**)
chain (**ch**)	inch or inches (**in.**)	remaining (**rem**)	yard (**yd**)
	increase(s), (d), (ing) (**inc**)		yarn over hook (**yo**)

Crocheting For Dummies®

Crochet Hook Conversion Charts

Aluminum Crochet Hooks

U.S. (American)	Continental (metric)	U.K. (English)
B-1	2½	12
C-2	3	11
D-3	3¼	10
E-4	3½	9
F-5	4	8
G-6	4¼	7
H-8	5	6
I-9	5½	5
J-10	6	4
K-10½	7	3
L-11	8	-
M-13	9	-
N-15	10	-
P-16	15	-
Q	16	-
S	19	-

Steel Crochet Hooks

U.S. (American)	Continental (metric)	U.K. (English)
00	3.5	-
0	3.25	0
1	2.75	1
2	2.25	1½
3	2.1	2
4	2.0	2½
5	1.9	3
6	1.8	3½
7	1.65	4
8	1.5	4½
9	1.4	5
10	1.3	5½
11	1.1	6
12	1.0	6½
13	.85	7
14	.75	-

by Karen Manthey and Susan Brittain

WILEY

Wiley Publishing, Inc.

Crocheting For Dummies®

Published by
Wiley Publishing, Inc.
111 River St.
Hoboken, NJ 07030-5774
www.wiley.com

Copyright © 2004 by Wiley Publishing, Inc., Indianapolis, Indiana

Published by Wiley Publishing, Inc., Indianapolis, Indiana

Published simultaneously in Canada

WILEY

About the Authors

Karen Manthey's first attempt at crocheting, while attending Mount Holyoke College, involved mixing wool and acrylic yarns to produce a granny square Afghan that (after washing and drying) resembled a relief map of the English countryside! Through the 1970s, while working as a graphic artist, Karen explored many arts and crafts, and her skill at crochet improved. In 1984, her training in art and understanding of crochet led her to a job illustrating the magazine *Crochet Fantasy.* Her task was to create the intricate crochet diagrams that accompany many patterns today, using the International Crochet Symbols. She soon moved on to editor of the magazine, while continuing to do the illustrations. Karen has also honed her skills by designing her own patterns and has had many of her creations published in *Crochet Fantasy* magazine. Her skill as an illustrator can also be seen in the book, *Crochet Your Way,* by Gloria Tracy and Susan Levin.

Susan Brittain's fascination with crochet began very early, around 4 or 5 years of age. She would watch her grandmother, who had lost her sight in midlife, spend hours crocheting beautiful Afghans for friends and family, counting the stitches with her fingers. By the age of 8, Susan was crocheting her own projects, starting with simple patterns such as scarves and moving on to Afghans, toys, and sweaters. Although her creative streak has led her to learn many different crafts, crochet has been a steady thread throughout. Susan combined work with pleasure as assistant editor for *Crochet Fantasy* magazine for a little more than two years, contributing as a designer as well. After moving west with her family, she continues to be a contributing editor and designer.

Dedications

To Karen's husband, Darryl Manthey, for teaching her the meaning of perseverance, and to her daughter, Tanya Manthey, for her patience and her sense of humor, which have kept her mother going through this project and everything else.

To Susan's husband, Paul Brittain, for his love, support, and understanding, and to her daughter, Angela, for putting up with the mess, the crazy schedule, and for waiting until I finished "just one more row."

Acknowledgments

Our thanks go out to Natasha Graf, our acquisitions editor, who had faith in us from the beginning and put us on the right track, providing encouragement and support when we needed it.

Thanks to Marcia Johnson, our first project editor who helped to make us look like Dummies in a good way, and to our other project editors, Kelly Ewing and Chrissy Guthrie. And last but not least, special thanks to Laura Peterson who grabbed hold of the reins and pulled it all together. Thanks to all the other editors and proofreaders at Wiley who helped to make this book a cohesive and professional endeavor.

Thanks to Kathleen Sams at Coats & Clark for her support both personally and professionally. Thanks also go to Margery Winter at Berroco, Inc., Cilene Martins-Castro at DMC Corporation, Jeanne Duncan at Fiesta Yarns, Nancy Thomas at Lion Brand Yarn Co., Catherine Blythe at Spinrite, Inc., Cheryl Schaefer at Schaefer Yarns, and Diane Friedman at Tahki/Stacy Charles for generously providing yarns for the projects featured in this book.

Thanks to Sean O'Brien for the beautiful photographs of our projects.

Thanks to the models who helped to make our crochet come to life: Angela Brittain, Rachel Gieniewski, and Alison Arnold.

Thanks to Jerry and Darren Cohen of All American Crafts for providing a proving ground for our talents, as well as an atmosphere that encourages creativity.

From Karen

Special thanks go to my husband Darryl for his encouragement, patience, love, and support. Also, thanks to my daughter Tanya for putting up with the mess, the late and (less than perfect) meals, as well as my lack of attention and focus. I couldn't have done it without you both.

Thanks go to Marie Arnold who gave me the encouragement I needed to get through this book. Throughout our 20-year relationship, she has provided a sturdy shoulder to see me through every crisis of my life.

Thanks to Michele Buchbauer who has helped me through it all and never let me quit.

Special thanks go to Janice Utter who taught me so much about crocheting that I could write a book! Through the years of our association, she has always given generously of her knowledge, help, and support, personally and professionally.

And finally, thanks to Susan, my partner in this project, for her optimistic approach to life. Thanks for giving me the courage to face this challenge and not letting me give up before we even began.

From Susan

Special thanks go out, first and foremost, to my husband Paul for his unfailing support throughout the whole writing process. Without his encouragement and support, this book may never have come to be.

Thanks also to my daughter Angela, who constantly urged me to "keep up the good work," her willingness to model the children's items, and her wonderful ideas for new designs.

To my mother-in-law, Angela, thanks for sharing special tips and tricks that she's learned during her many years of crocheting.

And finally, thanks to Karen for her expertise, and for providing a sounding board when deadlines approached and the words wouldn't flow.

Publisher's Acknowledgments

We're proud of this book; please send us your comments through our Dummies online registration form located at www.dummies.com/register/.

Some of the people who helped bring this book to market include the following:

Acquisitions, Editorial, and Media Development

Project Editors: Laura B. Peterson, Christina Guthrie, Kelly Ewing, Marcia L. Johnson

Acquisitions Editor: Natasha Graf

Copy Editors: Kristin DeMint, Esmeralda St. Clair

General Reviewers: Donna Scott, Vinette DePhillipe, Janice Utter

Editorial Managers: Jennifer Ehrlich, Michelle Hacker

Editorial Assistant: Melissa Bennett

Cover Photo: © Sean O'Brien Photography/2003

Cartoons: Rich Tennant, www.the5thwave.com

Composition

Project Coordinator: Nancee Reeves

Layout and Graphics: Karl Brandt, Jonelle Burns, Andrea Dahl, Brian Drumm, Kelly Emkow, Joyce Haughey, Stephanie D. Jumper, Michael Kruzil, Shelley Norris, Lynsey Osborn, Heather Ryan, Brent Savage, Jacque Schneider, Julie Trippetti, Mary Gillot Virgin

Special Art: Many illustrations in this book are based on illustrations published in *Crochet Fantasy* magazine, an All American Crafts publication; other illustrations based on the art of Karen Manthey.

Photos: Color insert by Sean O'Brien Photography; black and white photos by Karen Manthey.

Proofreaders: Laura Albert, TECHBOOKS Production Services

Indexer: TECHBOOKS Production Services

Special Help: Traci Cumbay, Michelle Dzurny, Laura Miller, Natalie Harris

---

Publishing and Editorial for Consumer Dummies

Diane Graves Steele, Vice President and Publisher, Consumer Dummies

Joyce Pepple, Acquisitions Director, Consumer Dummies

Kristin A. Cocks, Product Development Director, Consumer Dummies

Michael Spring, Vice President and Publisher, Travel

Brice Gosnell, Associate Publisher, Travel

Kelly Regan, Editorial Director, Travel

Publishing for Technology Dummies

Andy Cummings, Vice President and Publisher, Dummies Technology/General User

Composition Services

Gerry Fahey, Vice President of Production Services

Debbie Stailey, Director of Composition Services

Contents at a Glance

Table of Contents

Introduction

*N*o longer is crocheting considered something your grandmother or maiden aunt did while sitting on the front porch. Crocheted designs are popping up everywhere, from the racks in your favorite clothing store to fashion catalogs, even to the runways in Paris and Milan. Celebrities have started crocheting, and the craft even shows up in movies and TV shows. The reasons for this comeback are many, and we hope, by reading this book, that you discover some of those reasons and begin to enjoy a lifelong affair with crochet.

Even though crochet is a time-honored craft, that doesn't mean that it's behind the times. Advances in technology have made yarns softer and more colorful, with wonderful new textures appearing every time you turn around. No longer are we limited to solid or variegated colors; yarn is now hand-painted and space dyed. Although worsted-weight yarn is still a staple in every crocheter's yarn cache, so many varieties of weights and textures are available today that we're at a loss as to how to categorize them all.

Crocheting For Dummies gives first-time crocheters hands-on experience with new skills and serves as a reference tool for those of you who already have some crochet know-how. Start out with the chapters that show you the basic stitches or look farther in for more advanced (though still easy) techniques.

Each new person who masters the art of crochet is another person who helps keep this art form alive. You're never too old or too young to discover crochet. The skills that you master, the benefits that you get, and the beautiful heirlooms that you create can last a lifetime and, hopefully, be passed on to future generations.

How to Use This Book

If you're a novice crocheter, start at the beginning of this book and join us as we take you step by step from gathering your materials, to crocheting your first stitches, to finishing off a piece of crocheted fabric. You find detailed written instructions and easy-to-follow illustrations throughout this book.

Each part contains chapters full of information relevant to each other, with successive parts adding more building blocks to your crochet knowledge. If you already have some crochet experience and are looking to refine and expand your techniques, then the later chapters are for you. We include more advanced stitches and techniques there, with many tips to guide you.

Finally, each part contains several projects that allow you to practice your newfound skills, creating fun and useful designs while allowing you to feel a sense of accomplishment for a job well done.

Conventions Used in This Book

We use the following conventions throughout the book to make this whole new world easy to understand:

- New terms appear in *italic* and are closely followed by an easy-to-understand definition.

- **Bold** highlights the action parts of numbered steps.

- When we first introduce a new stitch or technique, we include its abbreviation in parentheses to help you become familiar with the shorthand used in crochet patterns. We also include the abbreviation the first time a stitch is mentioned in a set of numbered steps.

- The specific part of an illustration that relates to the step you're working on is shaded dark gray — for example, if you're inserting your hook in a certain stitch, only that stitch will be shaded so that you can clearly see where to go.

Foolish Assumptions

How does that saying about assuming something go? Well, never mind about that. We make every attempt to explain each step as clearly and concisely as possible, so you don't need any prior experience to understand the concepts introduced in this book.

We are assuming, however, that by picking up this book, you have a desire to master the art of crochet. Beyond that, all we ask is that you give it your best shot and don't give up. Everything you need to know to build a strong crochet base is in this book.

How This Book Is Organized

This book is divided into five parts, with a total of 21 chapters. Each part focuses on a different aspect of crochet. Together, they create a strong foundation for any skill level. If at any point you need prior knowledge in order to understand the concepts of a particular chapter, we refer you to the chapter that covers those particular basics.

Part 1: Crochet 101

Packed full of useful and necessary information, Part I tells you all about the craft and the many benefits you can derive from it. It describes the tools you need to get started and how to wade through the abundance of materials on the market. You can follow fully illustrated, step-by-step instructions on creating your first basic stitches upon which almost all crochet is based. Finally, we talk about what gauge is and why it's so important.

Part II: Basic Stitches and Techniques

Really getting down to the nuts and bolts, Part II shows you how to read and understand crochet instructions. It also opens the door to several basic techniques like increasing and decreasing your rows and rounds to shape your work, crocheting in-the-round, and working with more than one color at once.

Part III: Advanced Stitches and Techniques

Part III introduces you to the basics of sweater construction, with projects that include a simple vest and a pullover sweater. It also shows you how to combine the basic stitches to create a variety of common stitch patterns. Then you discover how to create different textures by working in different places within a stitch. Finally, you encounter two new techniques, the Afghan stitch and filet crochet.

Part IV: Putting It All Together

For those times when your pattern calls for separate sections, rather than crocheting something all in one piece, Part IV shows you the various methods for joining pieces of crocheted fabric to create a whole. You can see how to add special touches, embellishments, and final details. And last but not least, discover the secrets to turning your slightly rumpled piece into a smooth and shapely design.

Part V: The Part of Tens

Part V includes a list of useful resources to further expand your knowledge, as well as the do's and don'ts of crochet. You also find a list with brief descriptions of some of the many variations on crochet.

Icons Used in This Book

This icon clues you in on some tips of the trade that more experienced crocheters have discovered over time. They make your crocheting experience a bit easier.

When you see this icon, read carefully. It marks pitfalls along the way and helps you steer clear of frustrating and time-consuming mistakes.

This icon highlights important points. You should remember them and apply them when dealing with the skills shown at this point.

Where to Go from Here

Now that the introductions are over, it's time to begin. *Crocheting For Dummies* is written in a modular format, so you can start in whatever section best fits your skill level:

- ✔ If you're an absolute beginner, we suggest starting with Part I. It has all the essential information that you need to get started.

- ✔ If you already have some experience with the basics and want to expand your knowledge, then look ahead to the chapters on more advanced stitches and techniques. Whenever we feel that you should know something that was covered in a previous chapter, we refer you to that chapter.

- ✔ Finally, if you used to crochet and are coming back to it (sometimes life just gets too busy for stuff like this), skim through the chapters to reacquaint yourself with the techniques. The stitches themselves haven't changed, but the materials have, and you may come across some useful info.

Part I
Crochet 101

The 5th Wave — By Rich Tennant

"I use an Afghan hook most of the time, although there's nothing like a size H aluminum hook for cleaning nougat out of your molars."

In this part . . .

This is the beginning of a journey on a road to a whole new skill and a lifetime of crocheting pleasure. In this part, we introduce you to the tools and materials that you need to begin crocheting, and we unravel the mysteries of the basic stitches that you need to start making beautiful and useful crocheted projects. We also explain the importance of gauge and how it affects everything you crochet. By the end of this part, you're ready to make beginner projects, and you no longer look at crocheting as a deep dark mystery.

You can test out your new knowledge by making some simple coasters and placemats that use only the basic stitches.

Chapter 1

Hooking into a Life of Crochet

You don't have to be an expert to take advantage of crochet's many beneficial qualities. The soothing rhythm of creating stitches can calm even the most frazzled nerves. If you're one of those people who can't stand to be idle, crochet is a wonderful way to let your body get a bit of rest and not feel like you're wasting time. If your family is always clamoring for you to sit down and watch a TV show or a special movie at night, go ahead, but bring along your hook and yarn.

Crochet is also a wonderful take-along project. You can crochet on trains and planes as well, although these days, you'll have to use plastic hooks when using public transportation.

If you don't believe us, maybe you can believe the psychological studies that have been done on the benefits of crochet! The focus needed to create something takes your mind off the bazillion little things hollering for your attention and gives your brain some much-needed downtime. Crochet also serves as an outlet for your creativity and provides a sense of satisfaction when you complete your design and can look at it and say, "I created this myself."

Crochet has physical benefits as well. People suffering from various forms of arthritis have used it as a form of physical therapy. The constant movement required helps keep the hands limber and the joints from stiffening up. So you see, the reasons to enjoy this craft are many. We hope that at least one of these reasons is enough to get you on your way.

This book may start you on the path to an addictive hobby, so be warned.

Starting with a Hook and Skein

One of the greatest things about crochet is that you don't need to invest in many fancy, new materials or create a new room in your house to house a bunch of equipment. With just a simple hook, a skein of yarn, and a nice, comfy place to sit, you can begin enjoying the benefits that this craft provides. If you're like most people these days, finding the time to figure out something new can be a challenge. With crochet, you can pick it up when you have some time, put it down when you don't, or take it with you on the run. No mess to clean up and nothing to babysit. And you can easily find hooks and yarn in your local discount or craft store as well as the many specialty yarn stores that have cropped up in many towns — no need to wait while you special order some obscure item.

Gathering all your tools

All you need to get started are a couple hooks, preferably from different manufacturers so that you can find a style you're comfortable with, and a skein of yarn. The other stuff that you need, such as a pair of scissors and a bag to keep all this stuff in, you probably have at home.

Chapter 2 gives you the skinny on the various types of hooks and yarns, as well as on some of the other crochet gadgets available. As with any new undertaking, understanding the basics about the materials that you're working with is important.

Practice makes perfect

You don't learn to walk or ride a bike in a day, and the same is true with crochet. It takes practice, but probably not as much as you think. Start with the basic chain stitch (see Chapter 4) and practice until you're comfortable with the motions your hands must make, and then move on to another stitch. Each successive stitch, which we walk you through step-by-step in Chapters 4 and 6, builds on another, so try not to skip any of them, at least in the beginning. We don't want you to get frustrated and throw your work down. Believe us, in no time at all, you'll be moving right along.

The majority of the book deals with techniques from a right-hander's point of view, but we don't forget you lefties. All the information contained in this book (and there's plenty of it!) applies to you as well. Chapter 4 gets you started on the basics by giving you equal time with the righties. And then we give you a few tips to help you work your way through the rest of the book from your perspective.

Mastering Basic Crochet Techniques

Aside from figuring out the basic stitches, you need to understand a couple other techniques, all quite easy, in order to create your masterpiece. Adding and subtracting stitches, changing color, working in a circle, and reading those funny-looking patterns are all included.

Crocheting from a pattern

Even crocheters with years of experience work from patterns, so knowing how to read them is important. Chapter 5 tells you what the abbreviations and symbols in patterns mean and how to decipher the instructions. To ease you into the language of crochet, we provide an explanation beneath each line of instruction, although we urge you to take a stab at reading the "normal" instructions because this is the way all other crochet publications present them.

To help you get used to all the abbreviations and symbols, we include them in parentheses every time we introduce a new stitch or technique (which we fully explain in plain English, by the way). However, in the project patterns at the ends of the chapters, we slowly wean you from the English translations after Chapter 5. And you can always flip back to Chapter 5 if you don't remember something. The Cheat Sheet at the front of the book is also a handy reference guide to crochetese.

Adjusting tension

Making sure that your finished projects end up being the correct size is important. After all, who needs a doily the size of a coaster or a waist-length sweater that covers your knees? How about an Afghan that can double as a slipcover for your sectional couch?

Gibberish, anyone?

A while back, we had an experience that shows just how funny crochet instructions can look to one who's not familiar with the terminology. A young girl was leafing through a crochet magazine looking at the pictures, or so we thought. When we started to pay attention to the noises she was making, we both laughed so hard that our sides split. She was reading the instructions phonetically *(ch 3, dc in next sc, sc in next dc)*. Try this with one of the patterns at the end of the chapters, and you'll see what we mean. It can really look like a bunch of gibberish. Don't worry, though; crochet terminology is pretty simple.

By using some simple math and working a gauge swatch (see Chapter 3), you ensure that your stitches are the right size and tension for your design. So don't skip over the stuff at the beginning of the pattern directions — checking your materials and your gauge keeps you out of trouble.

Round and round you go

Because crochet stitches are so easily manipulated, you can go where other forms of needlework cannot, such as in circles. While the first few chapters have you going back and forth in rows, Chapter 8 throws the door to the world of crocheting wide open. All sorts of great projects, like doilies, Afghans, and sweaters, are worked in rounds. This basic variation is easy, so don't be afraid to try the projects in this book that are worked in rounds.

Color it in

Crochet is by no means monochromatic. Yes, we've all seen homes with white doilies scattered on every surface or the hat and scarf sets made in a single, dull color. But just wait until you walk into your local craft store or yarn shop. Your senses may be assaulted by the multitude of color and texture that's now available.

Changing color, carrying colors, and working with texture are all variables you can take into consideration to turn a ho-hum design into a work of art (and Chapter 9 shows you how to do this).

Adding New Stitches and Techniques to Your Crochet Vocabulary

After you have the basics down, you can move on to even more fun stuff. New techniques and stitch combinations add up to some creative works of art.

Many so-called specialty stitches (see Chapter 11) are nothing more than the combination of a couple of different basic stitches, just with a new name. So don't be intimidated if a new technique or stitch seems too complex. Broken down, it's nothing more than the basics you know.

Having fun with new stitches

You can do many things with your hook. Who says you have to work stitches in only one place? Because crochet is just a bunch of interlocking loops, you can stick your hook in myriad places to create stitches that are flat or textured, square or round — the variety is nearly endless. Chapter 12 has more on working your yarn in different spots.

Creating funky fabrics

Two types of crochet that create unique fabrics are filet crochet (see Chapter 14) and the Afghan stitch (see Chapter 13). You work them by using very specific stitch placements and by following a chart. Both of these techniques are easy to work, and the designs you create make you look like you've been a master for years.

Finishing Your Work: Taking Pride in What You've Made

More goes into finishing your work than weaving in that last end of yarn. You may need to sew pieces together, add a pretty border, or tack on a tassel. Often, after all that handling, your new creation looks a bit misshapen and you need to block or shape it. And although you may not have spent a fortune on materials, time's a pretty valuable commodity these days, so you don't want to waste it by ruining that new sweater on the first wash.

Putting the pieces together

Many crochet designs comprise several pieces that you need to put together to form the whole. Chapter 15 walks you through the various methods for joining, whether you sew pieces together with a yarn needle and yarn or use your hook and crochet the separate pieces together.

Final details

When you're finished crocheting, make sure that the piece looks its best. Does it need any special finishing touches? What about some pockets? Or maybe a fringe? (See Chapter 17.)

You may need to block or starch (see Chapter 18) your work to get it into shape. Blocking is a simple process that requires water, maybe a little heat, or some starch to help coax your design into place. Don't leave out this step. The instructions may not mention blocking, but if your piece looks a little off kilter, whipping it into shape by blocking it is probably all that's needed.

Taking care of crochet

Finally, you're finished. Now that you have this wonderful new piece, whether it's wearable or a home decor item, you want to take certain measures to ensure that it stands the test of time. If you care for it properly (see Chapter 18), you can pass down your crocheted work for generations, and hopefully, inspire new generations to take up this timeless craft.

A Few Tips to Keep You Going

Inevitably, you'll have highs and lows while you work to master a new skill. We hope your highs are more plentiful than your lows. Here are a few tips that may help make your journey to crochet mastery a happier one:

- ✔ **Hold the hook and yarn the way that feels the most natural and comfortable to you.** We've illustrated the most common ways, but you may feel better using a different method.

- ✔ **Always read the stitch descriptions at the beginning of each pattern.** Other publications may use different names for stitches. Crochet isn't standardized, so you may come across names that you're unfamiliar with.

- ✔ **Check to see whether you're working from a British or American pattern before you begin.** Patterns published in Great Britain or Canada use different terminology for even the basic stitches. For example, they call the American single crochet a *double crochet* and the American double crochet a *treble crochet!* You can end up crocheting something completely different from what you intended.

- ✔ **Pick a place to work where you have few distractions.** As when mastering any new skill, being able to focus is important.

- ✔ **Practice each new stitch or technique by working a swatch.** Crochet stitches often build on each other, so make sure you're comfortable with the stitch before moving on to the next one. Don't throw away your swatches — they can come in handy when you need something on which to practice making borders or buttonholes.

✔ **Put your hook and yarn down and come back later if you start to feel frustrated with a new stitch.** Sometimes, a little distance can clear up a previously difficult section.

✔ **Find an experienced crocheter to help explain a new technique that you're having a hard time with.** If you don't know anyone who crochets, try your local yarn shop. You can usually find someone there who's well versed in the craft and who'd be more than happy to help someone with a new skill.

✔ **Mark the pages of the books that you feel are most important or helpful to you.** That way, you can easily find the reference that you're looking for.

Getting Started

If you bought this book ten minutes ago and are already at the yarn shop, you probably just want to get a cheap hook and some yarn so you can start practicing stitches right away. You can read all the details about hook sizes and yarn content in Chapter 2. But here's what you need to get started (for less than $5):

✔ **A size H-8 U.S. crochet hook.** This size hook is comfortable to work with, and the size of stitch that it creates is easy to see.

✔ **A light and solid-colored, worsted-weight yarn, preferably made of acrylic fibers.** If the yarn is too dark or multicolored, you may have a hard time seeing the stitches, and the acrylic yarns are great for practicing with because they're inexpensive.

Chapter 2

Tools of the Trade

*A*s with any new project that you decide to undertake, you first have to figure out what tools and materials you need. For crocheting, your needs are pretty simple. Grab a hook and some yarn, find a comfortable seat, and you're ready to go.

In this chapter, we go over the different types of crochet hooks and when to use them, show you your yarn options and how to choose the right one for your project, and help you read a yarn label. We also include a list of other useful tools that aren't necessary all the time but can be useful (and sometimes essential) when crocheting different types of designs.

Choosing Your Weapon: The Crochet Hook

Your crochet hook is the single most important tool you use when crocheting. This section tells you everything you need to know about hooks: the reason they're shaped the way they are, the function of each part, and the purpose of different hook materials.

The anatomy of a crochet hook

Even though you may think a crochet hook is nothing more than a straight stick with a hook on one end, it actually has five distinct and necessary parts, as Figure 2-1 shows.

Figure 2-1:
Identifying
the five
parts of a
crochet
hook.

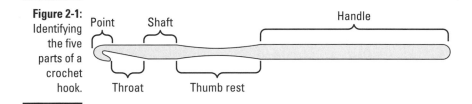

Each part of the hook performs a specific function.

- ✔ **Point:** You insert this part of the hook into previously made stitches. It must be sharp enough to slide easily through the stitches, yet blunt enough so that it doesn't split the yarn or stab your finger.

- ✔ **Throat:** The throat does the actual hooking of the yarn and pulls it through a stitch. It must be large enough to grab the yarn size that you're working with but small enough to prevent the previous loop from sliding off.

- ✔ **Shaft:** The shaft holds the loops that you're working with, and its diameter, for the most part, determines the size of your stitches.

- ✔ **Thumb rest:** The thumb rest should be sandwiched between your thumb and middle finger when you hold the hook, letting you easily rotate the hook as you do each stitch. Without the thumb rest, the hook can twist in the wrong direction, and you can find yourself gripping the hook too tightly — leaving you with hooker's cramp!

- ✔ **Handle:** The handle is used for balance or leverage. In the under-the-hook method of holding the hook (see Chapter 4), the handle helps keep the hook steady and well balanced. In the over-the-hook method of holding it, the handle is held against the heel or palm of your hand and provides the leverage needed to maneuver the hook properly.

Different brands of hooks have slightly different shapes. Some hooks have sharp points, while others have more rounded points. Some hooks have distinct flat, cutout throats, while others have smoother, rounded throats. Nowadays, most of the standard size and steel hooks have thumb rests, although the largest of the standard hooks don't. (See the next section for the lowdown on the different types of hooks.) Take some time to experiment with a couple different brands of crochet hooks to find the one that you're most comfortable working with. You'll be glad that you did. If you're happy with your hook, you'll be a happy hooker!

Sizing up your hook

Crochet hooks are made in a seemingly endless array of sizes and materials, but don't be overwhelmed by all the choices. Crochet hooks fall into two main categories:

- **Standard hooks** are most often made of aluminum or plastic (and sometimes wood); you normally use them when working with the larger sizes of yarn, such as sport weight, worsted weight, and those that are even thicker. They measure about 6 inches in length and vary in thickness from 2.5 mm to 19 mm.

- **Steel hooks,** which are the smallest of all crochet hooks, are used for crocheting with thread and fine yarns. They're made of — well, you know — steel, and measure about 5 inches in length and run from 0.75 mm to 3.5 mm wide.

In crochet, you work each stitch until only one loop remains on the hook, so you don't need a lot of space to hold loops (for the exceptions to the rule, see the Afghan stitch in Chapter 13). Therefore, the hooks are a convenient length, unlike the needles in our rival craft — knitting.

The size of a crochet hook refers to the thickness of the hook, which in turn determines the size of the stitches it creates. The photo in Figure 2-2 gives you an idea of the size variation in hooks. You'll run across three different systems for marking hook sizes — U.S. (American), which uses a letter/number combo, Continental (metric), which uses millimeters, and U.K. (English), which uses numbers. For standard hooks, using the U.S. or metric system, the higher the number or farther the letter is in the alphabet, the larger the hook. For example, a D-3 U.S. hook is smaller than a K-10½ U.S. hook. For steel hooks, which use only a number designation, the opposite holds true. The higher the number, the smaller the hook. But you don't need to worry about keeping the different systems straight — hooks are usually labeled with both the U.S. letter-number designation as well as the numeric metric designation. Table 2-1 is a conversion chart showing the most commonly used sizes of both steel and standard hooks. For a complete conversion chart, refer to the Cheat Sheet at the front of the book.

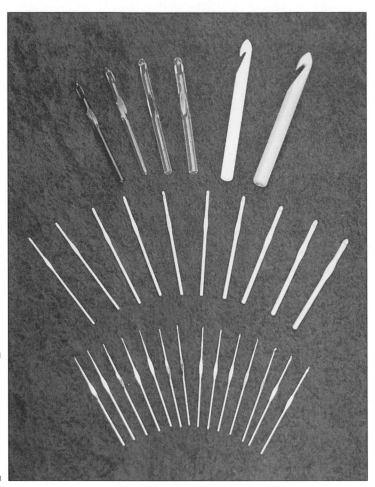

Figure 2-2:
Standard
and steel
hooks and
the range
of sizes
available.

Table 2-1	Common Crochet Hook Sizes	
Steel Crochet Hooks		
U.S. (American)	*Continental (Metric)*	*U.K. (English)*
6	1.8	3½
7	1.65	4
8	1.5	4½
9	1.4	5
10	1.3	5½

Standard Crochet Hooks		
U.S. (American)	*Continental (Metric)*	*U.K. (English)*
E-4	3½	9
F-5	4	8
G-6	4¼	7
H-8	5	6
I-9	5½	5
J-10	6	4
K-10½	7	3

When shopping for hooks, don't be afraid to try out lots of different brands and sizes. Hooks are inexpensive, and having extras of the most common sizes doesn't hurt. Even after you've found the style that you're comfortable with, hang on to other hooks you've collected as backups. You never know when you're going to lose your favorite hook and urgently need a replacement!

Plastic crochet hooks can bend or break with heavy use, so we recommend using aluminum hooks for the standard sizes simply because they literally last forever, provided that they don't disappear.

Ten handy household uses for crochet hooks

If you thought that crochet hooks were just for crocheting, guess again. Here are some more interesting uses for them:

- Pull a yarn snag to the inside of a sweater.
- Reweave a dropped stitch while knitting.
- Pull a drawstring through its casing.
- Fix a tangled necklace.
- Rescue a ring you dropped down the drain.
- Pull hair through the holes of the cap when highlighting your hair.
- Weave a potholder by using a loom.
- Weave anything through anything.
- Stake up a plant.
- Spear the last olive at the bottom of the jar.

Figuring Out Yarn Features and Functions

First things first: Forget about that scratchy, bulky yarn your grandmother used. The variety of yarn available today is astounding, to say the least. You can find everything from the basic solid-color acrylic yarns to silky soft wool blends, from long fringy eyelash yarn to sequined yarn. In addition to going over yarn weights, styles, and materials, this section shows you what to do with yarn packaging and labels and how to choose the right yarn for your projects.

Sizing up yarn weights

Although yarn *weight* or *size* (yarn thickness) doesn't have a standard classification system, you'll find several common weight descriptions that the majority of yarn companies adhere to. The following list, although not all-inclusive, outlines the most common sizes of yarn in order from the thinnest to the thickest strands. Check out Figure 2-3 to see how the different weights compare visually.

- **Fingering weight:** Also known as *baby weight,* this thin yarn is generally used to make lightweight garments, baby items, and designs with an open and lacy pattern.

- **Sport weight:** This medium-weight yarn is great for many different types of patterns, including sweaters, baby blankets, scarves, and shawls.

- **Double Knitting (DK) weight:** This yarn is slightly thicker than sport weight and can be used in the same patterns, but the resulting fabric is somewhat heavier.

- **Worsted weight:** Worsted weight is probably the most commonly used size of yarn and also the most readily available. It's great for Afghans, sweaters, scarves, hats, slippers, and toys.

- **Bulky weight:** This yarn is a thick, warm yarn and is generally used to make jackets, Afghans, rugs, and heavy outdoor sweaters.

Even though the different thicknesses of yarns are named by weight, as in worsted weight or sport weight, the size (diameter) of the yarn is actually what that name is referring to. The terms *size* and *weight* are interchangeable when referring to the thickness of the yarn.

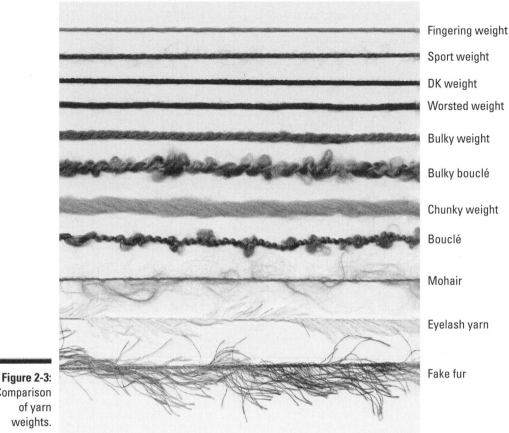

Fingering weight

Sport weight

DK weight

Worsted weight

Bulky weight

Bulky bouclé

Chunky weight

Bouclé

Mohair

Eyelash yarn

Fake fur

Figure 2-3:
Comparison
of yarn
weights.

Looking at yarn from the inside out

Yarns are made up of a wide variety of materials, ranging from natural fibers like wools, cottons, and silks to synthetics such as acrylic, rayon, and nylon. You can also find pretty much any combination or blend of these materials.

When choosing a yarn for a project, take into consideration how you'll use the piece after you complete it. If you're making a baby blanket, choose a yarn that will stand up to repeated washings. If you're making a tablecloth or bedspread that will someday be an heirloom piece, invest in good quality cotton that will withstand the test of time without falling apart. For a nice warm sweater, you can't beat wool for durability and warmth. After all, Mother Nature does know best! Go to the section "Matching your yarn to your project" for some tips on making an informed decision when picking out your yarn.

Wool

Of all the natural fibers used to make yarn, wool is the most popular choice to work with when you're creating a piece that you want to endure for years to come. Wool is resilient (which helps the stitches to retain their shape), soft, easy to work with, and relatively lightweight. It comes in many different sizes, from fingering weight to bulky. You can crochet with wool to make everything from beautiful, warm weather sweaters to cozy, wintertime pullovers, hats, scarves, mittens, socks, and Afghans. Wool is fairly low maintenance as well, but be careful to read the yarn label for specific washing instructions.

Although most wool comes from various breeds of sheep, you can get luxurious yarns from other animals as well. Fuzzy mohair and cashmere come from goats, and delicate, fluffy, Angora yarn comes from the Angora rabbit.

If you're allergic to wool, don't despair. Look for a synthetic instead. Many new synthetics mimic the real stuff so well that if you don't tell, no one will know.

Silk

Spun from the cocoon of the silkworm, silk yarn has a smooth, often shiny finish. It's lightweight and absorbent, and so a perfect choice for warm-weather garments. Silk's often combined with cotton or wool to increase its elasticity and durability.

Cotton

Once used mainly to make doilies, bedspreads, and tablecloths, cotton has become a versatile yarn. It comes in a wide range of sizes, from very fine threads to worsted-weight yarn. Garments made from cotton yarn are washable, durable, and have that great cotton comfort. Cotton yarn is also a good choice when making home decor items, such as placemats, potholders, and curtains.

Synthetics

Synthetic yarn is produced from man-made fibers such as acrylic, rayon, nylon, and polyester. Designed to look like the natural fiber yarns, synthetic yarns are readily available in a wide range of sizes, colors, and textures and are generally less expensive than their natural counterparts. These yarns, especially those made from acrylic, are good for making Afghans and baby blankets because they require little care. But be sure to check the label for instructions. Synthetic yarns are quite often used in combination with natural fibers, which gives you even more new textures, colors, and qualities of yarn to crochet with.

Novelty yarns

Novelty yarns are fun and funky and make your piece interesting without requiring complicated stitch patterns. From soft, fringy eyelash yarn to velvety chenille, bumpy boucle, glittering metallics, and slinky ribbon —

these yarns add a fresh and fashionable look to any piece that you create. Refer to Figure 2-3, earlier in the chapter, for a look at some novelty yarns.

Other materials

If you're really feeling adventurous, you can crochet with any material that resembles a string. You can use fine, colored wire and hemp to crochet cool jewelry, nylon cord for waterproof bags and outdoor seat cushions, and even embroidery floss and sewing thread to create appliqués and accents.

Sorting out yarn packaging: Hank, ball, or skein

Yarn is commonly packaged (*put up* in yarnese) in three different ways: as a *skein,* a *ball,* or a *hank.* You can crochet with balls and skeins of yarn as you buy them. However, hanks require a bit of preparation.

- ✓ **Ball:** If your ball of yarn is wound around a cardboard center, just grab the end on the outside of the ball, and you're ready to go. If the ball has an open center, your best bet is to find the end of the yarn from inside the ball. Using the inside end keeps the ball from rolling around the floor or becoming a new toy for your cat.

- ✓ **Skein:** The most common form of packaging, a *skein* is an oblong, machine-wound bundle of yarn. You start crocheting with the inside end, although finding it can be a little tricky. Sometimes, the end of the yarn is already pulled to the outside. Just give it a tug, and it'll pull out smoothly and evenly from the inside. If the yarn end isn't visible at either end of the skein, reach into the small indentation on either end of the skein and pull out a few strands. You'll find the end buried inside there. Sometimes, the label has an arrow pointing to the correct end of the skein to pull from, but more often than not, you have to guess. If the first end doesn't work, try the other end; it has to be in there somewhere! Working from the inside of the skein keeps the yarn tangle-free.

- ✓ **Hank:** A *hank* is a large circle of yarn twisted into a figure-eight shape. Trying to work from a hank soon results in a tangled mess and plenty of frustration, so you need to first wind it into a ball. Unfold, and then untwist the hank so that it's a circle of yarn. Place the large circle of yarn over a chair back or your knees, or have someone hold it with outstretched arms (remember seeing this method portrayed in old movies?). Find the outside end of the yarn and *loosely* wind it into a ball. Winding a ball too tightly can stretch your yarn, and you definitely don't want that. Stretched-out yarn may spring back into shape when your work is finished, and you may have to hand down your size-12 sweater to your size-10 daughter.

Deciphering yarn labels

Yarn labels contain a lot of valuable information that you need to take note of to make sure your project turns out right. Check out the label in Figure 2-4 and the following list for the lowdown on label info.

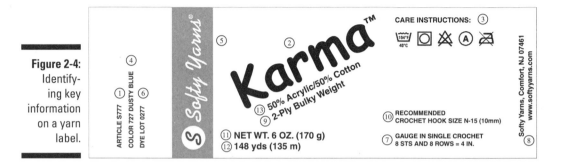

Figure 2-4:
Identifying key information on a yarn label.

Yarn labels include most if not all of the following information:

- **Article number (1):** Some manufacturers assign a number to each different type of yarn they produce for identification purposes. This number comes in handy when ordering yarn directly from the manufacturer or another mail-order source.

- **Brand name (2):** A yarn company may manufacture several different types or *brands* of yarn.

- **Care instructions (3):** As with any item that needs to be cleaned, yarn has specific care instructions. Some yarns require little care, and you can throw them in the washer and dryer; others need some TLC and should be handwashed and laid flat to dry. Still others should be sent to the dry cleaner. Be sure that the care instructions will work well for your finished work, or it may end up on the top shelf of the closet! Many manufacturers use the universal care symbols shown here. For more information on these symbols, see Chapter 18. Also, if you mix more than one type of yarn, the care requirements should be similar, or you may end up with a stretched (or shrunken) section after you launder it the first time.

- **Color name and number (4):** Yarn colors are identified in two different ways: by name and/or number.

- **Company name and logo (5):** This is the name of the company that manufactures the yarn. Sometimes contact information, such as address, telephone number, and Web site, is included as well.

- **Dye lot number (6):** The dye lot number identifies yarns that are dyed in the same batch. Although companies strive to match the colors as closely as possible, slight variations exist from lot to lot. Even if skeins of different dye lots look the same when you hold them together, you may end up with a distinct color difference in your finished project. To ensure an even color throughout your work, buy enough yarn from the same dye lot to complete the entire project. If you have to go back and buy more at a later date, chances are that you won't be able to find yarn from the same dye lot.

✔ **Gauge (7):** Gauge is a measurement that helps you keep your crochet stitches consistent. It's the number of stitches and rows in a given measurement that you should get with a particular yarn by using the recommended hook size for that yarn. If the label only gives a knitting gauge, you can use this gauge as a guide because crochet hook sizes correspond to knitting needle sizes. Check out Chapter 3 for more on gauge.

✔ **Manufacturer's address (8):** Sometimes the manufacturer's address is listed separately from the name, and it can come in handy if you have questions about the yarn or are having trouble locating a retail store that sells their product.

✔ **Ply (9):** *Ply* refers to the number of smaller strands twisted together to form the larger single strand of yarn. This number can be deceptive, though, because a fine yarn can be a 3- or 4-ply yarn, while a bulky yarn can be just 2 ply. Worsted-weight yarns are generally 4 ply, and some cotton yarns can be made up of 8 or more strands. The size or weight of the yarn may be included along with the ply on the label, too; for example, 4-ply worsted-weight yarn or 2-ply bulky-weight yarn.

✔ **Recommended hook size (10):** Sometimes the label suggests a certain hook size in order to work to the proper gauge for a specific yarn size. This size is a good place to start, although you may find that you need to use a smaller or larger size hook, depending on how you work your stitches and how loose you want them to be. You can get a lacy texture by using a much larger hook than recommended. On the other hand, if you want a tight, stiff fabric (if you're making a tapestry bag, for example), you should use a smaller hook than the one the label calls for.

✔ **Weight (11):** This number reflects the actual weight of the whole skein, ball, or hank of yarn, as opposed to the weight (size) of the yarn strand. The weight is usually quoted in ounces and/or grams.

✔ **Yardage (12):** The yardage is the length of the yarn in yards or meters that's in the ball or skein. This information is important because you don't want to get partway through your project and then realize that you don't have enough yarn.

✔ **Yarn content (13):** Yarn content is the stuff that your yarn is made of — wool or acrylic, cotton or silk, a blend of two or more fibers, or one of the many other fibers available.

Matching your yarn to your project

You need to take your project's design, pattern, color, and texture into consideration when choosing your yarn. Certain patterns work better with simple yarns and solid colors while others can showcase more exotic yarns.

Working with color and texture

A wide array of wonderfully colored yarns is available today, from bright jewel-toned solids to hand-painted, variegated ones. If your pattern is simple, try a multicolored yarn. Using colorful yarns allows you to create a beautiful work of art without having to work a more complex stitch pattern.

If you've chosen a design with fancier stitches, stick to a more basic yarn. A smooth, solid-color yarn adds definition to your stitches and allows them to stand out. You want your stitch work to be seen! Vibrant, solid colors are available today with both matte and shiny finishes. Both finishes work equally well, so choose what you like best.

Working with novelty yarns can be somewhat tricky. Seeing the stitches as you're crocheting is sometimes difficult. Don't let this put you off; just plan to take more time and effort to work up your creation. When first working with these yarns, such as eyelash yarn or fun fur, try using them as an accent to your piece in borders, edgings, and collars until you get used to them. This way, if you make a mistake, at least you won't have to take your whole design apart. Besides, these novelty yarns can be overwhelming when used in excess.

The more intricate that your stitch design is, the simpler the yarn should be. The more interesting the yarn is, the simpler the pattern should be.

Choosing natural or man-made fibers

When choosing your yarn, think about what your design will be used for. Soft wools and shimmery silks work beautifully for winter sweaters and dressy tops. High-quality cotton produces a wonderful summer cardigan or an heirloom doily, bedspread, or tablecloth. Natural fibers cost a little more and require more TLC than the man-made fibers, but they hold up well over a long period of time.

If you're making baby items or large designs, such as Afghans, opt for a good quality synthetic yarn, such as acrylic. Made to mimic the natural fibers, synthetic yarns come in a wide range of sizes and colors and can be smooth and soft to the touch. They're also easy to care for. In most cases, they can be thrown in the washer and dryer and still stand up well to the wear and tear of everyday use. Synthetic yarns are usually cheaper than their natural counterparts, which is a good thing when you're creating a design that uses a lot of yarn.

Substituting yarns

If you have your heart set on making the design exactly as you see it in the pattern picture, use the yarn listed in the pattern materials list. But if that gorgeous Afghan is made in shades of pink, and your decor is blue, don't be afraid to change the color scheme. Or if your budget doesn't accommodate the high-priced wool called for in that sweater design, look for a comparable synthetic or a less-expensive wool blend.

If you're substituting for more than just color, however, make sure that the yarn you choose is the same size or weight and can accommodate the same gauge. (See Chapter 3 for details on gauge.) For example, if the pattern calls for a worsted-weight yarn, make sure that you get another worsted-weight yarn. If you choose a bulky yarn instead, you'll end up with a design that's considerably larger than planned. If you're making something wearable, substitutions can cause disastrous results.

Another important consideration when substituting is total yardage. If the pattern calls for five skeins of a sport-weight yarn that has 400 yards to each skein for a total of 2,000 yards, make sure that you purchase enough of whatever sport-weight yarn you choose so that you have a total of 2,000 yards.

The manufacturer's gauge on the yarn label can help when you want to substitute one yarn for another. Just compare the gauge listed on the yarn label with the pattern gauge to determine the correct size yarn.

Creating your own yarn combinations

For even more variety, work with two or three different strands of yarn held together as one to create a unique blend of colors or textures. You can use two or more strands of the same weight of yarn to produce an extremely thick fabric. That's what those really big hooks are made for. If you want to use several strands in a pattern that only calls for one, make sure that the yarns you put together equal the same weight yarn that the pattern calls for. For example, if a design calls for a worsted-weight yarn, two or three strands of a fingering-weight yarn would approximately equal a worsted weight. If you're unable to come up with the correct weight, be sure to make a gauge swatch and adjust your hook size to achieve the proper gauge (see Chapter 3).

Working with more than one strand of yarn at a time can be tricky. Watch out for all those extra loops of yarn that you'll encounter.

Tool Time: Other Tools of the Trade

Although your crochet hook and yarn are your primary tools, several other items can come in handy. Some of these tools are necessary, and others, while not essential, are just nice to have. Some of our favorite tools include those in Figure 2-5. The following list describes each one, going clockwise from the scissors:

- ✔ **Scissors:** Small scissors with a sharp point work best. They're more manageable than large scissors, and you're less likely to snip at the wrong place. Don't try to break your yarn with your hands — doing so is almost impossible, and besides, it can stretch your yarn and hurt your hands. Craft and fabric stores carry a variety of scissors, and many come with carrying cases or are collapsible.

- ✔ **Ruler and tape measure:** These tools are necessary when measuring for gauge and for measuring your work in progress. Try to find a ruler and tape measure that have both standard and metric measurements.

- ✔ **Rustproof straight pins:** These pins are absolutely necessary when pinning down a project that you're going to *block* (meaning, shape — see Chapter 18). After putting so much time into your project, it'd be a shame to ruin it by not using rustproof pins and ending up with reddish-brown spots throughout your creation.

- ✔ **Safety pins:** Safety pins have a zillion uses, such as marking a spot in your work that you ripped out, holding two pieces together while sewing a seam, keeping track of increases and decreases, and marking the right side of your work. The ones without coils are the best. They slip in and out of your stitches easily, and the yarn doesn't catch.

- ✔ **Stitch markers:** You can find a variety of stitch markers at your local yarn or craft store. Although they're not absolutely essential, having some type of marker comes in handy when you have to mark the end of a specific row or a certain stitch within the row where you're going to work an increase or decrease. In a pinch, a piece of contrasting colored yarn, a safety pin, or a bobby pin works just as well.

- ✔ **Yarn bobbins:** These bobbins are usually plastic, and you use them to wrap different colors of yarn on when you're working a multicolored piece. (See Chapter 9 for working with more than one color.)

- ✔ **Yarn and tapestry needles:** Yarn and tapestry needles have larger eyes than regular sewing needles to accommodate the yarn. Yarn needles have a blunt point, which slips through the stitches without splitting the yarn. Tapestry needles are a bit smaller in diameter, have a sharper point, and are generally used when working with cotton thread. You use these needles often for weaving in ends, sewing motifs, or sewing seams. Yarn needles come in steel or plastic styles. Our preference is the steel variety because the plastic ones tend to bend and break over time.

Don't forget to keep a pad of paper and a pencil on hand. Keeping notes while you work is a must if you make any changes to a pattern or are designing your own piece. Even if you think you'll remember the changes you made, write them down. You'll be surprised how fast the smallest stitch change slips from your mind.

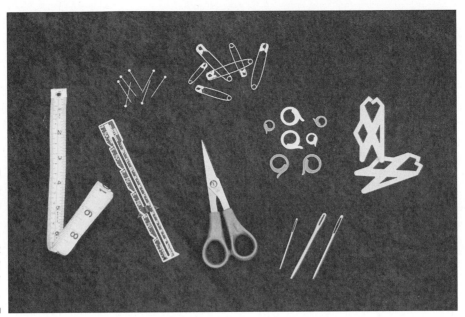

Figure 2-5:
More
crocheting
parapher-
nalia that
you may
need or
want.

You probably want to have a safe place to keep all this neat new stuff you
have. Most craft stores carry a variety of cases that you can use to store
everything. You can store smaller items in a small zippered case and place
it in a larger case or carrying bag along with your yarn.

Chapter 3

Creating Consistency with Gauge

. . . .

. . . .

Making sure that your stitches are consistently the right size is very important when crocheting. Otherwise, your sweater may be lopsided or your scarf may morph into a tablecloth. So in order to get the shape and size you want, you check the *gauge* provided in the pattern. Gauge is simply the ratio of a given number of stitches or rows to inches (or some other measurement), such as 7 stitches per inch or 4 rows per inch. You then use this ratio to keep your stitches consistent and the size of your design on track.

Gauge is particularly important when crocheting clothing, but you still need to keep it consistent in every crocheting project that you tackle. Working to the proper gauge ensures that the project you make is neat and attractive. Gauge also ensures that the amount of yarn the pattern specifies is sufficient to complete the project.

This chapter shows you how to test your gauge by crocheting a gauge swatch (sample) and how to adjust your gauge to equal the one that the pattern requires.

Why Bother with Gauge?

Although you can start a project without checking your gauge first, crocheting a sample gauge swatch to get a feel for the right ratio of stitches to inches is really important. If your gauge is off by even a little bit, your finished design may be off by several inches. You may spend beaucoup bucks on materials and many hours, days, or weeks crocheting, only to find that the sweater you made is a perfect fit for the neighbor's Chihuahua.

When you're making a design from a published pattern, the pattern almost always recommends a gauge for you to follow. The pattern designer determines this gauge by taking into account the recommended yarn and hook size, the type of stitches used in the pattern, and the desired result.

Look for the recommended gauge at the beginning of the pattern instructions. (A subtle hint to check your gauge first thing!) Although garment patterns usually mention both a stitch and a row gauge, the stitch gauge is the most important one to match. It determines the width of each piece of the design, which, when you sew the front and back together, adds up to the finished bust/chest measurement.

For example, say you're making a sweater and the required gauge is 8 stitches = 2 inches, and you want a finished bust measurement of 40 inches (or 20 inches across the back). The pattern may call for 80 stitches across the back (80 stitches ÷ 8 stitches × 2 inches = 20 inches). If your gauge measures 7 stitches = 2 inches, then working 80 stitches ÷ 7 stitches × 2 inches = 22 inches. Your sweater back would measure 22 inches, and the finished bust/chest would measure 44 inches! See how, with your gauge being off by just one stitch, your garment would end up 4 inches larger than intended? That's why gauge is so important.

Many sweater patterns allow for your row gauge being off a little by telling you to work to the desired length in inches, regardless of how many rows it takes you to get there. However, if your stitch gauge is off, your sweater may be too wide or too narrow, and that's something you can't adjust without tearing out all your hard work and at least some of your hair.

Note: The yarn manufacturer may also recommend a particular gauge on the yarn label. This gauge may be quite different from the one in your pattern, but that's okay. Sometimes, the pattern designer wants to create a looser or tighter stitch pattern than the standard that the yarn manufacturer set. Follow the pattern gauge to get the same results as the project pictured.

Working a Gauge Swatch

Working a gauge swatch may seem like a waste of valuable crocheting time, but it's worth the effort. In addition to making sure that your stitches and rows are the same size as the pattern's (which ensures a perfect-fitting garment), a gauge swatch lets you become familiar with the yarn you're using and practice any new stitches in the pattern.

Hand me that swatch

Although you may feel a little impatient when you have to spend your time crocheting a swatch, you can make that time and effort seem less painful if you find a use for all those practice swatches.

- ✔ Use them as coasters.

- ✔ Make your swatch large enough to use as a doll blanket.

- ✔ Sew several swatches together to form a pillow front or wallhanging sampler.

- ✔ Sew many swatches together to make a patchwork Afghan.

- ✔ Keep a scrapbook of your swatches to inspire future projects.

- ✔ Practice edgings and borders on the sides of your swatches.

- ✔ Use lacy cotton swatches as appliqués on sweatshirts or jeans.

Making your swatch

Different types of patterns call for different types of gauges. A simple pattern that uses just one stitch, like a single crochet stitch, states the gauge as a certain number of stitches and rows per a given number of inches. However, some patterns have a set of several different stitches that repeats across the row. In this case, the pattern states the gauge as one entire stitch repeat per a given number of inches.

Work the stitches for your gauge swatch according to the instructions in the pattern. However, you probably want to make it bigger than what the instructions specify in order to get an accurate measurement.

Crocheters tend to crochet tighter at the beginning and end of rows than in the body of their work. So if the gauge calls for 7 stitches = 2 inches and 8 rows = 2 inches, make your swatch at least 4 inches square. That way you can measure in the center of the swatch and get an accurate measurement of your normal pace. If you're working a gauge that has a repeated set of stitches, you may need to make it bigger than 4 inches square.

The swatches pictured in this chapter are made up of two colors so that you can identify the center stitches more easily, but you can just use a single color when working your own gauge swatch.

Blocking your swatch

To get an accurate measurement of your stitches, you have to treat your swatch just as you'll treat your finished project. Check to see whether your pattern requires you to *block* your final design. Blocking is a process that evens out the stitches and gets the final piece into the right shape. It usually involves getting the piece wet, whether you submerge it in a tub of water or just steam it, and then shaping the piece by hand into the correct measurements and allowing it to dry. After blocking your gauge swatch, you can measure your true gauge, therefore accurately predicting whether your finished design will be true to form. (See Chapter 18 to find out how to block your work.)

Blocking your gauge swatch is especially important if you're working with natural fibers, such as wool and cotton.

Measuring stitches and rows

After you make a swatch with the materials and hook size that the pattern recommends, measure the stitches and rows in your swatch to determine whether you have too many, too few, or just the right number for the given gauge.

The following swatches show you how to correctly measure gauge in a fabric made up of single-crochet stitches (see Chapter 4 for instructions on single crochet). Figure 3-1a shows that you have 7 stitches in 2 inches. Figure 3-1b shows that 8 rows of single crochet = 2 inches.

1 2 3 4 5 6 7

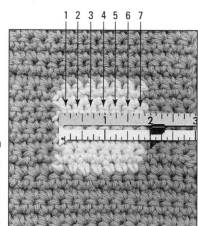

Figure 3-1:
Measuring gauge for a single-stitch pattern.

a.

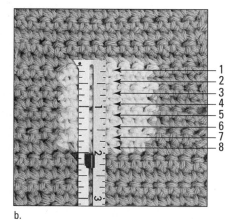

1
2
3
4
5
6
7
8

b.

Figure 3-2 shows you how to measure crocheted fabric that uses different stitches, worked in rows. When measuring a stitch gauge in a swatch that has a repeating pattern of combination stitches, be sure to include the total repeat in your measurement (see Figure 3-2a).

When measuring a row gauge, always measure the rows from the base of one row to the base of another row above it. If you measure to the top of a row, your gauge will be off because the base of the row lies in the valley of the previous row. (See Figure 3-2b.)

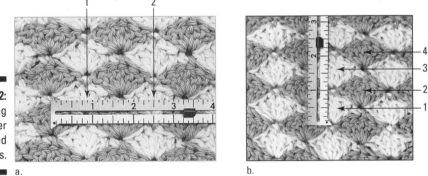

Figure 3-2:
Measuring
gauge over
patterned
stitches.

a.   b.

When working with a pattern such as the one in Figure 3-2, the gauge usually includes one or more repeats of the pattern. For example, if the stitch gauge = 3¼ inches, you need to work a swatch at least 6½ inches wide to get an accurate gauge. The row gauge for a pattern that has a 2-row repeat, such as this one, should be a multiple of 2 rows (2, 4, or 6 rows) to reflect how the pattern will work up in length. The gauge for this pattern is 4 rows = 2¼ inches. For an accurate row gauge, work a swatch at least 6 rows deep, or approximately 3½ inches.

Measuring stitches and rounds

If you're working a *round* (stitches crocheted in a circle instead of back and forth in rows), such as with a doily, you figure out the gauge by measuring the diameter of the swatch after you've made a certain number of rounds. The pattern usually states how many rounds to make for the swatch. Figure 3-3a shows 3 rounds of double crochet stitches that equal 3½ inches in diameter. Figure 3-3b shows the first 2 rounds of a hexagon motif that equal 3 inches in diameter across the widest point.

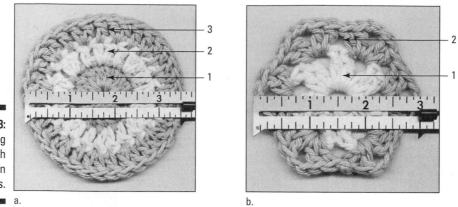

Figure 3-3: Measuring a stitch gauge in rounds.

a.   b.

If you're crocheting with cotton thread in rows or rounds, you can usually use a smaller gauge swatch than when you crochet with yarn, but you take the measurements the same way no matter what material or hook size you're using.

Over- or undershooting the mark

If your gauge is different from the one the pattern specifies, you can correct it by changing hook sizes and making another swatch. If you have more stitches than the pattern calls for, your work is too tight, and you should make another swatch with a larger hook. If you have fewer stitches than the pattern calls for, you're working too loosely, and you need to use a smaller hook to achieve the desired result. Figure 3-4 shows what a swatch looks like if you crochet too loosely (or if you use too large a hook). Notice how the white center section exceeds the required 2-inch gauge. Keep adjusting hook sizes and working swatches until you get the right gauge.

Everyone crochets a little differently. After you get to know your own crochet style (whether you tend to crochet tightly or loosely), you may be able to choose the proper hook size even before doing the first swatch. Changing hook size is the best way to compensate for your individual style of crochet. If you consciously try to tighten or loosen up your stitches to achieve the proper gauge, you invariably return to your natural style as you go along and then end up with the wrong gauge.

If you don't work on a project for several days or weeks or months, be sure to recheck your gauge before continuing with the project. Time away can affect your gauge, which varies depending on your stress level or other outside factors. You may need to adjust your hook size to maintain the original gauge.

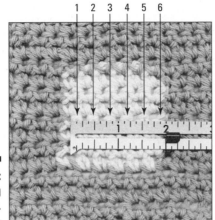

Figure 3-4:
Crocheting
too loosely.

Setting Out on Your Own: Establishing Your Own Gauge

After you get the hang of crocheting, your adventuresome side may kick in. You may want to try designing your own sweaters, scarves, and Afghans. Suppose you have a stitch pattern in mind and want to figure out how many stitches to work to create the size that you need — in other words, you want to set the right gauge for your project. The following steps make it easy:

1. **Work a swatch of the pattern, using the desired materials.**

2. **Change hook sizes as needed until the swatch has the look and feel you want.**

3. **Measure how many stitches your swatch has per inch (or several inches).**

For example, if your gauge measures 7 stitches = 2 inches and you want to make a sweater that measures 36 inches around, or 18 inches across the back, cross multiply to calculate the correct number of stitches you need to begin the back. (See the following equation.)

$$\frac{7 \text{ stitches}}{2 \text{ inches}} = \frac{x \text{ stitches}}{18 \text{ inches}}$$

Remember your cross multiplication? In order to find *x,* you first multiply 7 by 18, and then you divide that answer by 2: $7 \times 18 = 126$, and $126 \div 2 = 63$ stitches. Working 63 stitches produces a back width of 18 inches.

Never skip over the gauge stage when you create your own crochet master-piece. It's a necessary tool for creating a useful and beautiful final work of art.

Chapter 4

Getting Down to Basics

*W*hen you think about it, crocheting is nothing more than a series of loops made with a hook and some yarn, worked row on row or round after round. Piece o' cake! This chapter takes you through the basics of getting your loops right: from picking up your hook and holding your yarn to completing your first rows of stitches. It also includes diagrams and instructions for both lefties and righties.

In the Beginning: Preparing to Crochet

Before you even attempt your first stitch, you need to get some basic skills under your belt. This section shows you how to hold the hook and yarn and how to get the yarn on the hook.

Determining the right hand for hooking

The "right" hand for holding your crochet hook isn't necessarily the one on your right side. Your dominant hand — the one that you write with, eat with, and do just about everything else with — is the hand that you should hold your hook in. This is the hand that does most of the action, while the other hand guides the yarn and holds the work that you've already completed.

All the information in this book (and there's plenty of it!) deals with techniques from a right-hander's point of view, but it applies to you lefties as well. Don't get discouraged. Your motions are exactly the same. So if the instruction says right, you think left. If it says left, think right. In order to make sure that you get off on the right foot (or should we say left foot?), however, the beginning crochet techniques in this chapter include diagrams for both hands. See the sidebar "For southpaws only" for some more techniques to help you through the rest of the chapters.

Getting a grip on hook and yarn

Even though you crochet with only one hook, both hands are busy the whole time. Your dominant hand holds the hook, and your other hand holds the yarn.

Holding your crochet hook is pretty simple. You just gotta get the right grip on it. If your hand isn't comfortable, it can cramp up, and your stitches won't be even. Crocheting should be relaxing, not a continuous fight with the hook and yarn. Experiment with each of the following positions to see which one feels the most comfortable for you.

- ✔ **Over-the-hook position:** Position your dominant hand over the hook with the handle resting against your palm and your thumb and index finger grasping the thumb rest. (See Figure 4-1.)
- ✔ **Under-the-hook position:** Hold the hook as you would a pencil with the thumb rest between your forefinger and thumb. (See Figure 4-2.)

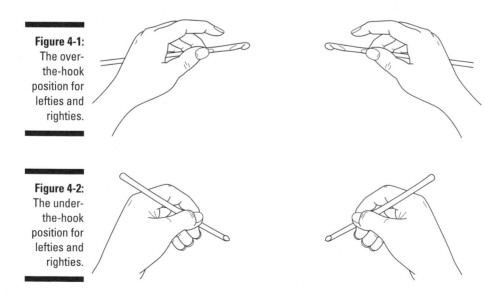

Figure 4-1: The over-the-hook position for lefties and righties.

Figure 4-2: The under-the-hook position for lefties and righties.

Both are common ways of holding the crochet hook that work just fine — for lefties or righties.

After you decide how you want to hold the hook, you're ready for the yarn. Your yarn hand — the hand not holding your hook — has an important job. Not only does it feed the yarn to your crochet hook, but it also controls the tension of the yarn.

Right-handed crocheters wrap the yarn over their left hand, and left-handed people wrap the yarn over their right hand. Figure 4-3 shows you what it should look like. (If it looks like your fingers have to be contortionists to get into position, don't worry — they can do it.)

The following steps offer one common method for wrapping the yarn around your hand:

1. **Starting from underneath your hand, bring the yarn up between your little finger and ring finger.**

2. **Wrap the yarn around your little finger to form a loop.**

3. **Draw the yarn under your ring finger and middle finger.**

4. **Bring the yarn up to the top of your hand between your middle finger and forefinger.**

5. **Finally, lay the yarn over your forefinger.**

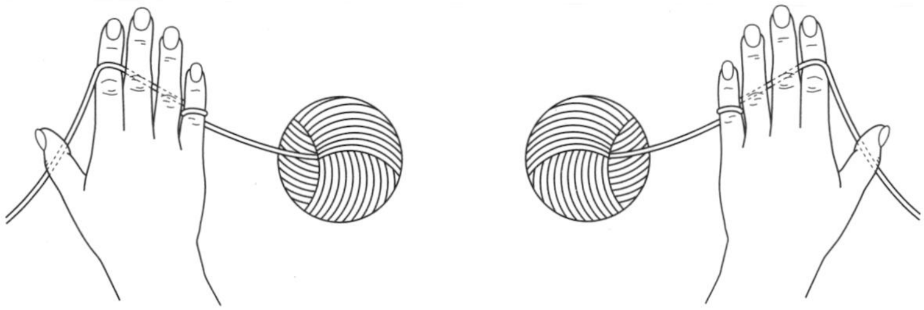

Figure 4-3:
Wrapping
the yarn
over your
yarn hand.

To keep the yarn in place, grasp the end of the yarn between your middle finger and thumb. By raising or lowering your forefinger, you can control the yarn tension. Practice wrapping and rewrapping the yarn around your yarn hand. If you ever feel that your working yarn is too loose or too tight, stop and rewrap to get the proper tension. This motion soon becomes an ingrained habit.

When you first start working with yarn, use a light solid-color, worsted-weight yarn. You can see the stitches more clearly and manipulate the yarn easier. Textured or variegated yarn takes a little more babying.

REMEMBER

From this point on, the diagrams in this chapter aren't marked "lefty" or "righty." But here's a clue: The left diagrams in the figures are for lefties, and the right diagrams are for righties.

Working a slipknot

To get started on any crocheted piece, you first have to join or tie the yarn to the hook with a *slipknot.* The standard slipknot is really simple — nothing magical. Follow these steps:

1. **Beginning about 6 inches from the end of the yarn, make a loop that looks somewhat like a pretzel.**

2. **Insert your hook through the center of the loop (see Figure 4-4) and draw the working end of the yarn through.**

Figure 4-4:
Pulling the
yarn through
the loop.

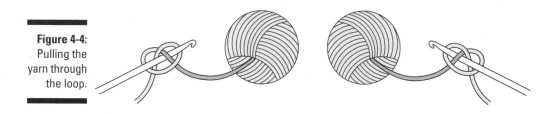

3. **Pull gently on both ends of the yarn to tighten the loop around the hook (see Figure 4-5).**

Figure 4-5:
Tightening
the loop
around
the hook.

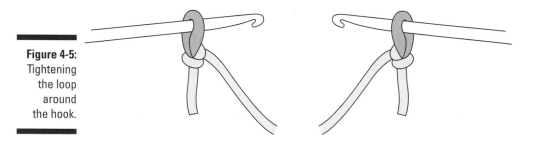

REMEMBER

The slipknot should slide easily up and down the shaft, but shouldn't be so loose that it slides off over the end of the hook. If it is too loose, gently pull on the working end of the yarn to snug it up. It also shouldn't be too tight because you have to pull your hook back through to make your first stitch. If your knot is too tight, simply tug on the loop to loosen it.

If pulling on the working end of the yarn doesn't tighten your slipknot on the hook and yanking on the cut end does, you made your slipknot backwards. Simply remove the loop from the hook, tug on both ends to release the knot, and try again.

Now that you have the yarn on the hook and are ready to begin making stitches, make sure that your hands are in the proper position, holding the slipknot with the yarn hand. If you're using the over-the-hook method for holding the hook, see Figure 4-6 for the proper position of both hands.

Figure 4-6: Proper position of both hands for the over-the-hook position.

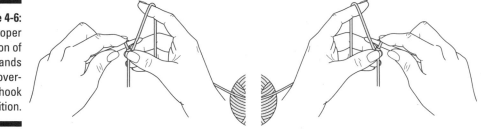

If you're more comfortable with the under-the-hook position, see Figure 4-7.

Figure 4-7: Proper position of both hands for the under-the-hook position.

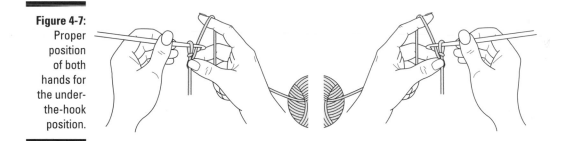

Wrapping the yarn over the hook

Wrapping the yarn over your hook, called a *yarn over* (abbreviated *yo*), is the most basic step to every stitch in crocheting. Sometimes you yarn over before you insert the hook into the next stitch, sometimes after, and sometimes you yarn over two or more times, depending on the stitch (check out the specific stitch sections later in this chapter). Yarning over is very simple, but you have to do it right, or you won't be able to draw the yarn smoothly through the stitch.

For southpaws only

If thinking left instead of right just isn't concrete enough for you, consider the following tips to help you work your way through from the opposite perspective:

✔ **Rely on a mirror image.** If you're a picture person and rely on the illustrations to help you understand a concept, hold the picture up to a mirror to view it as it should be for lefties. This may be a bit awkward, but a quick view from the correct angle may help. A makeup mirror that has a base and can sit on the open page works well and leaves your hands free to follow the image in the mirror.

✔ **Trace your way to success.** If you want a more permanent illustration or if the mirror

trick just doesn't cut it, trace the diagrams and illustrations on a piece of tracing paper and then flip the paper over. This gives you the view from the left side. Or if you have a scanner and a photo software application on your computer, you can scan the diagrams and illustrations and flip them horizontally.

✔ **Try to crochet the right-handed way.** If you're brand new to the craft and somewhat ambidextrous, you can try crocheting right-handed. You may be surprised that your hands do just what you tell them, thereby avoiding the extra work of having to translate the instructions.

To yarn over correctly, follow these steps:

1. **Make a slipknot.**

2. **Slide the slipknot onto the shaft of your hook.**

3. **With your yarn hand, hold the tail of the slipknot between your thumb and middle finger.**

4. **Using the forefinger on your yarn hand, bring the yarn up behind the hook.**

5. **Lay the yarn over the shaft, positioned between the slipknot and the throat of the hook, as Figure 4-8 shows.**

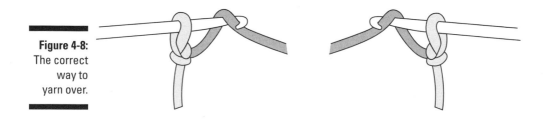

Figure 4-8:
The correct way to yarn over.

Practice the yarn over motion until you're comfortable with it.

If you try to wrap the yarn over your hook from front to back (see Figure 4-9), instead of from back to front, crocheting is more difficult and you end up with twisted, tangled stitches.

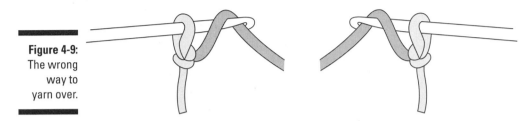

Figure 4-9:
The wrong
way to
yarn over.

Tied Up in Stitches: The Three Basics

This section takes you step-by-step through the three most basic stitches used in crocheting: The chain stitch, the slip stitch, and the single crochet.

Keep in mind that the first few stitches are often the hardest because you don't have much material to grasp onto with your yarn hand. But be patient; it gets easier.

Workin' on the chain stitch

The *chain stitch* (abbreviated *ch*) is the basis for all crochet. Almost every pattern begins with a chain stitch. If you're working in rows, your first row is a series of chain stitches, which is not surprisingly called a *foundation chain*. And when you're ready to start a new row, guess what, you use the chain stitch. Sometimes, you work just a few chain stitches and join them together to create a ring, which you use when working in rounds.

To make your first chain stitch, follow these steps:

1. **Make a slipknot.**

2. **Slide the slipknot onto the shaft of your hook.**

3. **With your yarn hand forefinger, yarn over (yo) the hook from back to front while holding the tail of the slipknot between the thumb and middle finger of your yarn hand.**

4. **Slide the yarn from the yarn over into the throat of the hook.**

5. **With your hook hand, rotate the hook toward you so that the throat faces the slipknot.**

6. **With gentle pressure upward on the hook, pull the hook, carrying the wrapped strand of yarn through the loop on your hook, as Figure 4-10 shows.**

One chain stitch (ch) is now complete, and one loop remains on your hook.

Figure 4-10:
Making a
chain stitch.

Whenever you're drawing the hook through a loop or stitch, rotate it so that the throat faces slightly downward, and apply gentle pressure upward on the hook so that the hook doesn't catch on any other loops of yarn.

Repeat Steps 3 through 6 until you feel comfortable with this motion. Each chain stitch should be the same size as the one before it, which means that you're keeping your yarn tension even for all your stitches. (See Figure 4-11.) If your stitches aren't the same size, don't get frustrated. If you find that your stitches are very tight and it's difficult to draw the hook through the stitch, try relaxing your hands. You're probably pulling too tightly on the yarn as you're drawing it through. If you find that your stitches are too loose, shorten up the distance between your yarn hand and hook hand, and lift the forefinger of your yarn hand, thus creating more tension. This stitch takes practice, but pretty soon, you'll find yourself moving right along.

As your chain gets longer and your hands get farther apart, you may have trouble controlling your work. Just let go of the bottom of your chain and, with the thumb and middle finger of your yarn hand, grab onto the chain closer to the hook, as Figure 4-12 shows. Holding the chain closer to the hook keeps your work stationary so that you can control your stitches and maintain even tension. As your work gets longer, keep readjusting so that you're always holding your completed work relatively close to the hook. This bit of advice applies to all your work as you're crocheting, not just chains. In fact, you'll probably find that you do it automatically without even thinking about it.

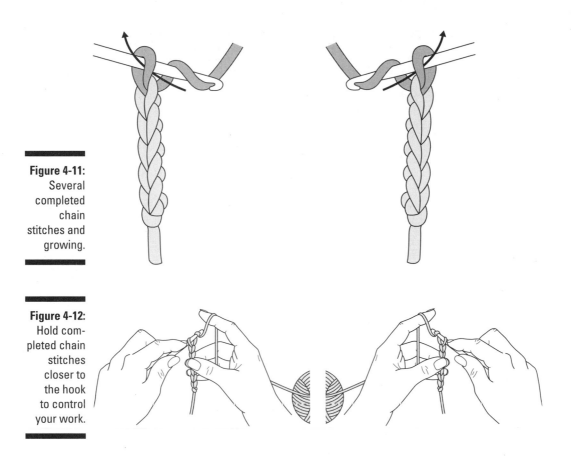

Figure 4-11:
Several completed chain stitches and growing.

Figure 4-12:
Hold completed chain stitches closer to the hook to control your work.

Telling right from wrong

Each stitch has a right side and a wrong side or a front and back. The right side of the chain is smooth, and you can see each stitch clearly. The wrong side has a small bumpy loop on each stitch. Figure 4-13 shows both the right and wrong sides of a chain.

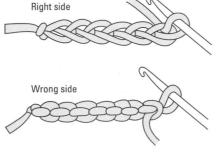

Figure 4-13:
Looking at the right and wrong (front and back) sides of a chain.

Right side

Wrong side

When you're talking about the right or wrong side of a piece of crocheted fabric, the first row of stitches (not counting the foundation chain) is generally considered the right side. You can always distinguish this by locating the tail of the foundation chain. If it's on your left (that is, if you're right handed), then the right side is facing you; if it's on the right, then the wrong side is toward you. (The reverse is true for lefties.)

A stitch it is, a stitch it's not: Counting stitches

Knowing what to count as a stitch is important when figuring out whether you've crocheted enough chain stitches for your foundation chain. It's easy. The loop on your hook doesn't count as a stitch. The first stitch is the one directly below your hook, and you begin counting from there, continuing down the chain until you reach the last chain stitch before the slipknot, which you don't count either. For example, Figure 4-14, in the next section, shows a chain of six chain stitches.

Working other stitches into chain stitches

To work your next row of stitches into the chain stitches, you have to know where to insert your hook. If you look at an individual stitch, you see that it consists of three separate loops or strands of yarn: two strands that create the V on the right side, which are called the *top loops,* and a third that creates the bump on the wrong side. You can insert your hook anywhere in the stitch and start stitching, but you get the best results like this: With the right side of the chain facing you, insert your hook between the top loops and under the back bump loop, catching both loops on your hook. (See Figure 4-14.) Working in the chain stitches like this gives you a neat base without any loose loops hanging down.

Figure 4-14:
Knowing where to insert your hook in the foundation chain.

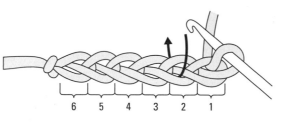

6   5   4   3   2   1

Slinking slip stitches

The *slip stitch* (abbreviated *sl st*) is the flattest (or smallest) of all the crochet stitches, and only the chain stitch is easier to make. Although you can use it to crochet a fabric, the slip stitch is really more of a utility stitch or a technique. Here are a few of its uses:

✔ **Making a seam:** Slip stitching is good for joining pieces of crocheted fabric. Because the slip stitch is relatively flat, it doesn't create a bulky seam. (See Chapter 15 for more on joining pieces of crochet.)

✔ **Shaping your work:** If you have to travel from one point to another to shape a crocheted item, such as for armholes in a garment, and don't want to fasten off your yarn and rejoin it, the slip stitch is ideal because it's almost invisible.

✔ **Joining a new ball of yarn:** When you have to join your yarn in a new place, whether for shaping purposes or to change colors, you use the slip stitch to attach it.

✔ **Creating a ring:** If you're working in rounds (like for a doily), the slip stitch joins one end of the chain to the other to create a ring.

✔ **Finishing the edges of your work:** Used as a final row or round on a design, the slip stitch creates a nice neat border.

✔ **Embellishing crocheted fabric:** You can slip stitch across the surface of a piece of crocheted fabric to create the look of embroidery. (Chapter 17 gives you lots of embellishment ideas.)

✔ **Forming combination stitches:** You can combine the slip stitch with other stitches to form fancy schmancy stitches. For example, you can combine the chain stitch with the slip stitch to form a *picot* stitch. (For more on combination stitches, see Chapter 11.)

The following steps show you how to make a slip stitch that forms a ring:

1. **Make a chain 6 chain stitches (ch 6) long.**

2. **Insert the hook into the first chain stitch made — the one farthest from your hook, as Figure 4-15 shows.**

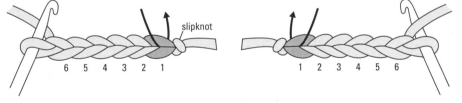

Figure 4-15: Inserting the hook into the first chain stitch made.

slipknot

6 5 4 3 2 1   1 2 3 4 5 6

3. **With your yarn hand, wrap the yarn from back to front over the hook (yo) and with your hook hand, rotate the throat of the hook toward you.**

4. **While applying gentle pressure upward, draw the hook with the wrapped yarn back through the stitch and then through the loop on the hook in one motion (see Figure 4-16).**

   One slip stitch is complete, and one loop remains on your hook. See Figure 4-17.

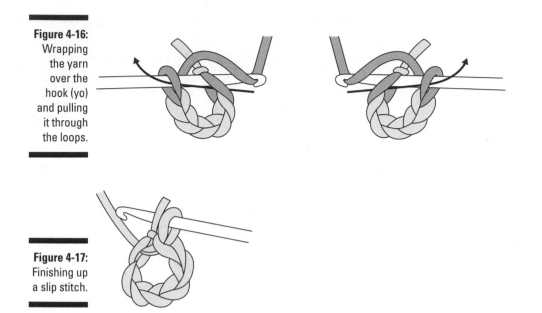

Figure 4-16:
Wrapping the yarn over the hook (yo) and pulling it through the loops.

Figure 4-17:
Finishing up a slip stitch.

The slip stitch forming a ring is all we show here, but no matter where you work the stitch, you always do it the same way.

The old standby: Single crochet

The *single crochet* (abbreviated *sc*) is the most fundamental of all stitches. A compact stitch, it creates a tight, dense fabric. You use this stitch over and over again, alone or in combination with other stitches. To begin your first row of single crochet:

1. **Make a foundation chain by doing 17 chain stitches (ch 17).**

2. **With the right side of the foundation chain facing you and your yarn hand holding the foundation chain, insert the hook from front to back into the second chain from the hook. (See Figure 4-18.)**

Figure 4-18:
Inserting the hook into the second chain stitch from the hook.

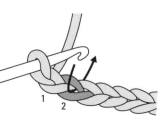
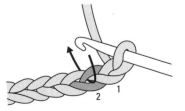

3. **With your yarn hand, wrap the yarn from back to front over the hook (yo).**

4. **Rotate the throat of the hook toward you with your hook hand.**

5. **Pull the hook with the wrapped yarn through the stitch, as Figure 4-19 shows.**

Figure 4-19: Drawing the yarn through the stitch.

You should have two loops on your hook.

6. **With your yarn hand, wrap the yarn from back to front over the hook.**

7. **Rotate the throat of the hook toward you with your hook hand.**

8. **Draw the hook with the wrapped yarn through both loops on the hook, as Figure 4-20 shows.**

One single crochet is now complete, and one loop remains on your hook.

Figure 4-20: Pull the yarn gently through both loops on the hook.

To work the next single crochet stitch and continue the row:

1. **Insert your hook into the next chain (ch) stitch, as shown in Figure 4-21.**

2. **Repeat Steps 3 through 8 from the first single crochet (sc) stitch instructions to complete the second stitch.**

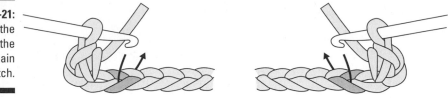

Figure 4-21:
Insert the hook in the next chain stitch.

3. **Work 1 single crochet stitch in each chain stitch across the foundation chain.**

    You should have 16 single crochet stitches, or one row of single crochet. See Figure 4-22.

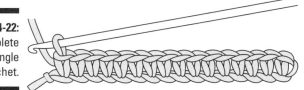

Figure 4-22:
Complete row of single crochet.

If you're wondering what happened to your 17th chain stitch, remember that you worked your first single crochet into the second chain from the hook. The skipped chain stitch is considered a turning chain that brings you up to the level needed to work your first stitch of the new row (see the "Climbing to new heights: Turning chains" section, later in this chapter).

Working stitches into the foundation chain isn't easy. Even experienced crocheters can have a tough time with this. But after the first few rows, you have more fabric to hold on to, which makes it easier to insert your hook.

Taking Things to the Next Level: Row Two

If you read the preceding section on the single crochet stitch and followed the steps, you now have a complete row of single crochet, and you're probably thinking, "Now what?" The answer is simple: You turn around and work back the same way that you came. This section shows you how to *turn* your work around so that the tops of the stitches in the previous row are in the proper position, which way to turn, and how to begin that first stitch of the new row.

Turning your work

To turn your work around so that you can start a new row of stitches, keep the last loop on your hook and simply take the completed work, which should be positioned under your hook hand, and turn it toward you until the work is positioned under your yarn hand (see Figure 4-23). This way, you hold the work between the middle finger and thumb of your yarn hand, your yarn is positioned behind your work, and the hook is in place to work the beginning stitches of the next row.

Keep in mind that each time you turn your work to crochet back across the previous row, a different side of the piece will be facing you. If the first row is designated as the right/front side of the piece, then when you turn to work the second row, the wrong/back side is facing you. The third row again has the right/front side facing you, and so on.

Figure 4-23:
Turning your
work in
order to
crochet
back across
the row.

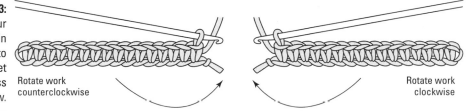

Rotate work
counterclockwise

Rotate work
clockwise

Climbing to new heights: Turning chains

After you turn your piece around, you're ready to crochet the *turning chain,* the one or more chain stitches that you make after you've turned your work and are about to begin your next row. The purpose of the turning chain is to bring your yarn to the height necessary in order to work the first stitch of your next row or round.

The number of chain stitches you make in the turning chain depends on what the next stitch in the row is because some stitches are taller than others. Figure 4-24 shows the height differences of several turning chains used for successively taller stitches. (See Chapter 6 for more info on taller stitches.)

Table 4-1 lists the number of chain stitches you need for several frequently used stitches.

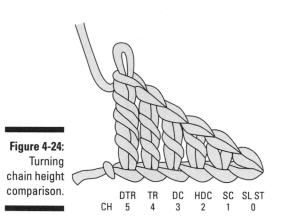

Figure 4-24:
Turning
chain height
comparison.

CH DTR TR DC HDC SC SL ST
     5   4   3   2   1   0

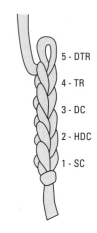

5 - DTR

4 - TR

3 - DC

2 - HDC

1 - SC

Table 4-1	How Many Chain Stitches Make a Turning Chain?
Stitch Name	*Number of Turning Chains Needed*
Slip stitch (sl st)	0
Single crochet (sc)	1
Half double crochet (hdc)	2
Double crochet (dc)	3
Triple crochet (tr)	4
Double triple crochet (dtr)	5

The turning chain almost always counts as the first stitch of the next row, except for the single crochet. The single crochet turning chain isn't wide enough to substitute for the first single crochet of the row and creates a rough edge to your rows. Working a single crochet stitch in the first stitch of the row fills out each row on the end.

Starting the next row

Going back and forth and back and forth may not get you places in real life, but it sure does when you're crocheting in rows. (You can also crochet in circles — check out Chapter 8 for that dizzying discussion.) So get ready to turn your work, make your turning chain, and start back across the row.

The following steps show you how to make your turning chain and begin a new row of single crochet, so grab your completed row of 16 single crochet stitches from the single crochet section:

1. **Turn your work to prepare for the next row.**

2. **Chain 1 (ch 1; turning chain for single crochet).**

3. **Insert your hook from front to back underneath the top two loops of the first stitch, as Figure 4-25 shows.**

Figure 4-25:
Inserting the hook under the top two loops of the first stitch.

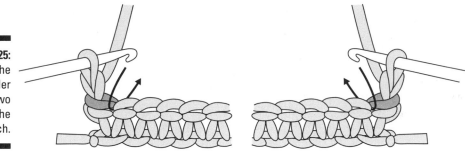

4. **Wrap the yarn over the hook (yo).**

5. **Draw your yarn through the stitch, as shown in Figure 4-26.**

Figure 4-26:
Drawing the yarn through the stitch.

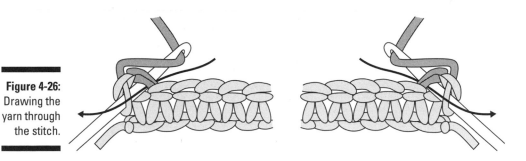

6. **Wrap the yarn over the hook.**

7. **Draw your yarn through the two loops on the hook.**

Now you have one single crochet in the second row completed, and one loop remains on the hook. (See Figure 4-27.)

Figure 4-27:
A new row with one complete single crochet.

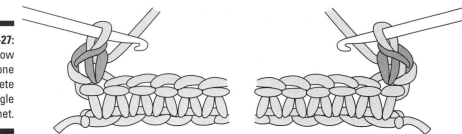

To complete the row, work one single crochet stitch in each single crochet stitch from the previous row all the way to the end. Make sure to count your stitches when you get to the end of the row. You should have exactly the same number of stitches in the second row as in the first.

Working across the row is that simple. You work the stitches exactly the same way as when you're working them into the foundation chain; you just place your hook in the top of a stitch from a previous row instead.

Some patterns like to change things up and may tell you to insert your hook in a different place in the previous row. But if no specific instructions are given, always work the stitches in each subsequent row under the top two loops of the stitch in the previous row. This is the best way to create a smooth, even fabric.

Working a practice swatch helps you figure out new stitches and start making them like a pro. Use worsted-weight yarn (it's easiest to work with) and a size H-8 hook (see Chapter 2 for more on hook sizes) to make a foundation chain approximately 4 inches long, and then chain 1 for your turning chain. Work as many rows of single crochet as you need to until you feel comfortable with the new stitch and your stitches have a smooth, even look. As you try out the other new stitches in this book, make a few practice swatches until you have the technique down cold.

All's Well That Ends Well: Fastening Off

Sooner or later, you're going to come to the end of your design and need to *fasten off* (cut) the yarn. Or maybe you're working with different colors and need to fasten off one color to join the new color.

This section shows you how and where to cut the yarn and what to do with the leftover tail.

Cutting the yarn

To fasten off your yarn, cut the yarn about 6 inches from the hook. (See the next section, "Weaving in the end," to find out why you leave this much yarn.) Using your hook, draw the cut end of the yarn through the last remaining loop on your hook, as Figure 4-28 shows. Pull gently on the tail of yarn to snug up the end. This action keeps your work from coming apart without having to make large unsightly knots.

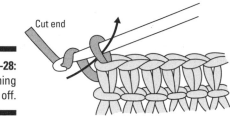

Figure 4-28:
Fastening
off.

Cut end

Weaving in the end

Now you weave those 6 inches of leftover tail through a few stitches to further secure the yarn and hide the end. To do this, thread the remaining yarn tail onto a yarn needle. Being careful not to split the yarn of the stitches, weave the 6-inch tail of yarn up and down through 3 or 4 stitches — kind of in a zigzag pattern. To really make the end secure, go back the way you came, weaving the end backwards through those same few stitches. When finished, cut the yarn about ¼ inch from the fabric and gently pull the fabric. The end disappears like magic, and your work is secure.

Colorful Coasters and Placemats Project

Nothing sets the mood at a table like a set of placemats and coasters. The following pattern lets you practice your newfound skills while at the same time creating a colorful set of tableware. The yarn used is a versatile worsted-weight cotton that's easy to work with and holds up well to everyday wear and tear. It comes in a variety of colors, so feel free to use the given colors (shown in the color insert) or choose your own to match your home decor. One skein contains enough yarn to make one coaster and one placemat.

Materials

The following is a list of materials you need to complete this project:

- ✔ **Yarn:** Lion Brand Yarn "Cotton-Ease" worsted-weight yarn (50% cotton/ 50% acrylic), Article #700 (3.5 oz [*100 gm*], 207 yds each skein). One skein each of
  - #102 Bubblegum
  - #113 Cherry
  - #133 Orangeade
  - #148 Popsicle
  - #158 Pineapple
  - #169 Pistachio
- ✔ **Hook:** Standard crochet hook size H-8 U.S. or size needed to obtain gauge.

Vital statistics

- ✔ **Size: Coaster:** 4 x 4½ in. excluding fringe. **Placemat:** 10½ x 16 in. excluding fringe.
- ✔ **Gauge:** 7 sts and 8 rows sc = 2 in.
- ✔ **Stitches used:** Chain stitch (ch), single crochet (sc).

Directions

The following directions are written in plain English, instead of crochetese, to help walk you through your first project. Refer back to the chain stitch section and single crochet section earlier in this chapter for details on each stitch.

Coaster

Make six coasters, one of each color given in the materials list.

1. **Create your foundation chain by working 17 chain stitches in a row (ch 17).**

2. **To complete Row 1, work 1 single crochet stitch (sc) in the second chain from the hook, then work 1 single crochet stitch in each chain across the row. You should have 16 complete single crochet stitches.**

3. **Turn your work, then chain 1 for the single crochet turning chain to prepare for the next row.**

4. **To complete the next row, work 1 single crochet stitch in each single crochet stitch across the row. You should have 16 complete single crochet stitches in this row.**

5. **Repeat Steps 3 and 4 until you have 16 rows on your work.**

6. **Fasten off your yarn.**

Fringe: Cut yarn into 3½-in. lengths. Using 2 strands of yarn held together as one for each fringe, single knot 1 fringe in each stitch across each short edge of the coaster. Trim ends even. For details on fringe, see Chapter 17.

Placemat

Make six placemats, one of each color given in the materials list. Figure 4-29 shows a completed placemat.

1. **Create your foundation chain by working 57 chain stitches in a row (ch 57).**

2. **To complete Row 1, work 1 single crochet stitch (sc) in the second chain from the hook, then work 1 single crochet stitch in each chain across the row. You should have 56 complete single crochet stitches.**

3. **Turn your work, then chain 1 for the single crochet turning chain to prepare for the next row.**

4. **To complete the next row, work 1 single crochet stitch in each stitch across the row. You should have 56 complete single crochet stitches.**

5. **Repeat Steps 3 and 4 until you have 42 rows on your work.**

6. **Fasten off your yarn.**

Fringe: Cut yarn into 3½-in. lengths. Using 2 strands of yarn held together as one for each fringe, single knot 1 fringe in each stitch across each short edge of the placemat. Trim ends even.

Figure 4-29:
Snazzy placemat in single crochet with fringe.

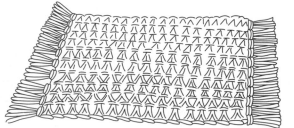

Part II
Basic Stitches and Techniques

The 5th Wave   By Rich Tennant

"I don't work with a pattern, man. I just make it up as I go along."

In this part . . .

This part gets down to the nitty-gritty techniques that you need for crocheting and also introduces four more basic stitches. If you've ever tried to read a crochet pattern and wondered, "What does all this gibberish mean?" wonder no more. We introduce you to the terminology, abbreviations, and symbolic language of crocheting in Chapter 5.

We also delve into the subjects of increasing and decreasing, how to crochet in circles, and working with more than one color of yarn.

To help demonstrate these new topics, we provide several new projects that you'll be crocheting in no time flat. To get you used to reading crochet patterns, the projects start out with both the crochetese and the plain-English translations, but by the end of the part, we slowly wean you from the translations. If you're not entirely comfortable reading the instructions, you can always refer to Chapter 5 and the Cheat Sheet at the beginning of the book.

Chapter 5

Decoding Crochet Patterns

Sometimes you may work thousands of stitches for one crochet project. If crochet instructions were all written out, stitch by stitch by stitch, without any abbreviations or shortcuts, one pattern would fill an entire book. Fortunately, crochet instructions have their own special abbreviations and a form of shorthand that simplify the written directions, saving space and a lot of tedious reading time.

Some patterns also use the International Crochet Symbols (see Figure 5-1 later in the chapter) to create pictorial diagrams of a crocheted design. For intricate patterns, you may find these diagrams easier to follow than the text. After you get a handle on the abbreviations and symbols of crochet design, reading a crochet pattern is a cinch. In this chapter, we help you decipher the unique language of crochet instructions.

Note: If you're reading this book in order, note that some of the stitches mentioned in this chapter aren't covered in Part I. If you want to know right away what a double crochet or a popcorn stitch is, flip over to the table of contents or the index to find the related chapter.

Gettin' the Lowdown on Crochet Patterns

Most crochet patterns that you find in a magazine or a book have several different sections that you need to be familiar with so you can concentrate on crocheting your masterpiece, rather than on deciphering the instructions.

The following list introduces the most common pattern sections (although some patterns will have more, others fewer):

- **Level of experience:** Most patterns give you a general idea of the complexity of the pattern and whether it's suitable for a beginner, advanced beginner, intermediate crocheter, or advanced crocheter. Don't let an advanced level put you off, though. Take a look at the pattern before you decide whether it's too complex for your ability.

- **Materials:** The materials section lists everything you need to complete the project:

  - **Yarn:** The materials list first lists all you need to know to get the right yarn for the project: the brand name, the specific yarn name, the fiber composition of the yarn, the size of the yarn (such as sport weight or worsted weight), the weight and yardage of each skein, and how many skeins (or hanks or balls) you need. (See Chapter 2 for complete details on yarn and reading the labels.)

  - **Hook:** The next item is the size crochet hook (or hooks) you need.

  - **Additional materials:** The materials list also includes any additional materials you need, such as a yarn needle, sewing thread, buttons, or beads.

- **Size information:** This part tells you the finished dimensions of the project or gives the size ranges if you're making a garment (check out Chapter 10 for full details on sweater sizing). It may also include a *schematic,* which is a diagram showing the dimensions of each piece used to make up the finished design.

- **Gauge:** The pattern always gives the gauge for a design. Make sure you work to the gauge specified to end up with the right size design.

- **Stitches:** Most patterns list the stitches used and give directions for any advanced stitches or techniques.

- **Crocheting directions:** The bulk of the pattern is the step-by-step instructions for crocheting the design. They may be written out row by row, or round by round, or include a pictorial diagram as well. If you make the project in several pieces, the pattern gives instructions for each piece. If keeping track of the right and wrong sides of a project is important for a certain pattern, the instructions will designate which row is which. For example, if the first row of the work is the right side, the instructions for the first row appear like this: Row 1 (RS). All subsequent odd-numbered rows are then considered right side and even-numbered rows are wrong side. See the sections "Figuring Out Written Instructions" and "Not Just a Pretty Picture: Symbols and Diagrams" for the nitty-gritty details of reading directions.

✔ **Assembly:** If a design is made in several pieces, this section shows you how to put it all together.

✔ **Finishing:** Here's where you add the final details, which can be as simple as sewing on buttons or as detailed as adding borders and collars. If an item needs to be blocked, you find the info here (see Chapter 18 for more on blocking).

Figuring Out Written Instructions

Written instructions are, by far, the most common way to present a crochet pattern. The various abbreviations and symbols — and combinations of the two — may seem like a foreign language to you in the beginning. The following sections serve as your dictionary, explaining each of the parts used in written instructions and how they all fit together.

Keep it short: Abbreviations

Most crochet stitches have shortened names or abbreviations. For example, instead of saying *double crochet stitch* throughout a pattern, the instructions abbreviate *dc*. As we introduce terms and stitches throughout this book, we also give you their abbreviations to help you become familiar with the short-hand. Table 5-1 lists the most common abbreviations. For a more complete list of crochet abbreviations, refer to the Cheat Sheet at the front of this book.

Table 5-1	Common Crochet Abbreviations
Abbreviation	*Spelled-out Term*
approx	approximately
beg	begin(ning)
bet	between
blp	back loop only
BP	back post
CC	contrast color
ch	chain

(continued)

Table 5-1 *(continued)*

Abbreviation	Spelled-out Term
dc	double crochet
dec	decrease(s)(d)(ing)
dtr	double triple crochet
flp	front loop only
foll	follow(ing)
FP	front post
hdc	half double crochet
inc	increase(s)(d)(ing)
MC	main color
pat	pattern
rem	remaining
rep	repeat
rib	ribbing
RS	right side
sc	single crochet
sl st	slip stitch
st(s)	stitch(es)
tog	together
tr	triple crochet
WS	wrong side
yo	yarn over hook

Crochet abbreviations don't have periods after them in order to keep the instructions as clutter-free as possible. If you do come across a period that isn't at the end of the sentence or action, it's probably attached to an abbreviation that is easily confused with another word, such as *in.* meaning inches as opposed to *in* — the word.

One other notation that you see quite frequently in instructions is the hyphen. Instructions commonly use the hyphen when referring to a chain loop — the hyphen denotes the number of chains you work to create a particular loop. For example, a *ch-5 loop* is a loop made up of 5 chain stitches. Don't confuse this instruction, however, with *ch 5,* which instructs you to make a chain of 5 chain stitches in a row.

Some patterns combine several basic stitches into a more complex stitch. For example, 5 double crochet stitches worked in the same stitch is called a *shell* because it resembles the shape of a clamshell. Besides having their own names, these special stitches may also have their own abbreviations. Chapter 11 defines many of these combination stitches and gives you their abbreviations.

Special stitches aren't standardized and may have different definitions in each pattern that you encounter. For example, one pattern may define a shell as 5 double crochet stitches, but another pattern may define it as only 3 double crochet stitches. Before you begin, be sure to check the beginning of the pattern's instructions for the definition of each special stitch.

Working terms and phrases

Crochet patterns often contain jargon that isn't abbreviated, such as the terms that follow:

- ✔ **Loop:** A *loop* is 3 or more chain stitches worked in a row. To work in the loop, insert your hook in the hole underneath the loop, not in any one stitch, and then complete the stitch indicated. Chapter 12 covers more information about where to work the stitches.

- ✔ **Space:** Usually, a *space* refers to the space created by working 1 or more chain stitches in between other stitches. To work in the space, insert your hook in the hole underneath the chain stitches and complete the stitch indicated.

- ✔ **Work across:** Crochet the designated stitch or stitches across the whole length of the row.

- ✔ **Work around:** Crochet the same stitch or stitch pattern repeatedly until you come back to the starting point.

- ✔ **Work across (or around) to within last 2 sts:** Crochet the designated stitches until you have 2 stitches left to work in at the end of the row or round; the instructions tell you what to do in the last 2 stitches.

Pondering parentheses

Instead of detailing each and every stitch or action involved in a row or round, instruction writers use parentheses to designate a repeated set of actions and stitches or to sum up a row. Here's a list of the different reasons instruction writers use these handy little arcs:

✏ **To isolate a set of 2 or more stitches that you work all in 1 stitch.** For example, you may find something like

> (2 dc, ch 2, 2 dc) in next sc

This means that in the next single crochet stitch, you want to crochet 2 double crochet stitches, chain 2, and then work 2 more double crochet stitches.

✏ **To enclose a set of stitches that you repeat a number of times in succession.** For example,

> (dc in next 3 sts, ch 2, skip next 2 sts) twice

In plain English, this means that you work a double crochet stitch in each of the next 3 stitches, chain 2, skip the next 2 stitches, and then repeat that by working a double crochet stitch in each of the next 3 stitches, chaining 2, and skipping the next 2 stitches again.

✏ **To sum up a completed row or round.** If you see (16 dc) at the end of the instructions for a row, you should have 16 double crochet stitches in that row. Likewise, (8 loops) means you've completed 8 loops, and (4 ch-3 loops made) means that you've made 4 loops that are each 3 chain stitches long. (For more on loops, see Chapter 12.)

✏ **To distinguish different sizes in a garment pattern.** If a garment pattern is written for three sizes, it includes separate instructions for the two larger sizes in parentheses. For example,

> dc in each of next 10 (12, 14) sts

So you work 10 double crochet stitches if you're going for the Small size, 12 double crochet stitches for Medium, and 14 double crochet stitches for Large. To make such a pattern easier to follow, you may want to highlight, underline, or circle the numbers that pertain to your size throughout the pattern.

Bracing yourself for brackets

Crochet instructions use brackets in the following ways:

✔ **Some patterns use brackets interchangeably with parentheses to isolate repeated phrases of stitches.** They may also appear as a set or phrase within another. For example,

> (2 dc, ch 5, sl st in 5th ch from hook forming a ring, [4 sc, ch 3, 4 sc] in ring just made, 2 dc) in next ch-2 space

In other words, start by working 2 double crochet stitches in the chain-2 space (see the section "Working terms and phrases," earlier in this chapter, to find out how to work in a chain-2 space). Next, chain 5 stitches and slip stitch in the fifth chain from the hook to form a ring; then, work 4 single crochet stitches, chain 3, and work 4 single crochet stitches again in the ring you just formed; finally, complete the operation by working 2 more double crochet stitches in the same chain-2 space you started out in.

✔ **Patterns use brackets within parentheses to sum up the number of stitches for different sizes.** For example, to sum up the number of stitches in each size, a numeric phrase at the end of a row on a sweater pattern might say

> (72 [76, 80] sts)

This means that when you reach the end of the row, you've worked a total of 72 stitches for a Small-size sweater, 76 for a Medium, and 80 for a Large.

Interpreting bullets and other special symbols

Patterns use symbols like bullets (•), asterisks (*), plus signs (+), and crosses (†) in instructions to show the repetition of a series of crochet stitches. Bullets and asterisks are the most common, but this depends on the preference of the publication. This book, however, uses only bullets.

Some patterns use only one symbol at the beginning of a phrase and then direct you to repeat from that symbol a designated number of times. For example:

> • Dc in each of the next 3 sts, ch 2, skip next 2 sts, rep from • 5 times.

In this example, you work all the information after the bullet once, and then repeat the same series of steps 5 more times for a total of 6 times.

You may also see bullet symbols marking both the beginning and end of a repeated phrase. The instructions may reference this repeat again if the phrase within the bullets is used at a different section of the row or round. For example:

> Ch 3, • dc in each of next 3 dc, ch 2, skip next 2 sts •, rep from • to • once, dc in each of next 6 sts, ch 2, skip next 2 sts, rep from • to • twice, dc in each of last 4 dc.

Just to make sure that you're interpreting crochet-speak properly, check out the following plain-English translation of the preceding example and see whether it jibes:

1. **Chain 3.**

2. **Double crochet stitch in each of the next 3 double crochet stitches, chain 2, and skip the next 2 stitches.**

3. **Repeat Step 2.**

4. **Double crochet stitch in each of the next 6 stitches, chain 2, and skip the next 2 stitches.**

5. **Repeat Step 2 twice.**

6. **Double crochet stitch in each of the last 4 double crochet stitches.**

In more complicated patterns, you may see two sets of symbols, such as single bullets (•) and double bullets (••), to designate two different repeats in the same row or round. For example:

> • Dc in dc, ch 2, skip next 2 sts •, rep from • to • 3 times, •• dc in next dc, 2 dc in next space ••, rep from •• to •• 3 times.

In plain English, this means that you want to

1. **Double crochet stitch in the double crochet stitch, chain 2, and then skip the next 2 stitches.**

2. **Repeat Step 1 three times.**

3. **Double crochet stitch in the next double crochet stitch and then work 2 double crochet stitches in the following space.**

4. **Repeat Step 3 three times.**

Or, you may find the single bullet phrase within the double bullet phrase, denoting a repeated phrase within the larger repeat. For example:

•• 5 dc in loop, ch 2, skip next 2 dc, • dc in next dc, ch 2, skip next 2 dc •, rep from • to • 5 times ••, rep from •• to •• 3 times.

In this case, you work the •• to •• phrase a total of 4 times to go around the entire piece, but within that phrase is another • to • phrase that you work a total of 6 times within each •• to •• repeat.

In plain English:

1. **Work 5 double crochet stitches in the loop, chain 2, and then skip the next 2 double crochet stitches.**

2. **Work 1 double crochet stitch in the next double crochet stitch, chain 2, and then skip the next 2 double crochet stitches.**

3. **Repeat Step 2 five times, which brings you to the next loop.**

4. **Repeat Steps 1 through 3 three times.**

Repeating rows and rounds

Sometimes a pattern includes several identical rows or rounds. To save space, the instructions may group these rows together and only write out the directions once, as follows:

Rows 2–7: Ch 1, sc in each sc across, *turn*.

This means that you chain 1, single crochet stitch into each single crochet stitch across the row, and then turn to complete one row. However, you work this row of single crochet consecutively for Rows 2 through 7 (a total of 6 rows).

If you're to repeat two (or more) different rows in the same order, you'll see the first 2 rows written out and then the subsequent rows written as a repeat, as follows:

Row 2: Ch 1, sc in each st across, *turn*.

Row 3: Ch 3 (turning ch for dc), dc in each sc across, *turn*.

Rows 4–9: Rep Rows 2–3 (3 times).

This means that for Row 2, you chain 1, single crochet in each stitch across the row, and then turn your work. For Row 3, you chain 3, double crochet in each single crochet stitch across the row, and turn. Then you go back and work Row 2 again and then Row 3, repeating Row 2 and Row 3 consecutively until you've worked them a total of 4 times each.

Not Just a Pretty Picture: Symbols and Diagrams

Some pattern books and crochet magazines give you a pictorial description of the pattern design — and may or may not have written directions alongside. These *stitch diagrams* are like a road map of the pattern, laying out each individual stitch in relation to the others so that you get the forest and the trees at once. The advantages of stitch diagrams are numerous:

- ✔ You can see the number and placement of the stitches at a glance.

- ✔ You can see what the design should look like so that, if your creation doesn't resemble the diagram, you can easily identify your mistake.

- ✔ You can highlight or outline the repeated pattern in each row or round to make it easy to follow.

- ✔ You can mark where you leave off when you put your work down, so you know where to begin the next time you crochet.

The beauty of these diagrams is that anyone can read them, regardless of what language she speaks. That's why the individual stitch symbols that make up the diagrams are called *International Crochet Symbols.* (See the following section.) So, if you come across a terrific pattern in a Japanese book, you can make it from the diagram. Although these symbols and diagrams may look like hieroglyphics to you now, you'll be reading them like a breeze in no time.

Deciphering International Crochet Symbols

Although they're called International Crochet Symbols, the symbols for crochet stitches aren't universally accepted yet. You may find slight variations in different publications. Nonetheless, we compiled a list of standard symbols that we use consistently throughout this book. Figure 5-1 lists the symbols for the most common crochet stitches. We include the symbols for more advanced stitches in their respective chapters, and you can check out the whole shebang on the Cheat Sheet at the front of the book.

Each symbol roughly resembles the shape and proportions of the stitch that it represents. The number of tick marks drawn diagonally across the middle of the symbols indicates the number of times that you yarn over at the beginning of the stitch. For example, the double crochet has 1 tick mark (yarn over once), the triple crochet has 2 tick marks (yarn over twice), and so on.

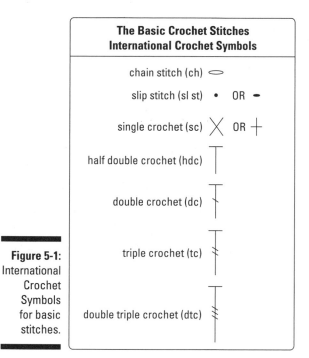

The Basic Crochet Stitches
International Crochet Symbols

chain stitch (ch)

slip stitch (sl st)   OR

single crochet (sc)   OR

half double crochet (hdc)

double crochet (dc)

triple crochet (tc)

double triple crochet (dtc)

Figure 5-1:
International
Crochet
Symbols
for basic
stitches.

Following a stitch diagram

The previous section introduces you to the individual stitch symbols and what they look like. In this section, we combine them all to make a stitch diagram like you'd see in a pattern, and then we deconstruct the diagram for you in plain English. But first, here's a quick rundown of stitch diagram basics:

- ✔ Each row or round in a diagram is numbered so that you know where to begin — Row 1.

  On a pattern done in rounds, the numeral in the center of the beginning ring indicates the number of chain stitches in the center ring.

- ✔ Because most crochet instructions are repetitive and most publications have limited space, a diagram may only show a repeated set of stitches a few times. But those few repeats are all you need to crochet the entire piece.

- ✔ When working in rows, the right side row number is placed on the right-hand side of the diagram, which means you work from the right side to the left side. On wrong side rows, the number is on the left-hand side, so you follow the diagram from left to right.

When working in rounds, you read the diagram counterclockwise, without turning between rows unless the instructions specifically instruct you to do so.

✔ Stitch diagrams are generally laid out from the right-handed crocheter's point of view, but a left-handed crocheter can read them just as well if he or she reverses the direction of the pattern, and works from left to right instead of right to left. To work in rounds, a lefty still follows the pattern counterclockwise, but works the piece clockwise, thus reversing the direction of the pattern.

✔ Because crochet is somewhat three-dimensional, the two-dimensional diagram has some limitations. So if a pattern also has written instructions, you want to check those out as well.

Now try your hand at reading an actual stitch diagram: The one in Figure 5-2 is for a lacy pattern that you work in rows. (To try out a stitch diagram for a design in rounds, see Chapter 8.) Notice that it doesn't look complete. Because this pattern is worked in identical rows consisting of repeated sets of stitches (the 8-stitch repeat in each row is shaded), the diagram shows only a few rows to save space. The pattern will tell you how many rows to make to get the exact result the pattern shows. If you want to go your own way and make a piece wider, narrower, longer, or shorter than the pattern specifies — for example, a runner that's 12 inches wide or a tablecloth that's 52 inches wide — just add more sets of repeats to each row and add more rows.

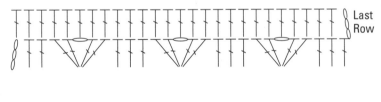

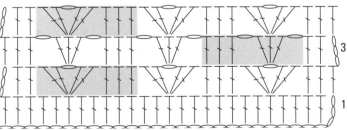

Figure 5-2: Stitch diagram of a repeated lacy row pattern.

To begin this design, you make a foundation chain (represented by the row of oval chain stitch symbols at the bottom of Figure 5-2) that's about the width you want, making sure it's a multiple of 8 stitches (to allow for the repeat), and then chain 2 more for the end of the row plus 3 more for the turning chain for the first double crochet of Row 1. For example, you could start with 21 chain stitches (2 x 8 + 2 + 3 = 21) or 85 chain stitches (10 x 8 + 2 + 3 = 85). The following steps take you from Row 1 to the last row, explaining each row in plain English and then giving the written intructions in crochetese so you can see how they correspond to the visual diagrams; Figure 5-3 shows you what it should look like when you're finished:

1. **Row 1: Dc in 4th ch from hook, dc in each ch across, *turn*.**

   This means to double crochet stitch in the fourth chain from the hook, double crochet in each chain going across, and then turn.

2. **Row 2: Ch 3 (turning ch for first dc), dc in each of next 2 dc, • skip next 2 dc (2 dc, ch 1, 2 dc) in next dc, skip next 2 dc, dc in each of next 3 dc •, rep from • to • across, ending with last dc of last rep in top of turning ch, *turn*.**

   For Row 2, chain 3 to make the turning chain for the first double crochet stitch and double crochet in each of the next 2 double crochet stitches. For the repeated part of this row (the instructions that are shown between the bullets), skip the next 2 double crochet stitches, work 2 double crochet stitches in the next double crochet, chain 1, work 2 more double crochet stitches in the same double crochet, skip the next 2 double crochet stitches, and then work 1 double crochet in each of the next 3 double crochet stitches. Repeat this section until you reach the end of the row, ending with a double crochet in the top of the previous row's turning chain. Turn your work.

3. **Row 3: Ch 3 (turning ch for first dc), dc in each of next 2 dc, • ch 1, skip next 2 dc, 3 dc in next ch-1 space, ch 1, skip next 2 dc, dc in each of next 3 dc •, rep from • to • across, ending with last dc of last rep in top of turning ch, *turn*.**

   To complete Row 3, chain 3 for your turning chain and then work 1 double crochet stitch in each of the next 2 double crochet stitches. For the repeated part of this row (the instructions that are shown between the bullets), chain 1, skip the next 2 double crochet stitches, work 3 double crochet stitches in the next chain-1 space, chain 1, skip the next 2 double crochet stitches, and then work 1 double crochet stitch in each of the next 3 double crochet stitches. Repeat this section until you reach the end of the row, ending with a double crochet in the top of the previous row's turning chain. Turn your work.

4. **Row 4: Ch 3 (turning ch for first dc), dc in each of next 2 dc, • skip next 2 sts, (2 dc, ch 1, 2 dc) in next dc, skip next 2 sts, dc in each of next 3 dc •, rep from • to • across, ending with last dc of last rep in top of turning ch, *turn*.**

   To complete Row 4, chain 3 for your turning chain and then work 1 double crochet stitch in each of the next 2 double crochet stitches. For the repeated part of this row (the instructions that are shown between the bullets), skip the next chain-1 space and the next double crochet stitch, work 2 double crochet stitches, chain 1, work 2 more double crochet stitches into the next double crochet stitch, skip the next double crochet stitch and the next chain-1 space, and then work 1 double crochet stitch into each of the next 3 double crochet stitches. Repeat this section until you reach the end of the row, ending with a double crochet in the top of the previous row's turning chain. Turn your work.

5. **Rep Rows 3–4 for desired length.**

   Repeat Row 3, then repeat Row 4, alternating these two rows until your piece is as long as you want it to be.

6. **Last Row: Ch 3 (turning ch for first dc), dc in each st and space across, ending with dc in top of turning ch. Fasten off.**

   Begin the last row from the right side, chain 3 for your turning chain and chain-1 space across the entire row. You should have the same number of double crochet stitches in this row as you have in Row 1. Fasten off your work.

Figure 5-3:
Swatch of lacy row pattern.

Chapter 6

Long, Longer, Longest: Four Common Crochet Stitches

In This Chapter

▶ Creating four of the most common stitches

▶ Joining a new ball of yarn

▶ Crocheting your first scarf

*T*he beauty of crocheting is that you can create so many patterns and textures by combining just three basic motions:

✔ Yarning over the hook

✔ Inserting your hook

✔ Drawing your yarn through

The first three stitches in this chapter, the double crochet, the triple crochet, and the double triple, are each made a step taller than the one before by yarning over an extra time. How simple is that? The fourth stitch, the half double crochet, is slightly different but makes sense after you master the other stitches in this chapter. Each of these stitches produces a slightly different textured fabric. And when you combine the stitches, the variety of possible patterns is endless. Of course, now that you're making so many stitches, you're going to run out of yarn, so this chapter shows you how to join a new skein without any unsightly lumps, bumps, or knots.

The sassy scarf project at the end of this chapter is not only an opportunity to practice each of the stitches this chapter features, but it's also a beautiful design that you'll be proud to show off.

Doing a Double Crochet

The *double crochet* (abbreviated *dc*) is one of the most common crochet stitches and is about twice as tall as a single crochet, which debuts in Chapter 4. A fabric made of all double crochet stitches is fairly solid but not stiff and is great for sweaters, shawls, Afghans, placemats, or any number of other home decor items. You can also combine the double crochet stitch with other stitches to produce many interesting patterns and textures.

First things first: Row 1

The following steps set you up to work your first double crochet stitch (see Chapter 4 for a refresher on foundation chains and turning chains):

1. **Make a foundation chain by doing 15 chain stitches (ch 15).**

2. **Chain 3 more stitches for the turning chain.**

Now for your first double crochet stitch:

1. **Yarn over the hook (yo).**

   Remember to yarn over from back to front.

2. **Insert your hook between the 2 front loops and under the back bump loop of the fourth chain from the hook. (See Figure 6-1a.)**

   Refer to Chapter 4 for details on working into the chain stitches.

Figure 6-1:
Beginning
a double
crochet
stitch.

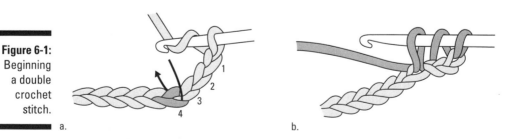

a.   b.

3. **Yarn over the hook.**

4. **Gently pull the wrapped hook through the center of the chain stitch, carrying the wrapped yarn through the stitch.**

   Now, you should have 3 loops on your hook. Refer to Figure 6-1b.

5. **Yarn over the hook.**

6. **Draw your yarn through the first 2 loops on your hook. (See Figure 6-2a.)**

Figure 6-2:
Drawing your yarn through the loops.

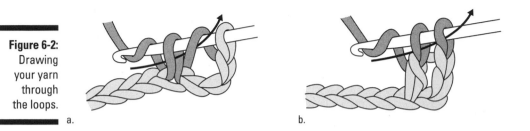

a.
b.

7. **Yarn over the hook.**

8. **Draw your yarn through the last 2 loops on the hook. (Refer to Figure 6-2b.)**

   One double crochet (dc) stitch is complete. You should have one loop remaining on your hook.

To finish your first row of double crochet, work 1 double crochet stitch in each successive chain stitch across the foundation chain, beginning in the next chain of the foundation chain as Figure 6-3a shows. You should have 16 double crochet stitches in Row 1 (counting the turning chain as the first double crochet).

Figure 6-3:
Finishing the first row of double crochet.

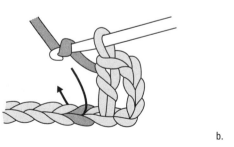
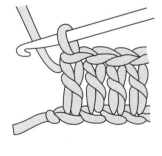

a.
b.

Take a look at Figure 6-3b to see what the end of the first row of double crochet looks like.

Turn around and begin again: Row 2

To work the second row of double crochet, follow these steps:

1. **Turn your work so that the back side is facing you.**

2. **Chain 3 (ch 3; for the turning chain).**

3. **Yarn over the hook (yo).**

4. **Skipping the first stitch of the row directly below the turning chain, insert your hook in the next stitch. See Figure 6-4a.**

   Figure 6-4b shows you the wrong place to insert your hook.

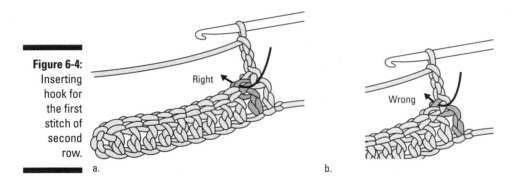

Figure 6-4: Inserting hook for the first stitch of second row.

a.   b.

5. **Repeat Steps 3 through 8 from the previous section in each of the next 14 double crochet (dc) stitches. Be sure to yarn over before inserting your hook in each stitch.**

6. **Work 1 double crochet in the top chain of the previous row's turning chain. See Figure 6-5.**

   You should have 16 double crochet stitches in Row 2 (counting the turning chain as 1 double crochet).

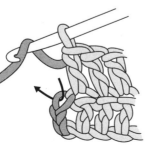

Figure 6-5: Insert the hook in the top chain of the turning chain.

Repeat these steps for each additional row of double crochet. Continue until you feel comfortable working this stitch. Figure 6-6 shows you how rows of double crochet look as a fabric.

Figure 6-6:
Several rows of double crochet.

Don't work a stitch into the first stitch of the row after the turning chain. Doing so produces an extra stitch, and if you continue to add a stitch in each row, your design gets wider and wider as it gets longer and longer. Be sure to count your stitches frequently to make sure that you haven't inadvertently gained (or lost) any stitches along the way.

Sometimes, especially when you're working with bulky yarn or a larger than usual hook, the turning chain on a double crochet row leaves a gap at the beginning of the row. To get a neater edge, try chaining 2 instead of 3 stitches for the turning chain.

Trying a Triple Crochet

The *triple crochet* (tr), also called a *treble crochet* in many publications, is slightly longer than the double crochet. These stitches create longer openings between the stitches and therefore produce a very loose fabric. For example, if you make a sweater with triple crochet, you'll want to wear a blouse under it or you risk revealing too much. However, the triple crochet is usually combined with other stitches for pattern variety and for producing interesting textures and fancier stitches.

First things first: Row 1

The following steps set you up to start working triple crochet (check out Chapter 4 to refresh your memory on chains):

1. **Make a foundation chain by doing 15 chain stitches (ch 15).**

2. **Chain 4 more stitches for the turning chain.**

To begin your first triple crochet stitch, follow these steps:

1. **Yarn over the hook (yo) 2 times.**

2. **Insert your hook in the fifth chain from the hook. (See Figure 6-7a.)**

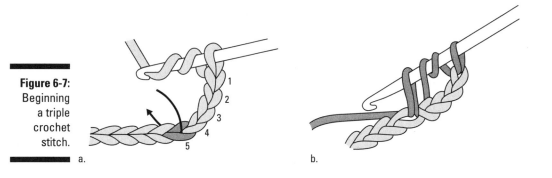

Figure 6-7: Beginning a triple crochet stitch.

a.   b.

3. **Yarn over the hook.**

4. **Gently pull the wrapped hook through the center of the chain stitch, carrying the wrapped yarn through the stitch.**

   You should have 4 loops on your hook. See Figure 6-7b.

5. **Yarn over the hook.**

6. **Draw your yarn through the first 2 loops on your hook. (See Figure 6-8a.)**

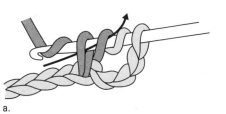

Figure 6-8: Drawing the yarn through the loops on your hook.

a.   b.

7. **Yarn over the hook.**

8. **Draw your yarn through the next 2 loops on your hook. (Refer to Figure 6-8b.)**

9. **Yarn over the hook.**

10. **Draw your yarn through the last 2 loops on your hook. (See Figure 6-9a.)**

    One triple crochet (tr) stitch is complete (see Figure 6-9b). You should have one loop remaining on your hook.

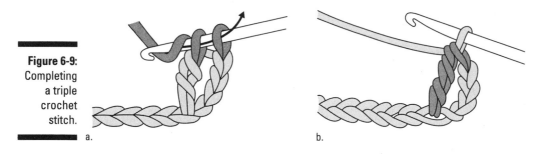

Figure 6-9:
Completing a triple crochet stitch.

a.   b.

To finish the row, yarn over twice and insert your hook in the next chain of the foundation chain, as Figure 6-10a shows. Work one triple crochet in each successive chain across the foundation chain. You should have 16 triple crochet stitches in Row 1 (counting the turning chain as 1 triple crochet). Figure 6-10b shows the end of the first triple crochet row.

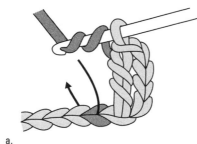 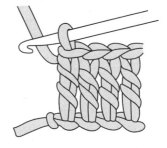

Figure 6-10:
Finishing the first row of triple crochet.

a.   b.

Turn around and begin again: Row 2

To begin your second row of triple crochet, follow these steps:

1. **Turn your work.**

2. **Chain 4 (ch 4) for the turning chain.**

3. **Yarn over your hook (yo) 2 times.**

4. **Skipping the first stitch of the row directly below the turning chain, insert your hook in the next stitch. (See Figure 6-11.)**

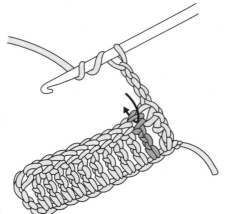

Figure 6-11:
Insert your
hook in the
second
stitch.

5. **Repeat Steps 3 through 10 from the previous section in each of the next 14 triple crochet (tr) stitches. Be sure to yarn over twice before inserting your hook in each stitch.**

6. **Work 1 triple crochet in the top chain of the previous row's turning chain.**

   You should have 16 triple crochet stitches in Row 2 (counting the turning chain as 1 triple crochet).

Repeat these six steps for each additional row of triple crochet. Continue working rows of triple crochet until you feel comfortable working this stitch. To see how rows of triple crochet look as a fabric, see Figure 6-12.

Figure 6-12: Several rows of triple crochet.

Diving into Double Triple Crochet

The *double triple crochet* (abbreviated *dtr*) is even taller than a triple crochet. As a fabric, it's loose and holey and commonly used in lacy designs, particularly doilies and other fine cotton crochet patterns.

First things first: Row 1

Before you begin a double triple crochet stitch:

1. **Make a foundation chain by doing 15 chain stitches (ch 15).**

2. **Chain 5 more stitches for the turning chain.**

   Check out Chapter 4 for the lowdown on chains.

To complete your first double triple crochet stitch:

1. **Yarn over the hook (yo) 3 times.**

2. **Insert the hook in the sixth chain from the hook. (See Figure 6-13.)**

3. **Yarn over the hook.**

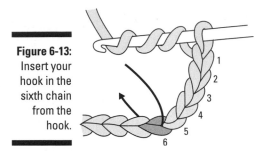

Figure 6-13:
Insert your hook in the sixth chain from the hook.

4. **Gently pull the wrapped hook through the center of the chain stitch, carrying the wrapped yarn through the stitch.**

   You should now have 5 loops on your hook.

5. **Yarn over the hook.**

6. **Draw your yarn through the first 2 loops on your hook (4 loops remain).**

7. **Repeat Steps 5 and 6 three more times until you have only 1 loop left on the hook.**

   One double triple crochet (dtr) stitch is complete.

To finish the row, begin a new double triple crochet stitch in the next chain of your foundation chain as indicated in Figure 6-14a. Work 1 double triple crochet stitch in each successive chain across the foundation chain. Make sure that you yarn over 3 times before inserting the hook in each chain. When you finish the row, you should have 16 double triple crochet stitches in Row 1 (counting the turning chain as 1 double triple crochet). Figure 6-14b shows the end of your first row of double triple crochet.

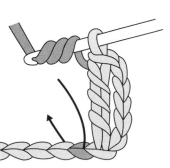

Figure 6-14:
Finishing the first row of double triple crochet.

a.

b.

Turn around and begin again: Row 2

To begin the second row of double triple crochet:

1. **Turn your work.**

2. **Chain 5 (ch 5) for the turning chain.**

3. **Yarn over the hook (yo) 3 times.**

4. **Skipping the first stitch of the row directly below the turning chain, insert your hook in the next stitch.**

5. **Repeat Steps 3 through 7 in the previous section in each of the next 14 double triple crochet (dtr) stitches. Be sure to yarn over 3 times before inserting your hook in each stitch.**

6. **Work 1 double triple crochet stitch in the top chain of the previous row's turning chain.**

   You should have 16 double triple crochet stitches in Row 2 (counting the turning chain as 1 double triple crochet).

Repeat these six steps for each additional row of double triple crochet. Continue working rows of this stitch until you feel comfortable with it. To see how rows of double triple crochet look as a fabric, see Figure 6-15.

Figure 6-15: Several rows of double triple crochet.

Making your stitches even longer

Each additional yarn over that you make at the beginning of a stitch adds length to the completed stitch. If you continue to add yarn overs, you produce longer and longer stitches. The longer stitches are used infrequently, but they do exist. This list gives you an idea:

- **Single crochet (sc):** No yarn over
- **Double crochet (dc):** Yarn over 1 time
- **Triple crochet (tr):** Yarn over 2 times
- **Double triple crochet (dtr):** Yarn over 3 times
- **Triple triple crochet (trtr):** Yarn over 4 times
- **Double triple triple (dtrtr):** Yarn over 5 times
- **Quadruple triple triple (quad):** Yarn over 6 times

The names may vary in different publications, but the theory remains the same. Theoretically, you can continue to make longer and longer stitches indefinitely, as long as your hook can hold all the loops.

Hooking a Half Double Crochet

The *half double crochet* (abbreviated *hdc*) is kind of an oddball stitch, and you make it differently from all the other stitches that you've seen so far. It falls in between a single crochet and a double crochet in height, but instead of working off two loops at a time, you draw the yarn through three loops on the hook. It produces a fairly tight fabric similar to one made with a single crochet stitch.

First things first: Row 1

Follow these steps to get started:

1. **Make a foundation chain with 15 chain stitches (ch 15).**
2. **Chain 2 more for the turning chain.**

   Check out Chapter 4 for the lowdown on chains.

To create your first half double crochet stitch:

1. **Yarn over the hook (yo).**
2. **Insert your hook in the third chain from the hook. (See Figure 6-16a.)**
3. **Yarn over the hook.**
4. **Gently pull the wrapped hook through the center of the chain stitch, carrying the wrapped yarn through the stitch.**

   You should have 3 loops on your hook. (See Figure 6-16b.)

Figure 6-16: Beginning a half double crochet.

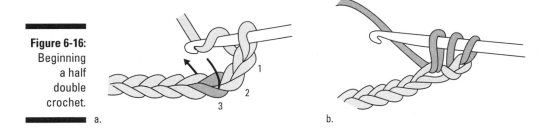

a.   b.

5. **Yarn over the hook.**

6. **Draw your yarn through all 3 loops on your hook. (See Figure 6-17a.)**

   Figure 6-17b shows a completed half double crochet (hdc).

Figure 6-17: Finishing a half double crochet.

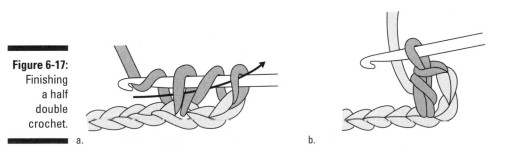

a.   b.

To complete a full row of half double crochet stitches, begin in the next chain of the foundation chain as Figure 6-18a indicates. Work 1 half double crochet stitch in each successive chain across the foundation chain. You have 16 half double crochet stitches at the end of Row 1 (counting the turning chain as 1 half double crochet stitch). Figure 6-18b shows what the end of your first row of half double crochet looks like.

Figure 6-18: Finishing the first row of half double crochet.

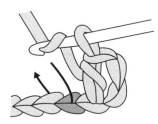

a.

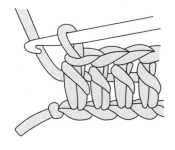

b.

Turn around and begin again: Row 2

To begin the second row of half double crochet:

1. **Turn your work.**

2. **Chain 2 (ch 2) for the turning chain.**

3. **Yarn over the hook (yo).**

4. **Skipping the first stitch of the row directly below the turning chain, insert your hook in the next stitch. (See Figure 6-19.)**

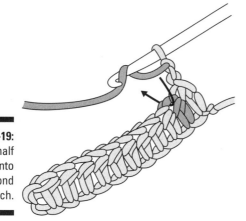

Figure 6-19: Work a half double into the second stitch.

5. **Repeat Steps 3 through 6 from the previous section in each of the next 14 half double crochet (hdc) stitches. Be sure to yarn over before inserting your hook in each stitch.**

6. **Work 1 half double crochet in the top chain of the previous row's turning chain.**

   You should have 16 half double crochet stitches in Row 2 (counting the turning chain as 1 half double crochet).

Repeat Steps 1 through 6 in the preceding list for each additional row of half double crochet. Continue working rows of half double crochet until you feel comfortable working this stitch. To see how rows of half double crochet look as a fabric, see Figure 6-20.

Stitch width: Mum's the word

Notice that crochet stitches vary in length or height, but no mention is made of varying stitch width. That's because all stitches are the same width when worked properly with the same yarn and hook. Whether you're making a row of 16 chain stitches or a row of 16 triple crochets, the width of your piece should be the same, even when you're working fancy three-dimensional stitches. After you complete the stitch and have one loop remaining on your hook, the top of the stitch is still the same width as all the other stitches. That's because the size of the hook you're using determines the size of that last loop as well as the width of the stitch.

Figure 6-20: Several rows of half double crochet.

Running on Empty: Joining a New Ball of Yarn

Each ball has a limited amount of yarn on it, so sooner or later you're going to run out of yarn in the middle of a project. You can join a new ball of yarn in any stitch of the row, but making the transition at the end of the row creates a neater appearance.

Don't give in to the temptation to just tie the beginning end of the new ball to the tail end of the first ball. This sloppy method produces an unsightly knot in your work.

Joining a new ball or skein of yarn correctly is as important to the appearance of your work as the actual stitches. You may find it awkward at first, but you'll be an old hand in no time. The following steps use a swatch of fabric made with double crochet stitches, so if you haven't already made a swatch, refer to the "Doing a Double Crochet" section, earlier in this chapter, to get ready. After you've got a few rows completed, follow these steps.

1. **Double crochet (dc) across the row, stopping before the last stitch of the row.**

2. **Work the last double crochet to the point where only 2 loops are left on the hook.**

3. **Wrap the cut end of the new yarn around the hook, from back to front.**

    The *working end* (the one that's attached to the ball or skein) should be the end closest to you.

4. **Draw the new yarn through the 2 loops on your hook. (See Figure 6-21.)**

    You have 2 strands of yarn hanging down.

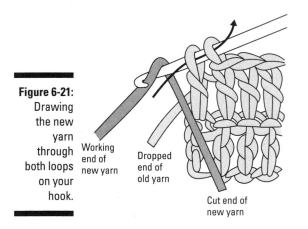

Figure 6-21: Drawing the new yarn through both loops on your hook.

Working end of new yarn

Dropped end of old yarn

Cut end of new yarn

5. **Tug on the dropped end of the old yarn at the base of the double crochet to tighten up the stitch.**

6. **Remove the loop from your hook.**

7. **Insert your hook into the top of the last double crochet down through the center of the stitch. (See Figure 6-22.)**

8. **Yarn over (yo), using the end of the old yarn at the bottom of the stitch.**

9. **Draw the tail end up through the stitch.**

10. **Stick your hook back through the loop and begin your next row.**

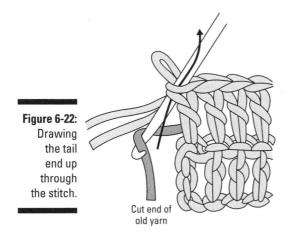

Figure 6-22:
Drawing
the tail
end up
through
the stitch.

Cut end of
old yarn

Sometimes you need to join a new ball of yarn in a different place from where you left off, such as when you shape necklines or armholes in a garment. To join a new ball in a different place, work as follows:

1. **Make a slipknot on the end of the new ball of yarn.**

   See Chapter 4 for details on making a slipknot.

2. **Insert your hook in the stitch designated for the new yarn to be joined in.**

3. **Place the slipknot in the new yarn on the hook.**

4. **Draw the slipknot through the stitch. (See Figure 6-23.)**

   One loop is on your hook, and you're ready to begin crocheting the new row.

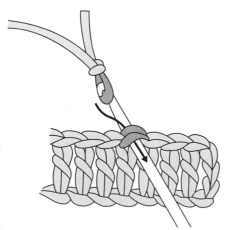

Figure 6-23:
Joining
yarn with
a slipknot.

You can weave the ends of the yarn in later with a yarn needle, but we recommend working over the strands while crocheting the next row because it saves time. To work over the strands, lay them down over the tops of the stitches in the current row; then when you work your stitches, the strands are captured in the bases of your stitches. Cut off any excess yarn after you've covered a few inches.

Weaving in yarn ends is a tedious and thankless job — and one you should avoid whenever you can. Some projects allow you to leave ends dangling off the side to be incorporated into fringe. You can also leave ends dangling on the side if they can be sewn into a seam later on. If you'll be working a border over the side of your piece, the border stitches will cover your ends as well. (For more information about borders, see Chapter 16.) But be sure you don't try to cover too many strands in one area or you create a messy lump along the edge.

Sassy Scarf Project

A scarf is a quick, easy, and versatile project that showcases your new skills. The pattern in this section incorporates all the stitches introduced so far and gives you the opportunity to practice each of them while creating a great fashion accessory.

You work the scarf lengthwise, progressing from rows of short stitches to rows of long and longer stitches, and then work back down again. Don't be intimidated by the number of stitches you need in each row. If you can count, you're good to go. Counting stitches, whether as you go or when you reach the end of a row, is as much a part of crocheting as the stitches themselves.

The instructions are written in crochet pattern lingo with plain English following each step. Figure 6-24 shows a reduced sample of the scarf pattern as a stitch diagram to give you the opportunity to try out reading diagrams. Flip back to Chapter 5 to refresh your memory on abbreviations and symbols or rip out the Cheat Sheet and keep it handy.

Feel free to let your creative impulses run wild. We give you the list of materials you need to make this scarf as it's shown in the color section of this book, but you can choose your own color or color combination using any worsted-weight yarn. Or you can add rows to make it wider.

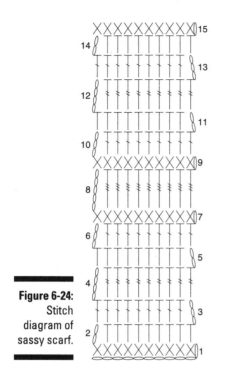

Figure 6-24:
Stitch
diagram of
sassy scarf.

Materials

For the lowdown on how to read the materials list and determine the type of yarn and hook to buy, refer to Chapter 2.

- ✔ **Yarn:** Berroco "Softwist" worsted-weight yarn (41% wool/59% rayon) (1.75 oz. [*50 gm*], 100 yds. each hank): 5 hanks of #9420 Nouveau Berry
- ✔ **Hook:** Crochet hook size H-8 U.S. or size needed to obtain gauge

Vital statistics

- ✔ **Size:** 8 x 68½ in.
- ✔ **Gauge:** 7 sts = 2 in.; 4 rows in pat = 2 in. (for information on gauge, flip to Chapter 3)
- ✔ **Stitches used:** Chain stitch (ch), single crochet (sc), half double crochet (hdc), double crochet (dc), triple crochet (tr), double triple crochet (dtr)

Directions

The following section gives you row-by-row instructions on how to crochet this scarf. To refresh your memory of the stitches, refer to the specific directions for each in this chapter and in Chapter 4.

1. **Foundation chain: Chain 241.**

   Create your foundation chain by working 241 chain stitches in a row.

2. **Row 1: Sc in second ch from hook, sc in each ch across (240 sc), *turn*.**

   To complete Row 1, work one single crochet stitch in the second chain from the hook, work 1 single crochet stitch in each chain stitch across the row, and then turn your work.

3. **Row 2: Ch 2 (counts as first hdc), hdc in each st across (240 hdc), *turn*.**

   To complete Row 2, chain 2 for your turning chain, skip the stitch directly below the turning chain, work 1 half double crochet stitch in each stitch across the row, and then turn your work.

4. **Row 3: Ch 3 (counts as first dc), dc in each st across (240 dc), *turn*.**

   To complete Row 3, chain 3 for your turning chain, skip the stitch directly below the turning chain, work 1 double crochet stitch in each stitch across the row, and then turn your work.

5. **Row 4: Ch 4 (counts as first tr), tr in each st across (240 tr), *turn*.**

   To complete Row 4, chain 4 for your turning chain, skip the stitch directly below the turning chain, work 1 triple crochet stitch in each stitch across the row, and then turn your work.

6. **Row 5: Ch 2 (counts as first hdc), hdc in each st across (240 hdc), *turn*.**

   To complete Row 5, chain 2 for your turning chain, skip the stitch directly below the turning chain, work 1 half double crochet stitch in each stitch across the row, and then turn your work.

7. **Row 6: Ch 3 (counts as first dc), dc in each st across (240 dc), *turn*.**

   To complete Row 6, chain 3 for your turning chain, skip the stitch directly below the turning chain, work 1 double crochet stitch in each stitch across the row, and then turn your work.

8. **Row 7: Ch 1, sc in each st across (240 sc), *turn*.**

   To complete Row 7, chain 1 for your turning chain, work 1 single crochet stitch in each stitch across the row, and then turn your work.

9. **Row 8: Ch 5 (counts as first dtr), dtr in each st across (240 dtr), *turn*.**

   To complete Row 8, chain 5 for your turning chain, skip the stitch directly below the turning chain, work 1 double triple crochet stitch in each stitch across the row, and then turn your work.

10. **Row 9: Ch 1, sc in each st across (240 sc), *turn*.**

    To complete Row 9, chain 1 for your turning chain, work 1 single crochet stitch in each stitch across the row, and then turn your work.

11. **Row 10: Ch 3 (counts as first dc), dc in each st across (240 dc), *turn*.**

    To complete Row 10, chain 3 for your turning chain, skip the stitch directly below the turning chain, work 1 double crochet stitch in each stitch across the row, and then turn your work.

12. **Row 11: Ch 2 (counts as first hdc), hdc in each st across (240 hdc), *turn*.**

    To complete Row 11, chain 2 for your turning chain, skip the stitch directly below the turning chain, work 1 half double crochet stitch in each stitch across the row, and then turn your work.

13. **Row 12: Ch 4 (counts as first tr), tr in each st across (240 tr), *turn*.**

    To complete Row 12, chain 4 for your turning chain, skip the stitch directly below the turning chain, work 1 triple crochet stitch in each stitch across the row, and then turn your work.

14. **Row 13: Ch 3 (counts as first dc), dc in each st across (240 dc), *turn*.**

    To complete Row 13, chain 3 for your turning chain, skip the stitch directly below the turning chain, work 1 double crochet stitch in each stitch across the row, and then turn your work.

15. **Row 14: Ch 2 (counts as first hdc), hdc in each st across (240 hdc), *turn*.**

    To complete Row 14, chain 2 for your turning chain, skip the stitch directly below the turning chain, work 1 half double crochet stitch in each stitch across the row, and then turn your work.

16. **Row 15: Ch 1, sc in each st across (240 sc). Fasten off.**

    To complete Row 15, chain 1 for your turning chain and then work 1 single crochet stitch in each stitch across the row. Fasten off your yarn.

Adding the fringe

After you finish the body of the scarf, it's time to add the finishing details. To add the fringe to your scarf, cut your yarn into 12-inch lengths. Using 2 lengths of yarn for each fringe, single knot one fringe in each stitch across each short edge of the scarf. For more about fringes, see Chapter 17.

Chapter 7

Shaping Up and Slimming Down: Increasing and Decreasing Stitches

C rocheting would be pretty boring if all you could make were squares and rectangles. Sure, you could make armloads of scarves or Afghans, but you probably want to branch out and create some shape. In this chapter, we show you how to widen and narrow your designs by simply adding or taking away a few stitches.

Note: This chapter shows you how to increase and decrease with single crochet or double crochet stitches, but you work increases and decreases with other stitches exactly the same way. Most patterns explain how to work the increases and decreases necessary for that particular design, so be sure to read all the pattern instructions before beginning.

When increasing or decreasing your stitches, always count your stitches to make sure that you have the correct number on your work.

Making It Grow: Increasing Stitches

Increasing stitches (abbreviated *inc*) is just what it sounds like. You add stitches to a row so that it has more stitches than the previous one. Depending on the type of design that you're making, you can increase stitches anywhere in the row: at the beginning, end, or middle; in every other stitch; or anyplace where you want the shaping to occur. If you're working from a pattern, it'll always tell you exactly where to place your extra stitches, so no guesswork is needed. Regardless of where the increase occurs, you always make it by working two or more stitches into one stitch.

If you're working in rounds, increasing usually occurs in each successive round to accommodate the larger circumference of the design. See Chapter 8 for more on working in rounds.

Increasing double crochet at the beginning

Adding a stitch at the beginning or end of a row is the most common way to increase stitches while working in rows. This method creates a smooth, tapered edge to your piece. To add 1 double crochet stitch at the beginning of a row, make a swatch of double crochet stitches and follow these steps:

1. **Chain 3 (ch 3).**

   This is the same number of chains required for a double crochet turning chain.

2. **Work your next stitch into the first stitch of the row.**

   This is the stitch directly below the turning chain, the one that you usually skip — see Figure 7-1a. Check out the completed stitch in Figure 7-1b and its symbol (Figure 7-1c) as you'd see it in pictorial crochet diagrams.

3. **Finish the rest of the row as you normally do, working 1 double crochet stitch in each stitch across the row.**

Increasing double crochet in the middle or end

You work an increase in the middle or at the end of a row the same way. Follow these steps:

1. **Work across your row until you get to the designated increase stitch or the last stitch of the row.**

2. **Work 2 stitches into the designated stitch. (See Figure 7-2a.)**

   Figure 7-2b shows a completed increase in the middle of a row and Figure 7-2c gives its symbol as you'd see it in pictorial crochet diagrams.

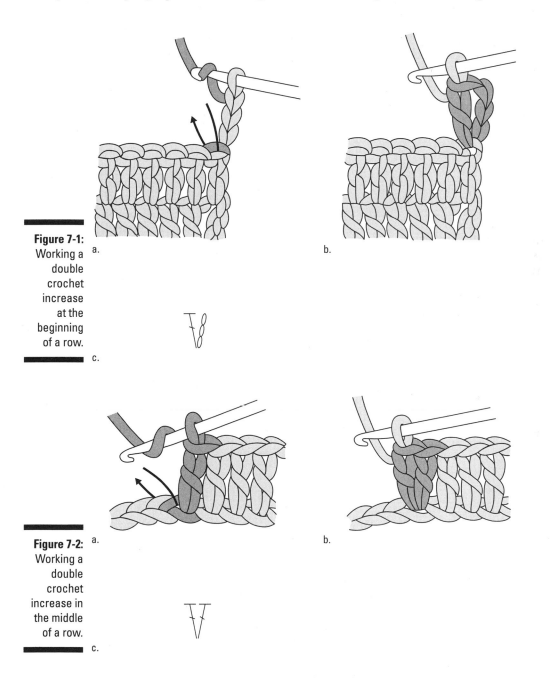

Figure 7-1:
Working a
double
crochet
increase
at the
beginning
of a row.

a.

b.

c.

Figure 7-2:
Working a
double
crochet
increase in
the middle
of a row.

a.

b.

c.

Increasing with single crochet

Because the turning chain in a single crochet row doesn't count as a stitch, increasing one single crochet at the beginning of the row is the same as doing it in the middle or at the end of a row. Wherever you want to increase 1 single crochet, just work 2 single crochet stitches in the designated stitch, as Figure 7-3a shows. Figure 7-3b shows a completed single crochet increase and Figure 7-3c shows the stitch symbol you'd see in a diagram.

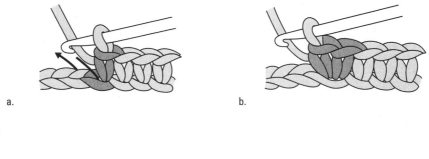

a.   b.

Figure 7-3:
Increasing
with single
crochet.

c.

Diminishing Results: Decreasing Stitches

Sometimes, you want to shape your design so that it gets smaller. You can *decrease* a stitch (abbreviated *dec*), which is really just subtracting a stitch, in the same places that you increase stitches — at the ends of the row or somewhere in the middle. Decreasing takes a few more steps, but it's just as simple as increasing.

Decreasing with double crochet

You decrease stitches in the middle or end of a row by turning 2 separate stitches into 1, which is a two-step process. But because of these two steps, you have to think ahead and start the first part 1 stitch before the actual decrease is designated in your pattern. Begin the first part of the decrease by starting the first double crochet as you would for a normal double crochet stitch:

1. **Yarn over the hook (yo).**

2. **Insert your hook into the next stitch.**

3. **Yarn over.**

4. **Draw the yarn through the stitch.**

5. **Yarn over.**

6. **Draw the yarn through the first 2 loops on your hook.**

   Two loops remain on the hook, as Figure 7-4 shows.

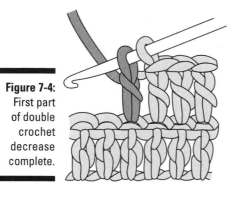

Figure 7-4:
First part
of double
crochet
decrease
complete.

In the second part of the decrease, you work the second double crochet stitch and join it with the first to complete the decrease. With the 2 loops still on your hook (at this point, the first stitch is a *half-closed stitch*), start to work the second double crochet stitch as you would a regular stitch:

1. **Yarn over the hook (yo).**

2. **Insert your hook into the next stitch. (See Figure 7-5.)**

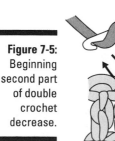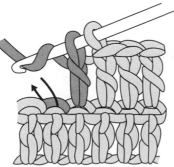

Figure 7-5:
Beginning
second part
of double
crochet
decrease.

3. **Yarn over.**

4. **Draw the yarn through the stitch.**

5. **Yarn over.**

6. **Draw the yarn through the first 2 loops on your hook.**

   You should have 3 loops remaining on your hook.

7. **Yarn over.**

8. **Draw the yarn through all 3 loops on your hook. (See Figure 7-6a.)**

   If you look at the tops of the stitches in Figure 7-6b, you see only 1 stitch across the top of the two underlying stitches. This is 1 complete double crochet stitch decrease.

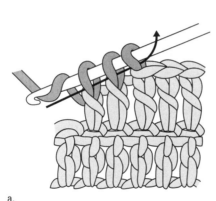 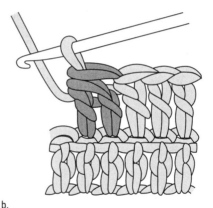

a.   b.

Figure 7-6:
Finishing
a double
crochet
decrease.

c.

 If you want to decrease at the very beginning of a row and you're working with a stitch that requires a turning chain (which is a double crochet and anything taller), you work the decrease a little differently than one in the middle or at the end of a row. Make your turning chain 1 stitch shorter than you normally would (for example, chain 2 instead of 3 for a triple crochet), and then continue across the row as normal. When you work the next row, don't work a stitch in the shortened turning chain. This process takes care of the decrease and leaves a smooth edge.

Decreasing with single crochet

The single crochet decrease is similar to the double crochet decrease, only you have one less step. That's always good news.

To begin the two-part process of turning 2 single crochet stitches into 1, start the first single crochet as you normally would:

1. **Insert your hook into the next stitch.**

2. **Yarn over (yo).**

3. **Draw the yarn through the stitch.**

   You should have 2 loops remaining on your hook.

With the 2 loops still on your hook, begin the second part of the decrease by working the second single crochet:

1. **Insert your hook into the next stitch. (See Figure 7-7.)**

Figure 7-7:
Beginning
the second
part of
a single
crochet
decrease.

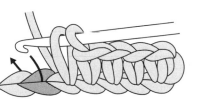

2. **Yarn over (yo).**

3. **Draw the yarn through the stitch.**

   You should have 3 loops on your hook.

4. **Yarn over.**

5. **Draw the yarn through all 3 loops on your hook. (See Figure 7-8a.)**

   Figure 7-8b shows one complete single crochet stitch decrease and Figure 7-8c shows its stitch symbol.

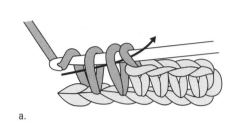
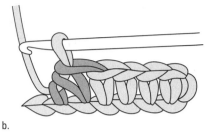

a.   b.

Figure 7-8:
Finishing
a single
crochet
decrease.

c.

Decreasing with slip stitches

Another method for decreasing at the beginning of the row is to slip stitch across the number of stitches that you want to decrease. When you reach the stitch designated to be the first stitch of the row (see Figure 7-9), you make the turning chain and work across the row as you normally would. You use this method when you need to decrease more than just one or two stitches, typically for shaping the armholes or neck edges in a garment. The resulting look is a squared-off corner. Check out Chapter 4 for more on the slip stitch.

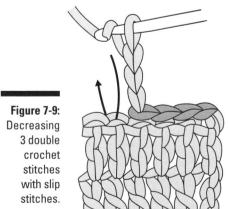

Figure 7-9:
Decreasing
3 double
crochet
stitches
with slip
stitches.

The simplest decrease: Stopping before you reach the end

An alternate method of decreasing stitches at the end of a row is to just stop before you get to the last stitch. This method gives you a rather squared off look and is quite often used when shaping garments. Pretty simple. Here's how:

1. **Work across the row until you have the number of stitches that your work requires.**

2. **Stop crocheting and turn your work, leaving the remaining stitches on the current row unworked.**

3. **Make your turning chain, and then work back across the previous row in the same manner as if you had crocheted all the way to the end.**

   Figure 7-10 shows this decrease after you've turned your work.

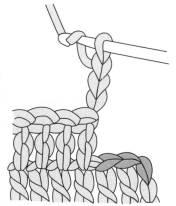

Figure 7-10: Decreasing double crochet by stopping and turning your work.

Simple Bandana Project

This fun, simple bandana pattern starts with a long chain of stitches and decreases 1 stitch at each end of every row until you have only 1 stitch left. You then crochet a couple of chains to attach to the corners for ties. Or if you're feeling a little more ambitious, you can work a simple edging around the outside, which includes the ties. The bandana shown in the color section has the edging. The yarn used to make this bandana is a multicolored ribbon yarn, which is easy to work with and comes in a variety of colors.

You can make the bandanas in this chapter with any colors you like and with any brand of yarn. Just remember to make sure that the yarn you buy is the same size and weight (see Chapter 2 for more on yarn substitution) and that you can come up with the right gauge. (Find out all about gauge in Chapter 3.)

Materials

- **Yarn:** Paton's "Fresco" worsted-weight ribbon yarn (100 percent acrylic), Article #242001 (1.75 oz. [*50 gm*], 81 yds. each skein): 1 skein of #01741 Oasis
- **Hook:** Crochet hook size I-9 U.S. or size needed to obtain gauge

Vital statistics

- **Size:** 13½ in. wide x 6½ in. deep, excluding ties and tassel
- **Gauge:** 7 sts and 8 rows sc = 2 in. (For info on gauge, see Chapter 3.)
- **Stitches used:** Chain stitch (ch), single crochet (sc), dec 1 sc • (insert hook in next st, yo, draw yarn through st) twice, yo, draw yarn through 3 loops on hook •

Directions

We give you the directions for the following project in two forms — as you'd see them in the real world of crochet, complete with abbreviations, as well as in plain-English format. Feel free to follow whichever set you're most comfortable with (check out Chapter 5 to brush up on the abbreviations). Your design will turn out super no matter which format you follow.

1. **Foundation chain: Chain 47 for the front edge of your bandana.**

   Create your foundation chain by working 47 chain stitches in a row. This is the front edge of your bandana.

2. **Row 1: Sc in second ch from hook, sc in each ch across (46 sc),** *turn.*

   To complete Row 1, work 1 single crochet in the second chain from the hook, continue to work 1 single crochet in each chain stitch across the row, and then turn your work. You'll have 46 single crochet stitches.

3. **Row 2: Ch 1, dec 1 sc in first 2 sc, sc in each sc across to within last 2 sc, dec 1 sc in last 2 sc (44 sc), *turn*.**

   To complete Row 2, chain 1 for your turning chain, and then decrease 1 single crochet stitch in the first 2 single crochet stitches. Work 1 single crochet stitch in each single crochet stitch across the row until you reach the last 2 single crochet stitches, decrease 1 single crochet stitch in the last 2 single crochet stitches, and then turn your work. You'll have 44 single crochet stitches.

4. **Rows 3–23: Ch 1, dec 1 sc in first 2 sc, sc in each sc across to within last 2 sc, dec 1 sc in last 2 sc (2 sc at end of last row), *turn*.**

   To complete Rows 3 through 23, chain 1 for your turning chain, and then decrease 1 single crochet stitch in the first 2 single crochet stitches. Work 1 single crochet stitch in each single crochet stitch across the row until you reach the last 2 single crochet stitches, decrease 1 single crochet stitch in the last 2 single crochet stitches, and then turn your work. Each row will decrease the number of stitches you have by 2. You'll have 2 single crochet stitches at the end of Row 23.

5. **Row 24: Ch 1, dec 1 sc in 2 sc (1 sc), do not turn. Fasten off.**

   To complete Row 24, chain 1 for your turning chain and then decrease 1 single crochet stitch in the remaining 2 single crochet stitches. You'll have 1 single crochet stitch left. Don't turn your work. Fasten off the yarn.

Note: If you're making the optional edging and ties, then don't fasten off your work as described in Step 5 of the above directions. Skip to the "Optional edging with ties" section.

Adding the ties

1. **Foundation chain: With the right side of the bandana facing, join the yarn with a sl st in the right-hand corner stitch at the front edge of the bandana, ch 51.**

   With the right side of the fabric facing you, join the yarn in the corner stitch on the right-hand side of the front edge of the bandana with a slip stitch, and then chain 51 for the foundation chain for the first tie.

2. **Row 1: Sc in second chain from hook, sc in each chain across (50 sc).**

   To complete Row 1, work 1 single crochet in the second chain from the hook, continue to work 1 single crochet in each chain stitch across the row. You have 50 single crochet stitches.

3. **Sl st in the same stitch as joining. Fasten off.**

Slip stitch in the same corner stitch that you used to join the yarn to make the first tie, as shown in Figure 7-11a. Figure 7-11b shows the completed slip stitch. Fasten off the yarn.

4. **Repeat Steps 1 through 3 for the left side tie, joining the yarn in the corner stitch on the left-hand side of the front edge of the bandana.**

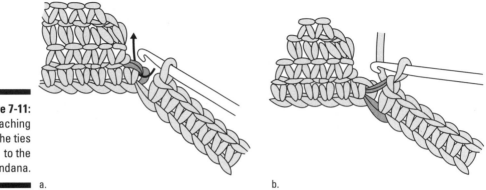

Figure 7-11:
Attaching
the ties
to the
bandana.

a.

b.

Optional edging with ties

If you want a more finished look to your bandana, you can make a simple but decorative edging with single crochet stitches. For more detailed info on edgings, see Chapter 16. Here are the edging directions as you'd see them in a pattern:

> Ch 1, working across left side edge of bandana, sc in first row-end sc, •
> ch 1, skip next row-end sc, sc in next row-end sc •, rep from • to • across
> to next corner, ch 51 (for first tie), sc in second ch from hook, sc in each
> ch across to front edge of bandana, working across opposite side of foun-
> dation chain, sc in each ch across to next corner, ch 51 (for second tie),
> sc in second ch from hook, sc in each ch across to next side edge, ch 1, sc
> in first row-end sc on side edge, rep from • to • across to bottom point of
> bandana, 2 sc in sc at bottom point, sl st in first sc to join. Fasten off.

Here are the instructions in everyday English:

1. **To create the edging, chain 1, and then, working across the left side edge of the bandana, work 1 single crochet stitch in the first row-end single crochet stitch.**

2. **Chain 1, skip the next row-end single crochet, and then work 1 single crochet stitch into the following row-end single crochet stitch.**

3. **Repeat Step 2 until you reach the next corner.**

4. **At the corner, make 51 chain stitches for the first tie.**

5. **Turn your piece, work 1 single crochet stitch into the second chain from the hook, and then work 1 single crochet stitch in each chain stitch across until you reach the body of the bandana.**

6. **Working across the opposite side of the foundation chain (the front edge of the bandana), work 1 single crochet stitch in each stitch across until you reach the next corner.**

7. **At the corner, make 51 chain stitches for the second tie.**

8. **Repeat Step 5.**

9. **Chain 1 and then, working across the right side edge of the bandana, work 1 single crochet stitch in the first row-end single crochet stitch.**

10. **Repeat Steps 2 and 3 until you reach the bottom point of the bandana.**

11. **Work 2 single crochet stitches in the 1 single crochet stitch at the bottom point.**

12. **Work 1 slip stitch in the first single crochet stitch to join the round. Fasten off your yarn.**

Finishing off with a tassel

Now all you need to complete this bandana is a fun and funky tassel. (See Chapter 17 for complete instructions and illustrations for creating a tassel.)

1. **Cut yarn into ten 8-inch lengths and lay them together.**

2. **Cut 2 more strands of yarn, each 10 inches in length.**

3. **Tie the first length of yarn securely around the center of the bundle, leaving equal lengths on each side.**

4. **Fold the bundle in half, with the tie at the center top.**

5. **Wrap the second length of yarn several times around the folded bundle of yarn approximately ¾ inch below the folded end.**

6. **Tie tightly to secure. Using remaining ends of yarn from first tie at center top of tassel, tie to the end of point at back of bandana.**

7. **Weave in extra lengths of yarn after tassel is attached.**

Ruffled Bandana Project

This bandana is worked by increasing stitches in each row. It's made using three different solid colors of a light sport-weight yarn, but feel free to change the colors or make it in one solid color to match your own wardrobe. If you want a funky look that's not much extra work, you can add a ruffled border around the outside, as shown in the color section of this book.

Materials

- **Yarn:** Schachenmayr nomotta "Catania" light sport-weight yarn (100% mercerized cotton) (1.75 oz. [*50 gm*], 125 m. each skein): 1 skein each of blue, green, and white
- **Hook:** Crochet hook size E-4 U.S. or size needed to obtain gauge

Vital statistics

- **Size:** 12½ in. wide x 10½ in. deep, excluding ties
- **Gauge:** 11 sts and 13 rows sc = 2 in.
- **Stitches used:** Chain stitch (ch), single crochet (sc)

Directions

This section walks you through each step to crochet the body of the bandana. You can follow the bold instructions, which are what you'd see in a normal crochet publication, or the plain English.

1. **Foundation chain: Starting at bottom point of bandana, chain 2.**

   Create your foundation chain by working 2 chain stitches in a row.

2. **Row 1: (right side): Work 2 sc in second ch from hook (2 sc),** *turn.*

   To complete Row 1, work 2 single crochet stitches in the second chain from the hook, and then turn your work.

3. **Row 2: (wrong side): Ch 1, sc in each sc across (2 sc),** *turn.*

   To complete Row 2, chain 1 for your turning chain and then work 1 single crochet stitch in each single crochet stitch across the row. You'll have 2 single crochet stitches. Turn your work.

4. **Row 3: Ch 1, 2 sc in each sc across (4 sc),** *turn.*

   To complete Row 3, chain 1 for your turning chain and then work 2 single crochet stitches in each single crochet stitch across the row. You'll have 4 single crochet stitches. Turn your work.

5. **Row 4: Ch 1, sc in each sc across (4 sc),** *turn.*

   To complete Row 4, chain 1 for your turning chain and then work 1 single crochet stitch in each single crochet stitch across the row. You'll have 4 single crochet stitches, and then turn your work.

6. **Row 5: Ch 1, 2 sc in first sc, sc in each sc across to within last sc, 2 sc in last sc (6 sc),** *turn.*

   To complete Row 5, chain 1 for your turning chain and work 2 single crochet stitches in the first single crochet stitch. Next, work 1 single crochet stitch in each stitch until you reach the last one, and then work 2 single crochet stitches into the last stitch. You'll have 6 single crochet stitches. Turn your work.

7. **Row 6: Ch 1, sc in each sc across (6 sc),** *turn.*

   To complete Row 6, chain 1 for your turning chain and then work 1 single crochet stitch in each stitch across the row. You'll have 6 single crochet stitches. Turn your work.

8. **Rows 7–58: Rep Rows 5–6 (26 times) (58 sts at end of last row).**

   To complete Rows 7 through 58, repeat Rows 5 and 6 a total of 26 times. Every 2 rows adds 2 single crochet stitches. At the end of Row 58, you'll have 58 single crochet stitches, and then turn your work.

9. **Row 59: Ch 1, 2 sc in first sc, sc in each sc across to within last sc, 2 sc in last sc (60 sc),** *turn.*

   To complete Row 59, chain 1 for your turning chain and work 2 single crochet stitches in the first single crochet stitch. Next, work 1 single crochet stitch in each stitch until you reach the last one, and then work 2 single crochet stitches into that last stitch. You'll have 60 single crochet stitches, and then turn your work.

   Note: If you choose not to make the optional border, then proceed to Step 10, and your bandana will be completed. If you do choose to make the border, then skip Step 10, and go on to work Step 11, which will set you up for working the border.

10. **Row 60: Ch 1, sc in each sc across, ch 51 (first tie),** *turn,* **sc in second ch from hook, sc in each ch across, sl st in next sc on bandana to join. Fasten off. With right side facing, join blue in first sc in Row 60, ch 51 (second tie),** *turn,* **sc in second ch from hook, sc in each ch across, sl st in next sc on bandana to join. Fasten off.**

    To complete Row 60 and add the ties, chain 1, work 1 single crochet stitch in each single crochet stitch across the row, and then chain 51 chain stitches in a row for the first tie, turn your work, then work

1 single crochet in the second chain from the hook, and 1 single crochet in each chain stitch across, slip stitch in the next single crochet stitch on the bandana to complete the tie. Fasten off the yarn. With the right side of the bandana facing you, join the blue yarn in the first single crochet stitch made in Row 60 and work 51 chain stitches in a row for the second tie, turn your work, then work 1 single crochet in the second chain from the hook, and 1 single crochet in each chain stitch across, slip stitch in the next single crochet stitch on the bandana to complete the tie. Fasten off your yarn.

11. **Row 60: Ch 1, sc in each sc across, ch 50 (first tie). Fasten off. With right side facing, join blue in first sc in Row 60, ch 50 (second tie). Fasten off.**

To complete Row 60 and add the ties, chain 1, work 1 single crochet stitch in each single crochet stitch across the row, and then chain 50 chain stitches in a row for the first tie. Fasten off the yarn. With the right side of the bandana facing you, join the blue yarn in the first single crochet stitch made in Row 60 and work 50 chain stitches in a row for the second tie. Fasten off your yarn.

Adding an optional ruffled border

The contrasting colors in the border of this bandana add color and interest to what could be a plain piece of fabric. The second round of the border adds a bit of feminine ruffle. While the ruffle may seem a bit complex, it's really nothing more than a bunch of stitches worked into one. The extra stitches give the appearance of a ruffle. (See Chapter 16 for details on adding borders.)

Rnd 1: With right side facing, join green in first ch at bottom point of bandana, ch 1, work 3 sc in sc at point of bandana, working in row-end sts, sc in each row-end st across side edge of piece to next corner, working across ch sts of first tie, sc in each ch st across tie to within last ch, work 3 sc in last ch, working across opposite side of ch, sc in each ch across to front edge of bandana, sc in each sc across front edge to next tie, sc in each ch across next tie to within last ch, work 3 sc in last ch, working across opposite side of ch, sc in each ch across to next side edge, sc in each row-end st across side edge to point, sl st in first sc to join. Fasten off green.

If you find the preceding instructions hard to follow, then take a peek at these instructions in plain English:

1. **With the right side of the bandana facing you, join the green yarn in the first chain stitch at the bottom point of the bandana with a slip stitch (see Chapter 4 for info on how to join a new color).**

2. **Chain 1 and then work 3 single crochet stitches in the single crochet stitch at the bottom point.**

3. **Working across one side edge of the bandana, work 1 single crochet stitch in each row-end stitch until you reach the first tie.**

4. **Working across the chain stitches of the tie, work 1 single crochet stitch in each chain stitch until you reach the next-to-last stitch of the tie. Work 3 single crochet stitches in the last chain stitch, and then, working across the opposite side of the chain, work 1 single crochet stitch in each chain stitch across until you reach the body of the bandana.**

5. **Working across the front edge of the bandana, work 1 single crochet stitch in each stitch across to the second tie.**

6. **Repeat Step 4.**

7. **Working across the last side edge, work 1 single crochet stitch in each stitch across until you reach the bottom point, and then slip stitch in the first single crochet stitch to join. Fasten off the yarn.**

Rnd 2: With right side facing, join white in center sc at bottom point of bandana, ch 1, sc in first sc, ch 3, • sc in next sc, ch 3 •, rep from • to • across to first tie, working behind tie, sc in first sc on front edge, ch 3, rep from • to • across front edge to next tie, working behind next tie, sc in first sc on next side edge, ch 3, rep from • to • across side edge to bottom point, sl st in first sc to join. Fasten off.

In other words:

1. **With the right side of the bandana facing you, join the white yarn in the center single crochet stitch at the bottom point of the bandana with a slip stitch (see Chapter 4).**

2. **Chain 1 and then work 1 single crochet stitch in the first single crochet stitch.**

3. **Chain 3.**

4. **Work 1 single crochet stitch in the next single crochet stitch and then chain 3.**

5. **Repeat Step 4 in each stitch across until you reach the first tie.**

6. **Working behind the tie, work 1 single crochet stitch in the first single crochet stitch on the front edge of the bandana.**

7. **Chain 3.**

8. **Repeat Step 4 in each stitch across to second tie.**

9. **Working behind the tie, work 1 single crochet stitch in the first single crochet stitch on last side edge.**

10. **Chain 3.**

11. **Repeat Step 4 in each stitch across until you reach the bottom point.**

12. **Slip stitch in the first single crochet stitch to join. Fasten off the yarn.**

Chapter 8

I've Been Here Before: Crocheting in Circles

*W*ho says that going in circles doesn't get you anywhere? Obviously, that person has never crocheted. Whether you want to make a lacy doily to adorn your tabletop, a stylish hat to keep your head warm in cold weather, or motifs that you'll join together to make an Afghan or vest, you need to be able to crochet in a circle, or in *rounds*.

Crocheting rounds is no more difficult than working in rows. Instead of working back and forth, you work around in a circle, increasing the number of stitches you work in each round to accommodate the growing circumference. This chapter shows you the two most common methods for creating a center ring, which is the basis for all rounds, and how to work rounds of stitches off of it. We also describe how to morph your simple rounds into squares and how to work in a spiral and make three-dimensional shapes.

You can practice your new skills on the cute cloche hat project at the end of this chapter. Or try out the simple three-dimensional appliqué flower project.

Lord of the Center Rings

To begin a design that you work in rounds, you first have to create a *center ring.* The center ring is the foundation for all crocheted designs that are worked in rounds — just like the foundation chain you use when working in rows. The center ring is the circle created by several chain stitches joined together to form a circle, or it can be just a single chain stitch. This section shows you the two most common methods for creating the center ring, when you want to use each, and how to end a round and be in the proper position to start the next round. The two most frequently used methods are making a ring of chain stitches or working a round of stitches into one chain stitch.

Working stitches in the hole

The most common method for creating a center ring is to make a chain and close it into a ring with a slip stitch. (Refer to Chapter 4 for the how-to on making chain stitches and slip stitches.) You would use this method when your first round is made up of a fairly large number of stitches and you need the room in which to fit them, or if the design calls for an obvious hole in the center. The following steps show you how to create a simple center ring.

To make a center ring of 6 chain stitches:

1. **Chain (ch) 6.**

2. **Insert your hook into the first chain stitch you made, forming a ring. (See Figure 8-1.)**

Figure 8-1: Making the center-ring chain.

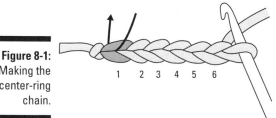

1 2 3 4 5 6

3. **Yarn over your hook (yo).**

4. **Draw the yarn through the stitch and through the loop on your hook, as Figure 8-2a shows.**

   Your center ring is now complete. (See Figure 8-2b.)

Figure 8-2:
Completing
the center
ring.

a.

b.

REMEMBER

The number of stitches in the beginning chain determines the size of the hole that the center ring creates as well as how many stitches you can work into the center ring. Make sure the ring is large enough to accommodate the number of stitches that you'll be working in it. On the other hand, make sure it's not so long that you have a big loose hole in the center. When you're working a pattern, it tells you how many chain stitches you need for the proper size center ring.

After you make the center ring, you're ready for the first round. Just as when you're beginning a new row, you first have to determine the number of turning chain stitches that you need in order to bring your hook up to the proper level for the next round of stitches. (The number of turning chain stitches you need depends on the stitch you're about to work — flip back to Chapter 4 for a chart on how many turning chain stitches the basic crochet stitches require.) Now here's the really easy part about working with a center ring: Instead of inserting your hook into the actual stitches of the center ring, you just go through the center hole. The following steps show how to work single crochet stitches into the center ring:

1. **Chain (ch) 1 to make the turning chain for single crochet (sc).**

2. **Insert your hook into the center ring. (See Figure 8-3a.)**

Figure 8-3:
Working
a single
crochet in
the center
ring.

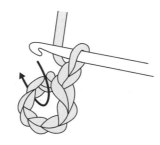

a.

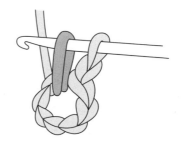

b.

3. **Yarn over your hook (yo).**

4. **Draw the yarn through the center ring. (Refer to Figure 8-3b.)**

5. **Yarn over your hook.**

6. **Draw the yarn through the 2 loops on your hook.**

   One single crochet stitch is complete. (See Figure 8-4a.)

Figure 8-4:
Working a
round of
single
crochet.

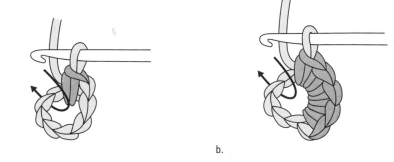

a.   b.

Continue to work single crochet stitches into the ring until you can't fit any-more. (Refer to Figure 8-4b.) The center ring will stretch somewhat, and you'll probably be surprised at how many stitches you can fit in.

Working stitches in the chain stitch

The second most common method for creating a center ring is to work all the stitches for the first round in one chain stitch. You generally use this method when the design calls for a small hole in the center of the pattern or almost no hole at all. To start a center ring this way, you always chain 1 (this is what you work the stitches in) plus the number of stitches required for the turning chain, depending on which particular stitch you work in the first round (see Chapter 4 for a list of the most common turning chain lengths). Follow these steps to work your first round of double crochet stitches into a chain stitch:

1. **Chain (ch) 1.**

2. **Chain 3 more for the double crochet (dc) stitch's turning chain.**

3. **Yarn over your hook (yo).**

4. **Insert your hook in the fourth chain from the hook. (See Figure 8-5.)**

   This is the first chain stitch you made and becomes your center ring chain stitch.

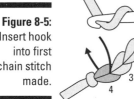

Figure 8-5:
Insert hook
into first
chain stitch
made.

5. **Work 1 complete double crochet stitch in the center ring chain stitch.**

   Continue to work double crochet stitches in the same chain stitch until
   you're comfortable with the process. Figure 8-6a shows you how to
   begin the second stitch, and Figure 8-6b shows several completed
   stitches and growing.

Figure 8-6:
Making
first round
of double
crochet in
center-ring
chain stitch.

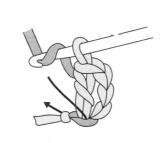

a.

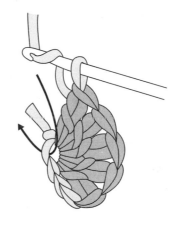

b.

Uniting the Ring

After you complete the number of stitches you need for your first round, you
have to join the first and last stitch of the round to complete the circle. The
most popular method is to work a slip stitch in the top of the round's first
stitch; this puts you in the proper position to begin the next round. You join
each successive round in the same place, which creates a slightly visible
seam (to make a round without a seam, see the section "Spiraling Up and
Up"). You join single crochet rounds a little bit differently than rounds of
other stitches, so we show you one example of each here.

To join a round of single crochet stitches:

1. **After completing the last single crochet (sc) of the round, insert your hook under the top 2 loops of the first single crochet stitch you made.**

   The chain-1 turning chain at the beginning of a single crochet round doesn't count as a stitch, so you ignore it (skip over it) and work the slip stitch in the first single crochet.

2. **Yarn over your hook (yo).**

3. **Draw the yarn through the stitch and the loop on your hook to complete 1 slip stitch (sl st). (See Figure 8-7a.)**

   You've just joined the first round of single crochet. Figure 8-7b shows a stitch diagram depicting the placement of the joining slip stitch, which is the dot at the top. (See Chapter 5 for more on reading stitch diagrams.)

Figure 8-7:
Joining the single crochet round with a slip stitch.

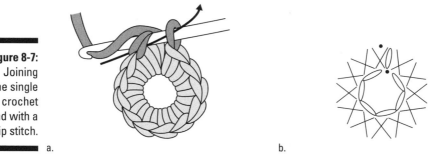

a.   b.

To join a round of double crochet (or any other stitch):

1. **After completing the last double crochet (dc) of the round, insert your hook in the top of the turning chain. (See Figure 8-8a.)**

   The turning chain counts as the first stitch of the round.

2. **Yarn over your hook (yo).**

3. **Draw the yarn through the turning chain and the loop on your hook to complete 1 slip stitch (sl st), as Figure 8-8a shows.**

   You've just joined the first round of double crochet. Figure 8-8b shows a stitch diagram depicting the placement of the joining slip stitch, which is the dot at the top by the turning chain. (See Chapter 5 for more on reading stitch diagrams.)

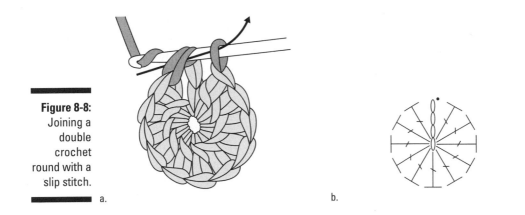

Figure 8-8:
Joining a double crochet round with a slip stitch.

a.   b.

To the Outer Circles and Beyond: Adding Rounds

Adding more rounds to your work is similar to adding rows, except that you usually don't turn your work and you increase the number of stitches you work in each round so that it lies flat. (See Chapter 7 for info on working an increase.) To work a second round of double crochet stitches, follow these steps:

1. **After joining the first round, chain (ch) 3 for the turning chain.**

2. **Without turning your work, work 1 double crochet (dc) stitch under the top two loops of the first stitch, the stitch directly below the turning chain.**

3. **Work 2 double crochet stitches in each stitch around.**

4. **Join the first and the last stitch of the round with a slip stitch (sl st).**

   You should have twice as many stitches in the second round as in the first round.

For your piece to lie flat, the number of stitches in each round should increase by the number of stitches worked in the first round. (If you don't increase enough stitches, your piece will begin to cup up.) For example, if your first round has a total of 6 stitches, then your second round should increase by 6 stitches, for a total of 12 stitches at the end of round 2. The third round should again increase by 6 stitches, giving you a total of 18 stitches at the end of the round. Table 8-1 gives you three different examples of round increases as well how to work the increase.

Table 8-1	Increasing Stitches in Rounds			
Round #	Number of Stitches in Round			How to Work the Increase
Rnd 1	6	8	12	N/A
Rnd 2	12	16	24	Inc 1 stitch in each stitch around
Rnd 3	18	24	36	Inc 1 stitch in every other stitch around
Rnd 4	24	32	48	Inc 1 stitch in every 3rd stitch around
Rnd 5	30	40	60	Inc 1 stitch in every 4th stitch around
Rnd 6	36	48	72	Inc 1 stitch in every 5th stitch around

These guidelines apply to one specific form of increasing in rounds. You can increase rounds many different ways, although the principle of increasing in a regular sequence remains the same. Always follow the increasing instructions in the pattern you're making.

Because you don't turn your work at the end of each round, you get a definite front and back to your piece. Figure 8-9a shows the right (front) side of a round. Notice how the stitches lean toward you. Figure 8-9b shows the wrong (back) side. It's a little smoother and the stitches angle away from you somewhat.

Figure 8-9:
Two definite sides: (a) the right side (front); (b) the wrong side (back).

a.

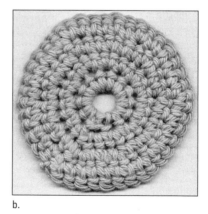
b.

Sometimes, though, you want to avoid this front-and-back business and create a reversible fabric — especially for projects such as an Afghan that you want to look good on both sides. To do this, you just turn your piece after each round. If you're working a pattern that requires a reversible fabric, the directions will show you how to turn and where to work the stitches.

Great Granny's a Square: Cornering Your Rounds

Just because you're working in rounds doesn't mean you can only make circles. Turning a circle into a square is very simple to do: All you do is add four short chain loops to your round. The granny square is a very common circle turned square. Figure 8-10 is the stitch diagram for the granny square and shows you how the rounds square off. To start a typical granny square, follow these steps:

1. **Chain (ch) 4.**

2. **Close into a ring with 1 slip stitch (sl st) in the first chain.**

   This is the center ring.

Then follow these instructions to complete the first round of your granny square:

1. **Chain (ch) 3 for your first double crochet (dc) and then work 2 more double crochet stitches into the ring. Chain 2.**

   This is your first corner.

2. **Work 3 more double crochet stitches in the ring and chain 2.**

3. **Repeat Step 2 two times.**

   You now have your four corners.

4. **Join the round by working 1 slip stitch in the top of the turning chain. Don't turn your work.**

To go on to the second round, follow these steps:

1. **Slip stitch (sl st) across to the first ch-2 space and then chain (ch) 3 for the first double crochet (dc).**

   See Chapter 4 for info on traveling across stitches with the slip stitch.

2. **Work 2 double crochet stitches in the first ch-2 space, chain 2, then work 3 more double crochet stitches in the same ch-2 space. Chain 1.**

3. **Work 3 double crochet stitches, chain 2, work 3 more double crochet stitches all in the next chain-2 space. Chain 1.**

4. **Repeat Step 3 twice, which brings you to the last side of the motif. Work 1 slip stitch in the top of the turning chain to join.**

You can add as many rounds as you want to the granny square — you could make it as big as an entire Afghan if you wanted to. Just remember that each successive round will have additional chain-1 spaces across the sides. Simply work 3 double crochet stitches in each space across the sides and work your corners the same. Figure 8-11 shows a granny square with four rounds.

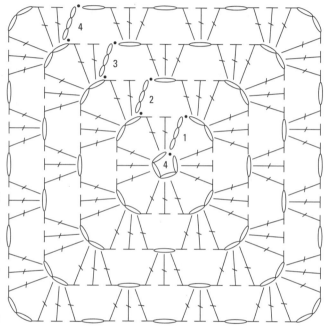

Figure 8-10:
Stitch
diagram of
a basic
granny
square
motif.

Figure 8-11:
Granny
square
swatch.

Spiraling Up and Up

Working in a spiral is another way to crochet in rounds when you prefer not to have a visible seam. Most often, you work in a spiral to make hats, mittens, bags, and toys with a three-dimensional shape. Another advantage of working in a spiral is that you don't have to join the end of each round or make a turning chain, and this perk makes crocheting items faster and neater. In this section, we give you spiral basics and show you how to work one from a stitch diagram, such as you may find in a pattern you want to try.

Working tall stitches (like triple crochet) in a spiral gives your work an uneven (and unattractive) edge. We recommend you use this technique only for single crochet stitches.

Working in a spiral

The first round of a spiral design begins the same way as any other round. You create a center ring by using either of the two methods described earlier in this chapter, and then work the required number of stitches in the first round. The stitch diagram in Figure 8-12 shows a center ring of 6 chain stitches and a first round of 12 single crochet stitches. (See Chapter 5 for more on how to read a stitch diagram.) The twist comes in at the end of the round.

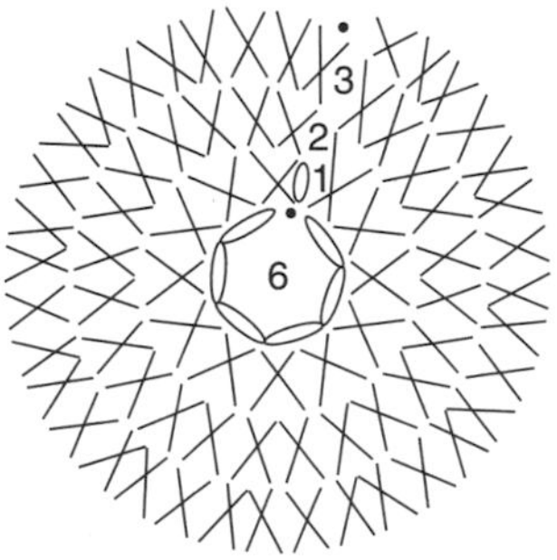

Figure 8-12:
Single crochet stitch diagram: Working in a spiral.

Instead of joining the round, you work the first stitch of the next round into the first stitch of the last round, and so on for each successive round. The only time you'll slip stitch to complete the round is when you've finished the required number of rounds for the design. Reading the diagram in Figure 8-12 counterclockwise, you work the 13th stitch in the first stitch of round 1. This now becomes the first stitch of the second round.

Before continuing on with round 2, mark the first stitch of the second round with a stitch marker or a safety pin because losing your place or miscounting the stitches in each round is easy to do. (Stitch markers are a handy gadget that we mention in Chapter 2.) When you work your way back around, you work the first stitch of round 3 into the marked stitch. Remove the marker from round 2 and place it in the first stitch of round 3. Continue spiraling until you're too dizzy to go any further or until your design is the size you want.

Ending the spiral

The last stitch in the last round on a spiral design will be raised above the level of the previous round. To finish the round and make the edge smooth, you need to slip stitch in the next stitch (the first stitch of the previous round) before fastening off.

Adding Another Dimension

Not all designs that you work in the round have to be flat. A perfect example is the design at the end of this chapter, a cloche hat. It's a flat round at the top, but then it takes on a tubular shape to fit over your head. If you're worried that making a round go tubular is a difficult technique, don't be — it's actually easier than getting the darn round to lie flat.

In the section "To the Outer Circles and Beyond: Adding Rounds," you find out how to keep a round flat by increasing the number of stitches in each successive round. To get the round to start curving up, you simply stop adding new stitches in each round. Here's how:

1. **Make a center ring of 6 chain (ch) stitches and work a complete round of 12 single crochet (sc). Join with a slip stitch (sl st).**

   See the sections "Working stitches in the hole" and "Uniting the Ring," earlier in the chapter.

2. **Work 2 more rounds, increasing 12 stitches for round 2 and 12 more stitches for round 3, and joining after each round.**

   See the section "To the Outer Circles and Beyond: Adding Rounds" for how to make the turning chain and add new rounds. You don't have to stop after 3 rounds. Add more rounds to make a larger design, but remember to keep increasing the stitches for each round.

3. **To start adding depth, don't add any extra stitches to round 4. Work 1 single crochet stitch in each stitch of the previous round. Join with a slip stitch.**

   Working 1 stitch in 1 stitch like this causes the edges of your work to turn in. Repeat Step 3 until the piece is as deep as you want.

If you want your piece to start curving in more gradually, don't add as many increase stitches to the rounds in Step 2. You need to add a few so that the circumference grows, but not enough to keep it lying flat. Try adding just 8 stitches to each round. Play around with the number of increases: The fewer you add, the more dramatic the curve; the more you add, the shallower the curve.

After your work is as deep (or long) as you want, you have three choices:

✔ **Fasten off your work.** You now have something that looks like a cap or a tube sock, depending on how big you made the initial flat round and how many rounds you added for depth.

✔ **Begin increasing stitches in each round.** This makes your piece begin to widen and flatten out, kind of like the brim on a hat.

✔ **Begin decreasing stitches in each round.** Decreasing the number of stitches starts to close up the edges of your piece, creating a spherical design. You decrease rounds the same way you decrease rows, by combining 2 stitches into 1. (Refer to Chapter 7 for more on decreasing.) Decreasing evenly in each successive round creates a smooth, even curve, but if you work a large number of decreases in one round, the work will pull in sharply. If you want your design to be symmetrical in shape, decrease at the same rate as you increased on the first half of your piece.

You can make some fun three-dimensional projects with this shaping technique, such as crocheted dolls and animals. You crochet the pieces into the proper shape and then stuff them with filling to make them soft and plump. Christmas ornaments, mittens, slippers, and leg warmers are just a few of the other designs that you shape by working in rounds.

Flower Power Project

The three-dimensional flowers in this project are quick and easy to make and show off your new skills. They make great package toppers, which is what they're used as in the color insert. Or you can eliminate the ties and sew them onto garments, bags, or Afghans. This project gives two different color options: You can use a variegated yarn for the whole flower or use two different solid colors to create different-colored petals. You can also make the flowers larger by using a heavier weight yarn such as worsted weight with an H-8 hook, or smaller, using cotton thread and a size 7 steel hook.

Materials

- ✔ **For variegated flowers:** Patons "Bumblebee" baby-weight yarn (100% cotton), (1.75 oz [*50 gm*], 123 yds each skein): 1 skein of #02413 Flowers Variegated

- ✔ **For solid and 2-color flowers:** Coats & Clark(r) Red Heart "LusterSheen(r)" sport-weight yarn (100% acrylic), Article E721 (4 oz [*113 gm*], 325 yds each skein): 1 skein each of #1 White, #206 Crystal Pink, and #227 Buttercup

- ✔ **Hook:** Size F-5 U.S. or size needed to obtain gauge

- ✔ **Yarn needle**

Vital statistics

- ✔ **Measurements:** Approximately 3 inches in diameter

- ✔ **Gauge:** First 3 rnds = 1¾ in. in diameter

- ✔ **Stitches used:** Chain stitch (ch), slip stitch (sl st), single crochet (sc), half double crochet (hdc), double crochet (dc), triple crochet (tr)

Directions

One-color flower

Center ring: Leaving a 6-in. length, ch 6 and close into a ring with 1 sl st in first ch.

Rnd 1: Ch 1, work 15 sc in ring, sl st in first sc to join.

Rnd 2: Ch 1, • sc in sc, ch 3, skip next 2 sc •, rep from • to • around, sl st in first sc to join (5 ch-3 loops made).

Rnd 3: Sl st in first ch-3 loop, ch 1, (sc, hdc, 3 dc, hdc, sc) in each ch-3 loop around (5 petals made), sl st in first sc to join.

Rnd 4: • Ch 4, skip next 6 sts, sl st in next sc •, rep from • to • around (5 ch-4 loops made).

Rnd 5: Sl st in first ch-4 loop, ch 1, (sc, hdc, 2 dc, tr, 2 dc, hdc, sc) in each ch-4 loop around (5 petals made), sl st in first sc to join.

Rnd 6: • Ch 5, skip next 8 sts, sl st in next sc •, rep from • to • around (5 ch-5 loops made).

Rnd 7: Sl st in first ch-5 loop, ch 1, (sc, hdc, 2 dc, 3 tr, 2 dc, hdc, sc) in each ch-5 loop around (5 petals made), sl st in first sc to join. Fasten off.

Two-toned flower

Work the stitches the same as in the one-color flower: Work the center ring and round 1 in the first color. Fasten off the first color and join the second color. Work rounds 2–5 in the second color. Fasten off and join the first color to work rounds 6–7.

Ties

If you want to tie the flower to a package, make a tie in your desired color.

Make a chain 2 inches longer than the combined circumference of the package in both directions. Fasten off, leaving a 6-in. sewing length. Wrap the tie around the package in both directions with the ends meeting at the center top. Tie the ends in a knot at the center top.

Curlicues

Make as many as desired in colors to match or contrast with flowers.

Make a chain long enough to reach from the flower to the edge of the package.

Row 1: 3 sc in second ch from hook, 3 sc in each ch across. Fasten off, leaving a 6-in. sewing length. With yarn needle and sewing lengths, sew one end to wrong side of Rnd 1 of flower as desired.

Finishing

Arrange flowers on top of the package as desired. With a yarn needle and the extra sewing lengths, sew the flowers to the ties.

Cloche Hat Project

The pattern for this versatile hat incorporates both single crochet and double crochet stitches and allows you to practice increasing and decreasing in rounds and see how shaping occurs. The beautiful hand-painted yarn in this design, shown in the color photo section, allows you to create a pretty accessory with a fairly simple stitch pattern.

Materials

- **Yarn:** Schaefer Yarns "Marjaana" 4-ply worsted-weight yarn (50% merino wool/50% tussah silk) (4 oz. [*113 gm*], 550 yds. each hank): 1 hank of Eleanor Roosevelt

- **Hook:** Size H-8 U.S. or size needed to obtain gauge (refer to Chapter 3 for information on gauge)

Vital statistics

- **Size:** One size fits most adults; circumference = 21 in.

- **Gauge:** First 3 rnds = 2¼ in. in diameter

- **Stitches used:** Chain st (ch), slip stitch (sl st), single crochet (sc), double crochet (dc); **dec 1 sc:** • (insert hook in next st, yo, draw yarn through st) twice, yo, draw yarn through 3 loops on hook •

Directions

The instructions for this project are just as you'd see them in any regular crochet publication, complete with abbreviations. Figure 8-13 gives you a partial stitch diagram for extra guidance. If you need more info on how to read crochetese or the stitch diagram, see Chapter 5 for the whole kit and caboodle on what each abbreviation means and how to work with bullets. The Cheat Sheet at the front of the book also provides a handy reference tool. For complete instructions on how to increase and decrease stitches, refer to Chapter 7.

Center ring: Ch 4 and close into a ring with 1 sl st in first ch.

Rnd 1: Ch 3 (counts as first dc), work 7 dc in ring, sl st in top of ch-3 to join (8 dc).

Rnd 2: Ch 1, 2 sc in top of ch-3, 2 sc in each rem dc around, sl st in first sc to join (16 sc).

Rnd 3: Ch 3 (counts as first dc), 2 dc in next dc, • dc in next sc, 2 dc in next sc •, rep from • to • around, sl st in top of ch-3 to join (24 dc).

Rnd 4: Ch 1, sc in top of ch-3, sc in next dc, 2 sc in next dc, • sc in each of next 2 dc, 2 sc in next dc •, rep from • to • around, sl st in first sc to join (32 sc).

Rnd 5: Ch 3 (counts as first dc), dc in each of next 2 sc, 2 dc in next sc, • dc in each of next 3 sc, 2 dc in next sc •, rep from • to • around, sl st in top of ch-3 to join (40 dc).

Rnd 6: Ch 1, sc in top of ch-3, sc in each of next 3 dc, 2 sc in next dc, • sc in each of next 4 dc, 2 sc in next dc •, rep from • to • around, sl st in first sc to join (48 sc).

Rnd 7: Ch 3 (counts as first dc), dc in each of next 4 sc, 2 dc in next sc, • dc in each of next 5 sc, 2 dc in next sc •, rep from • to • around, sl st in top of ch-3 to join (56 dc).

Rnd 8: Ch 1, sc in top of ch-3, sc in each of next 5 dc, 2 sc in next dc, • sc in each of next 6 dc, 2 sc in next dc •, rep from • to • around, sl st in first sc to join (64 sc).

Rnd 9: Ch 3 (counts as first dc), dc in each of next 6 sc, 2 dc in next sc, • dc in each of next 7 sc, 2 dc in next sc •, rep from • to • around, sl st in top of ch-3 to join (72 dc).

Rnd 10: Ch 1, sc in top of ch-3, sc in each of next 7 dc, 2 sc in next dc, • sc in each of next 8 dc, 2 sc in next dc •, rep from • to • around, sl st in first sc to join (80 sc).

Rnd 11: Ch 3 (counts as first dc), dc in each of next 8 sc, 2 dc in next sc, • dc in each of next 9 sc, 2 dc in next sc •, rep from • to • around, sl st in top of ch-3 to join (88 dc).

Rnd 12: Ch 1, sc in top of ch-3, sc in each rem dc around, sl st in first sc to join (88 sc).

Rnd 13: Ch 3 (counts as first dc), dc in each sc around, sl st in top of ch-3 to join (88 dc).

Rnd 14: Ch 1, sc in top of ch-3, sc in each of next 8 dc, dec 1 sc in next 2 dc, • sc in each of next 9 dc, dec 1 sc in next 2 dc •, rep from • to • around, sl st in first sc to join (80 sc).

Rnd 15: Ch 3 (counts as first dc), dc in each sc around, sl st in top of ch-3 to join (80 dc).

Rnd 16: Ch 1, sc in top of ch-3, sc in each of next 7 dc, dec 1 sc in next 2 dc, •
sc in each of next 8 dc, dec 1 sc in next 2 dc •, rep from • to • around, sl st in
first sc to join (72 sc).

Rnd 17: Ch 3 (counts as first dc), dc in each rem sc around, sl st in top of ch-3
to join (72 dc).

Rnd 18: Ch 1, sc in top of ch-3, sc in each rem dc around, sl st in first sc to
join (72 sc).

Rnd 19: Ch 3 (counts as first dc), ch 2, skip next 2 sc, • dc in next sc, ch 2, skip
next 2 sc •, rep from • to • around, sl st in top of ch-3 to join (24 ch-2 spaces).

Rnd 20: Ch 1, sc in top of ch-3, 2 sc in next ch-2 space, • sc in next dc, 2 sc in
next ch-2 space •, rep from • to • around (72 sc). Fasten off.

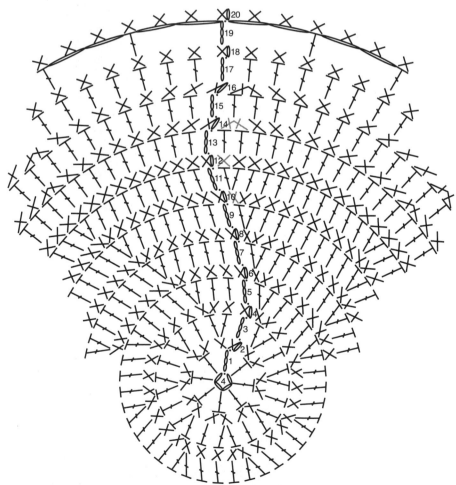

Figure 8-13:
Partial
stitch
diagram of
cloche hat.

Chapter 9

Crocheting in Technicolor

- -

In This Chapter

▶ Changing from one color to another

▶ Avoiding the snipping and rejoining part

▶ Decoding color codes

▶ Decorating with a colorful pillow

- -

*H*ave you ever stopped to imagine what the world would be like without color? Everywhere you look, from outside your windows to inside your home to the clothes on your body, color shapes your life and the way you view things. Well, the same holds true for the designs you crochet. Take, for example, an Afghan made out of motifs. Worked in a single color, it provides warmth but not much else. Add one or more colors, though, and not only do you have a warm blanket to snuggle up with, but you also have a work of art to display.

Whether you want to create a simple stripe pattern or a complex mosaic design in many colors, this chapter explains the various techniques for working with color and reading color charts. If you work the fun strawberry pillow project at the end of this chapter, you can practice your newfound techniques.

Bringing Things to Life: Joining New Colors

Working color changes properly gives your finished project a smooth, clean appearance with no unsightly bumps and knots. You usually switch colors at either of two different places within your design:

✔ At the beginning (or end) of a row or round

✔ In the middle of a row or round

You typically change colors at the beginning of a row when working a striped pattern. For *charted patterns,* those with a picture in the middle of the design, you need to change colors in the middle of a row. This section shows you how to create a smooth, clean transition between colors wherever you need to switch.

Changing color at the beginning

If you're going for stripes, master changing colors at the beginning of a row because you'll be doing this a lot. Fortunately, you change colors at the beginning of a row or round the same way you join a new strand of yarn of the same color. (Need a refresher on joining yarn? See Chapter 6.) Practice this technique by crocheting a swatch of double crochet several rows long with your first color; then follow these steps to join the new color:

1. **Using the first color, double crochet (dc) in each stitch across to the next-to-last stitch of the row.**

2. **Work the last double crochet to the point where only 2 loops are left on the hook.**

3. **Drop the first yarn color and pick up the second color.**

4. **Wrap the end of the second yarn color around the hook.**

5. **Draw the second yarn color through the 2 loops of the first yarn color that are on your hook. (See Figure 9-1a.)**

   At this point, you should have two strands of yarn hanging down.

Figure 9-1:
Joining a
new color
at the
beginning
of a row.

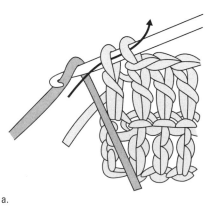
a.

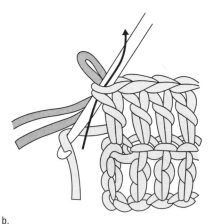
b.

6. **Tug on the end of the first color at the base of the double crochet to tighten up the stitch.**

7. **If you plan to pick up the first color in a later row, leave the first color yarn hanging and continue on with the second color.**

   See the section "Hitching a Ride: Carrying the Yarn," later in this chapter, to find out what to do with the unused first color strand of yarn.

If you don't plan to pick up the first color in a nearby row, fasten off the first color as follows:

1. **After joining the second color of yarn, remove the loop of the second color from your hook.**

2. **Cut the first color yarn, leaving a 6-inch tail.**

3. **Insert your hook into the center top of the last double crochet (dc) down through the center of the stitch. (Refer to Figure 9-1b.)**

4. **Yarn over (yo) with the first color's tail end at the bottom of the stitch.**

5. **Draw the tail end up through the stitch.**

6. **Place the loop of the second color back on the hook and begin your next row with the second color.**

To hide the tail end of the first yarn color, lay it across the tops of the stitches in the previous row and work over it or weave it in with a yarn needle when you finish crocheting.

When you join a new yarn color, always finish the last stitch of the first color with the second color, regardless of the type of stitch you're working. Doing so gets you ready to start the first stitch of the second color with the correct color loop on your hook. This prevents *color drag,* which happens when part of a stitch is one color, and the rest of the stitch is another color.

Changing color midstream

If you're making a design with a picture in the middle (a charted design), you usually change colors in the middle of a row. As when changing colors at the beginning of a row, correctly switching to a new color is important in order to prevent color drag. To add a new color within a row, follow these steps:

1. **Work the last stitch prior to the stitch where you're going to make the color change up to the point where only 2 loops are left on the hook.**

2. **Drop the first yarn color to the wrong (back) side and pick up the second color.**

3. **Wrap the end of the second yarn color around the hook.**

4. **Draw the second yarn color through the 2 loops (of the first yarn color) on your hook, thus completing the stitch with the second yarn color. (See Figure 9-2a.)**

   If you don't plan to use the first color yarn in the next few rows, cut the yarn, leaving a tail. Fasten off the first color by drawing the tail end through the current stitch as described in "Changing color at the beginning." Then work over this tail with the new color or weave it in later with a yarn needle.

5. **Continue to work with the new color yarn. (See Figure 9-2b.)**

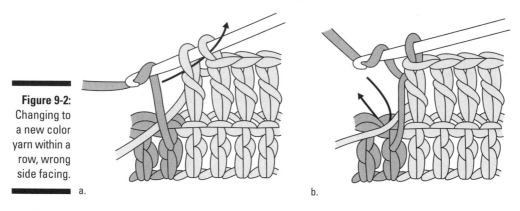

Figure 9-2:
Changing to a new color yarn within a row, wrong side facing.

a.

b.

You can change color with either the right side or the wrong side of the work facing you. Just remember to drop the tail end of the first color yarn to the wrong side, even if it's the side of the work facing you.

Hitching a Ride: Carrying the Yarn

When you're crocheting with two or more colors, you often carry the yarn that you're not presently working with to avoid having to fasten it off and rejoin a new strand each time you make a color change. You have several different options for carrying the yarn, each of which produces a different result.

If you're carrying several different colors, you can end up with a tangled mess in no time at all. The simple act of turning your work at the end of each row becomes a nightmare if you have many different balls of yarn attached to your work at the same time. For small areas of color, cutting off a few yards of the required color and winding it around a bobbin alleviates this mess. (See Chapter 2 for more on yarn bobbins.) Leave the whole skein intact for the most prominent colors, however.

Careful coloration

"Does this green really work with that brown?" Choosing different colors for a design may turn into a more daunting process than you originally bargained for. The following list provides some tips for combining them:

✔ **Use a color wheel.** This handy little gadget is available in most craft and yarn stores. Choose colors within the same segment to get several tones that work well together, or for a more vibrant look, choose colors that are exactly opposite each other on the color wheel.

✔ **Pick a multicolored yarn and a solid color yarn.** Many yarn companies create variegated or multicolored yarns to coordinate with their solid colors. Choose a multicolored yarn that appeals to you and then match it up with a solid color yarn. This gives the appearance of using many different yarns, when you actually use only two or three.

✔ **Rely on basic white or off-white to add contrast.** White or off-white works well with almost any other color. If you're looking for a stark contrast, go with a dark secondary color. If you want something subtler, a lighter color works fine.

✔ **Use dark and light tones of the same color.** If you favor a particular color, why not use its many shades?

Carrying on the wrong side

Carrying the yarn across the row on the wrong side of the fabric is probably the easiest method to use when working with different colors. When you're working a design that changes colors fairly frequently, such as vertical stripes or multicolored charted designs, fastening off each color each time you have to change is too much work and too sloppy.

To carry a strand on the wrong side of the fabric, work over the strand every few stitches with the second color, as shown in Figure 9-3. Please note that Figure 9-3 shows the wrong side of the fabric.

Every other row the wrong side of your piece is facing you, so make sure that you're always carrying the yarn on the same side. If you're changing color on a right side row, you carry the first color on the wrong (back) side of your work.

If you'll be switching back to the carried color several times across the row, then carry the yarn all the way across. If the design is only in a particular section of the work, such as a picture in the middle of a sweater back, then carry the yarn only in the part of the row where the design is featured and then let it drop while you finish the row. When you work back across the row, the color will be available for you to pick up in the correct place as the design dictates.

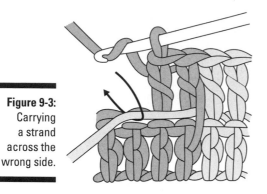

Figure 9-3:
Carrying a strand across the wrong side.

Keep the carried strand tight enough so that it lies flat against the wrong side of the fabric and doesn't catch on anything, but don't pull the strand too taut, or the fabric can pucker.

Working over the strand

Working over the carried strand produces a neater appearance on the wrong side of the fabric, which is especially important on a design where the backside is visible, such as an Afghan or a scarf.

The technique for working over the strand is basically the same as working over the end of the yarn when joining a new ball (see Chapter 6). All you do is lay the unused strand of yarn across the tops of the stitches of the previous row. Then, using the new color, work the stitches in the current row and encase the strand, as Figure 9-4 shows.

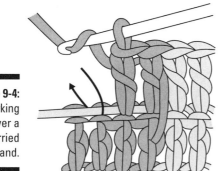

Figure 9-4:
Working over a carried strand.

The carried color is sometimes slightly visible, depending on the type and color of the yarn and the stitches you're using. But don't worry because more often than not this visibility adds depth and contrast to the design.

Carrying on the right side

The only reason you ever carry the yarn on the right side is if the carried strand is an integral part of your design. For example, carrying a thin strand studded with sequins or mirrors across the right side can add fancy flash to a project made with otherwise simple yarn.

You carry the yarn across the right side the same way you carry it across the wrong side of the work (see the earlier section, "Carrying on the wrong side"). You may want to catch the strand every other stitch or even every stitch, depending on the pattern, to make sure that no long, loose loops are hanging around. If your pattern calls for this carrying method, the instructions will indicate how often to catch the yarn.

Carrying up the side

Carrying the yarn up the side comes in handy when you're working a horizontal stripe pattern. However, this technique works only when you're crocheting stripes in even numbers of rows. If you're working a stripe pattern that changes color every row, the carried yarn won't be on the side you need it to be when you want to pick it up in the next row.

To carry a strand of yarn up the side edge of your work, work through the following steps:

1. **Work 2 rows in the first color, switching colors of yarn in the last stitch of the second row.**

   To switch colors of yarn, follow the first set of steps in the section "Changing color at the beginning," earlier in this chapter.

2. **Work 2 rows with the second color.**

3. **Draw up the first color from 2 rows below to complete the last stitch of the second row and drop the second color, which you'll pick up later. (See Figure 9-5.)**

   If you pull the strand too tightly up the side, your design will pucker.

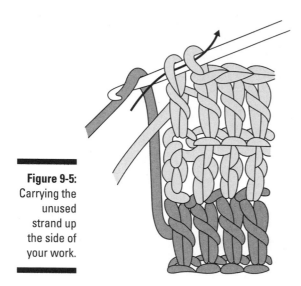

Figure 9-5:
Carrying the unused strand up the side of your work.

Demystifying Color Codes

Working with color has its own special language. To make the instructions more compact and concise, most instruction writers use abbreviations when referring to colorful designs. This section gives you the skinny on color codes and reading charts.

Abbreviating color names in patterns

When you first look at the instructions for a particular pattern, you obviously check to see what materials you need, including how many different colors of yarn the pattern uses. If the pattern involves two or more colors, you may see some funny letter designations after each color name.

Pairing up: Main color and contrasting color

If a pattern requires only two colors, the *main color* (abbreviated MC) is usually the first and most prominent color within the pattern. The *contrasting color* (CC) is the secondary color.

If the materials call for three skeins of white as the main color (MC) and two skeins of red as the contrasting color (CC), and the instruction is for a striped pattern, you may see something like this:

1. **Row 2: With MC, ch 1, sc in each sc across, complete last st with CC, *turn*. Fasten off MC.**

   Working with the main color (white), chain 1 and then work 1 single crochet stitch in each single crochet stitch across until you reach the next to last stitch, completing the last stitch of the row with the contrasting color (red). Fasten off the main color (white). Then, turn your work.

2. **Row 3: With CC, ch 1, sc in each sc across, *turn*.**

   Working now with the contrasting color (red), chain 1, work 1 single crochet in each single crochet stitch across the row, and then turn your work.

Three's a crowd: Letter abbreviations

When a design calls for three or more colors, patterns use letters of the alphabet to designate the colors. For example, a materials list that calls for six different colors may appear like this:

> 4 balls of Yellow (A); 3 balls each of White (B), Green (C), and Blue (D); 1 ball each of Pink (E) and Lilac (F).

Some patterns may use the initials of color names to abbreviate, such as (G) for green, (W) for white, and so on. Sometimes, a pattern has a main color (MC) along with several other colors designated A, B, C, and so on. As with MC and CC, patterns usually list the yarns in order of appearance in the pattern or by the quantity required. Be sure to read through the materials list at the beginning of each project so you're familiar with the color abbreviations. You may want to write out a separate list of the abbreviations and the color names to help keep things straight.

Charting color change

Many patterns use a color chart rather than written instructions to show designs that have frequent color changes or use several different colors. A color chart is a grid, with each square representing 1 stitch (see Figure 9-6a). Because most publications are in black and white, symbols in each square indicate the different colors. So always refer to the chart key to find out which symbol stands for which color (see Figure 9-6b).

When reading a chart, you generally read the odd-numbered rows from right to left and the even-numbered rows from left to right, unless otherwise specified. This is simply because you work your first row after the foundation chain from right to left and the second row from left to right. Figure 9-7 shows a swatch made from the chart in Figure 9-6.

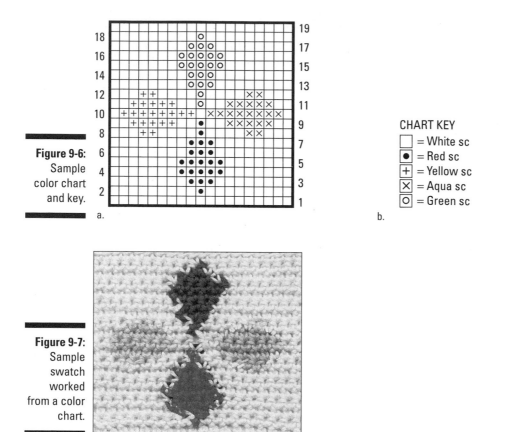

Figure 9-6:
Sample
color chart
and key.

CHART KEY

| | = White sc
● = Red sc
+ = Yellow sc
× = Aqua sc
○ = Green sc

a.   b.

Figure 9-7:
Sample
swatch
worked
from a color
chart.

Strawberry Pillow Project

Mastering the technique of changing color is a breeze with this charming strawberry pillow, which you can see in the color photo insert. Working with bulky-weight yarn and a large crochet hook makes it easy to see the stitches and work the color changes. This great beginning project makes a darling accent for any decor.

Materials

✔ **Yarn:** Coats & Clark "Red Heart Grande," bulky-weight yarn (100% acrylic), Article E720 (2 oz [*57 gm*] each skein):

• 2 skeins of #2101 White (MC)

• 1 skein of #2915 Spanish Cranberry (A)

- 1 skein of #2675 Dark Thyme (B)

Coats & Clark "Red Heart Classic" 4-ply worsted-weight yarn (100% acrylic), article E267 (3.5 oz [*99 gm*], 198 yds each skein): 1 skein of #0012 Black (C)

✔ **Hook:** Crochet hook size N-15 U.S. or size needed to obtain gauge (see Chapter 3 for info on gauge)

✔ **Yarn needle**

✔ **Pillow form:** 12 x 12 in. square

Vital statistics

✔ **Measurements:** 12 x 12 in.

✔ **Gauge:** 8 sts and 8 rows sc = 4 in.

✔ **Stitches used:** Chain stitch (ch), single crochet (sc)

✔ **Embroidery stitches used:** French knot

Directions

Work the pillow back in the main color. Work the pillow front following the chart in Figure 9-8. Read all odd-numbered rows from right to left, all even-numbered rows from left to right. To change color, complete the last single crochet of the first color with the next color. Drop the first color to the wrong side to be picked up later. Don't carry colors for more than 3 stitches. Attach separate balls of color as needed. Fasten off colors when they're not needed in the following row.

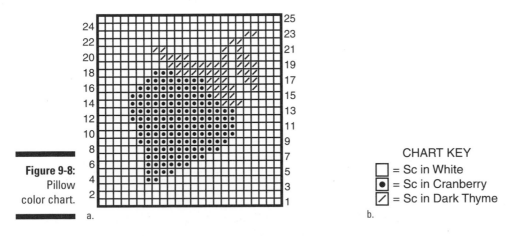

Figure 9-8:
Pillow
color chart.

a.

b.

CHART KEY

☐ = Sc in White

⊡ = Sc in Cranberry

◪ = Sc in Dark Thyme

Back

With MC, ch 25.

Row 1 (right side): Sc in second ch from hook, sc in each ch across (24 sc), *turn.*

Row 2: Ch 1, sc in each sc across (24 sc), *turn.*

Rows 3–25: Rep Row 2. Fasten off.

Front

With MC, ch 25.

Row 1 (right side)**:** Sc in second ch from hook, sc in each ch across (24 sc), *turn.*

Row 2: Ch 1, sc in each sc across (24 sc), *turn.*

Rows 3–25: Work in sc foll chart. *Do not* fasten off.

Embroidery

With yarn needle and C, randomly embroider French knots over the surface of the strawberry on the front to resemble seeds.

Joining round

With wrong sides of front and back facing, aligning top edges, working through double thickness, matching sts all around, ch 1, • sc in each sc across to next corner, work 3 sc in next corner •, rep from • to • around, inserting pillow form into cover before joining last side, sl st in first sc to join. Fasten off.

Part III
Advanced Stitches and Techniques

The 5th Wave   By Rich Tennant

Ch4, trc in 1 next 2 trc *ch10...?

That's the programming code for my mom's laptop.

In this part . . .

If you want to delve into more advanced crochet techniques, you came to the right spot. In this part, we introduce a number of more complex stitches to broaden your crochet expertise. To demonstrate the diversity you can achieve with a crochet hook, we take a look at two completely different variations on the craft: Afghan stitch and filet crochet. You also become well versed in the subject of sweater construction. We demonstrate each new stitch and technique that you encounter through a fun and practical project that may pique your interest.

Chapter 10

Design 101: Crocheting Your First Sweater

So you want to crochet a sweater? Although this may seem a bit daunting, it's really easier than you think. Many sweater designs are nothing more than squares sewn together. The simple shaping involved in these designs is as easy as increasing or decreasing a few stitches in the designated places. (Chapter 7 gives you a refresher on increasing and decreasing.) Of course, you'll want to take a few points into consideration before you dig in. You want to choose a design that you like and that suits your physique. And if you're new to the craft, you also need to consider the difficulty of the pattern. You want to choose your materials carefully, too, picking a yarn that's easy to work with so you don't become frustrated and give up before you finish.

This chapter shows you various sweater styles and how to construct them. You also see how sweaters are sized so that you can adjust patterns to suit your needs. And at the end of the chapter, we give you instructions for a simple sweater that you can crochet in no time flat.

Sweater Basics: Choosing Stitches and Yarn

To make sure that your first sweater attempt isn't your last, choose your stitch pattern and yarn carefully. You can crochet beautiful sweaters with simple stitch patterns and readily available yarns. This section gives you a heads up on what to keep in mind.

Making the right pattern choice

Make sure that the pattern you're considering isn't too complicated for your skill level before you buy it or any of the materials. (Refer to Chapter 5 for more info on reading patterns.) Here are some things to consider:

- ✔ If you want a sweater design that has an open, lacy pattern, try a pattern that uses yarn (it's easier to use than the cotton thread many lacy patterns call for) and a simple stitch repeat.

- ✔ If you want to crochet a sweater with more than one color, choose a pattern that has stripes or many different-colored *motifs* (crocheted rounds — see Chapter 8). Crocheting a pattern with color changes throughout is much more difficult than working a sweater in simple stripes or motifs. Another option is to use a multicolored or variegated yarn. This gives you color variation without your having to worry about changing yarn colors throughout (see Chapter 2 for info on substituting yarns).

- ✔ As a newbie, you also want to avoid a pattern that calls for crocheting with two strands of yarn held together as one. Working with more than one strand of yarn can be confusing.

- ✔ For your first sweater, find a pattern that suggests a smooth yarn, such as wool or a wool blend, or a synthetic yarn, such as acrylic. These yarns are easier to work with than highly textured novelty yarns, such as *boucles* or *eyelash* yarn. (Refer to Chapter 2 for more on the types of yarn.) The extra tufts on some novelty yarns make for a bumpy crochet experience, and if you happen to make a mistake and have to tear out some stitches, you may end up tearing out your hair as well.

- ✔ Choose a pattern that you like or you'll lose interest within the first ten minutes.

If you're brave enough to go ahead and buy a pattern with new stitches, be sure to work a practice swatch to get a feel for them before beginning the sweater.

Finding the right yarn

Choosing the right yarn to work with means more than just picking your favorite color. Select a yarn that complements the pattern and yet won't tie you up in knots while you're crocheting with it. Of course, the pattern usually recommends a yarn so you have a ballpark idea of the yarn weight you need, such as sport weight or worsted weight, and the yarn material, such as acrylic or wool blend.

Keep in mind the following factors when you go yarn shopping:

- **Feel:** For a softer sweater, choose a lighter-weight yarn or a pattern with looser stitches. Crocheting with the heavier weights of yarn can produce a stiff sweater that feels a bit like a cardboard box.

- **Fiber content:** Generally, natural fibers make for a more attractive and comfortable garment; however, they can be quite expensive and may require hand washing or dry cleaning. For your first sweater, acrylic may be more practical and easier to work with. Acrylic yarns tend to be really soft and come in a variety of textures and colors.

    Mixing materials can lead to disastrous results when you wash your sweater, so if a pattern calls for two or more yarn types or colors, be sure to compare the care instructions on the yarn labels. Always choose yarns with the same laundering requirements.

- **Twist:** Use yarns with a nice twist to the strand; yarns without much twist have a tendency to split while you're crocheting.

- **Quantity:** When buying yarn for a project, be sure to purchase enough for the entire project. The materials list at the beginning of the pattern specifies the amount you need in order to complete the design. If you run out, you may not be able to find the color you need in the same dye lot (see Chapter 2), and you may end up with an unplanned two-tone sweater.

- **Quality:** Don't skimp on materials. You get what you pay for, and after all your hard work, you want a sweater that retains its beauty for years to come. (See Chapter 2 for the ins and outs of yarn selection).

Sweater Construction: Selecting a Super Style

You work most sweater designs in separate pieces — the back, the front (or fronts for a cardigan), the sleeves, and any borders desired — and sew or crochet them together after you complete them. (See Chapter 15 for more on joining pieces of crochet.) How you make these pieces and put them together determines the sweater's style. The simpler styles have little or no shaping to the pieces. More-complicated designs may have shaping or decreasing around the armholes and at the neck. This section shows you several basic designs that you may want to consider.

For your first sweater, choose a pattern with simple shaping. Most sweater patterns include a *schematic* — a diagram of the sweater construction. The schematic includes the important measurements, such as the width of the back and front(s), the *armhole depth* (the size of the opening that you put your arms through), the sleeve length, and the finished back length.

Baring arms: Sleeveless sweaters

The simplest sleeveless styles have two panels that you join at the center back and center front, producing a V-neck with a small overhang at the shoulder (see Figure 10-1a). You can make a shell by merely skipping stitches at the side seams to make armholes and skipping across the center to make the neck opening. (See Figure 10-1b.)

Figure 10-1:
Sleeveless sweater styles: (a) two-panel V-neck and (b) simple shell.

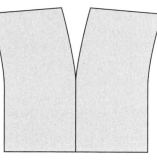
a.

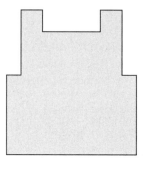
b.

With only minor shaping at the armholes and around the neck, you can make a simple tank top. (See Figure 10-2a.) The classic sleeveless vest cardigan usually requires a bit more shaping at the armholes and neck, but you can still make it with relative ease. (See Figure 10-2b.)

Figure 10-2:
More sleeveless sweater styles: (a) tank top with shaping and (b) classic vest cardigan.

a.

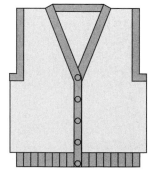
b.

Pretty in pullovers

You can make a pullover with almost any combination of sleeve and neck styles. Figure 10-3 shows you one of the simplest combinations. It has drop shoulders, wide cuffs, and a boat neck without borders or ribbing to complicate the design. A long sweater with no ribbing at the bottom is a *tunic* style, and a short sweater is sometimes called a *crop top*.

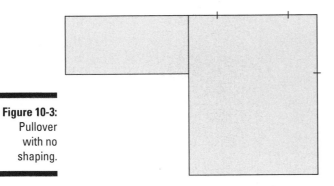

Figure 10-3:
Pullover
with no
shaping.

Sweaters with tapered sleeves and some shaping at the neck are more common. Both sweaters in Figure 10-4 have tapered sleeves. (Tapered sleeves are easier than they look: You just start at the cuff edge and increase on each side until the sleeves reach the desired circumference or start at the top edge and decrease until you get to the cuff.) The crew-neck sweater in Figure 10-4a has no armhole shaping and subsequently has dropped shoulders; the V-neck sweater in Figure 10-4b has inset sleeves for a more tailored look.

Frequently, ribbing or borders edge the bottom, cuffs, and neck opening. (See Chapter 16 for more on ribbing and borders.)

Figure 10-4:
Pullover
styles: (a)
drop-
shoulder
crew-neck
and (b) inset
sleeves with
a V-neck.

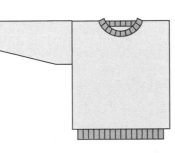

a.

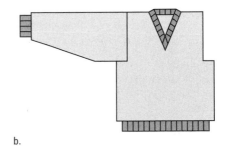

b.

The cap sleeve is fitted to the shape of the body and produces less bulk under the arms. (See Figure 10-5a.) The upper sleeve edge is shaped in a curve to fit into the shaped armholes. This cap-sleeve sweater sports a scoop neck and fold-down collar. You usually work the raglan-sleeve style (see Figure 10-5b) in one piece, starting at the neck and increasing at the "seam" point between the sleeves and the body of the sweater as you work down. This style has the advantage of having few, if any, seams to sew.

Figure 10-5:
Pullover styles: (a) cap sleeves with a scoop neck and (b) raglan styling.

a.   b.

Buttoning up with cardigans

Cardigans can have tapered sleeves or straight sleeves, inset sleeves or dropped shoulders, scooped necks, V-necks, or boat necks, just like pullovers. The only difference is that cardigans have two fronts, so you sew the front to the back a little differently. Figure 10-6 shows a V-neck cardigan and a hooded cardigan, both with tapered sleeves.

Figure 10-6:
Cardigan styles: (a) V-neck and (b) hooded.

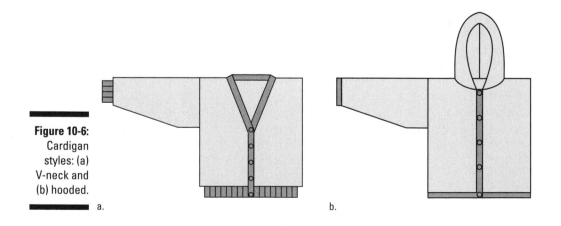

a.   b.

TIP

Think flatter, not fatter

Before you buy a pattern, consider the style of the sweater that you hope to crochet. Does it flatter you or does it make you look like a pumpkin? Vertical lines can make you look thinner, but the construction of the sweater also affects how it looks on you. For example, dropped shoulders can look rather sloppy, but inset sleeves look tailored. The length of the sweater is important to consider, too. Not everyone is cut out to wear a crop top. A sweater with ribbing that tends to cut you across the waist may be ideal for a thin, tall shape; a long tunic style, on the other hand, has a streamlining effect on a fuller figure. A boat neck can take away the look of sloped shoulders, and if you have narrow shoulders, wearing a cap sleeve with a slight puff can beef them up.

Making sweater magic: Motifs and vertical rows

Motifs and vertical rows are two fairly common design methods that can create a sweater with a lot of visual interest without you having to learn a bunch of complex stitch patterns.

Motifs are small crocheted pieces worked in rounds (see Chapter 8 for details) that you sew or crochet together (see Figure 10-7a). You can use square or hexagonal, round or triangular motifs of almost any size, providing that all parts add up to the sweater measurements.

You can also crochet a one-piece sweater in vertical rows (see Figure 10-7b), starting at one cuff edge, working to the shoulder, and then increasing for the length of the body of the sweater in the front and the back. Even though it seems a bit more complex, this technique is great for making a flattering sweater.

Figure 10-7:
Unique construction:
(a) motif sweater and (b) vertical-stripe cardigan.

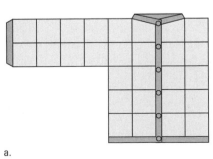
a.

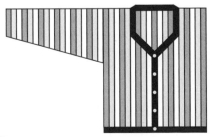
b.

Sizing Up the Sweater Situation

When is a Small not a Small? When your sweater pattern lists it as a Medium — and it may do just that. So far, no industry sizing standard exists, so you need to look carefully to determine your size when picking out a pattern. As if that weren't enough, each type of sweater will fit your body differently. One size may be right if you want a snug sweater, but that same size is all wrong if you're setting out to crochet a sweater so baggy it could hold you and a friend. Even if you can't find the perfect pattern, you may be able to alter the next best thing to get what you want. This section shows you how to read the sweater sizes, determine the right size for you, and adjust the pattern accordingly.

Understanding sweater pattern sizes

Most sweater patterns list the size ranges (and one pattern may include several sizes) at the beginning of the instructions. You may find the back length and sleeve length listed as well. And you may even find a schematic diagram showing the measurements of the different pieces.

Sweater patterns also include the instructions for making all the listed sizes. Usually, patterns list the directions for the smallest size first, followed by changes for the larger sizes in parentheses. For example:

Sc in each of next 50 (54, 58) stitches.

In this example, you work 50 single crochet stitches if you're making a size Small, 54 single crochet stitches for size Medium, and 58 single crochet stitches for Large. To make such a pattern easier to follow, highlight all the numbers for your size before you begin.

Figuring out fit

Choosing the right size depends on the kind of fit you want. Some sweater styles are specifically designed to be loose fitting, but others are supposed to be snug. So if you normally wear a size Medium, don't assume that the Medium in the pattern is automatically the fit you want.

The best way to ensure a great-fitting sweater is to first decide what fit you want: body hugging, close fitting, normal fitting, loose fitting, or oversized. Then forget what the pattern labels as Small or Large, measure your own bust line, and add to or subtract from it to get your desired fit. Table 10-1 tells you how many inches to add to (or subtract from) your own bust measurements to come up with a finished bust measurement that achieves the fit you desire. (The _finished bust measurement_ is the total number of inches around the bust of the finished sweater — which isn't necessarily the same as your own bust measurement.) You then take this adjusted bust measurement and find the pattern size that matches it.

Table 10-1	Determining Sweater Fit
Fit You Want	_Number of Inches to Subtract from or Add to Your Bust Measurement_
Body hugging	–1–2
Close	+ 1–2
Normal	+ 2–4
Loose	+ 4–6
Oversized	+ 6–8

For example, if you have a 36-inch bust and want to make a normal-fitting sweater, add 2 to 4 inches to your bust measurement for a total finished bust of 38 to 40 inches. Now look at the pattern for the finished bust measurement closest to this range. If you don't find an exact measurement, choose the next larger size for a comfortable fit. Usually patterns offer sizes in 4-inch increments. However, that's not always the case. You may have a pattern that offers the bust sizes of 36 inches, 41 inches, and 46 inches. In this case, the 41-inch size is your best choice for a comfortable fit.

Working to the designated gauge is especially important when making sweaters. The gauge determines how many stitches you use for a given finished bust size. If your gauge is off, then your finished garment will be as well. The sweater that's supposed to have a 38-inch finished bust measurement may very well end up being a 34 if your gauge is too tight, or a 42 if it's too loose.

Customizing your pattern

If you find a sweater that you want to make, but it doesn't have directions for your size, you may be able to alter it on your own. This section shows you how to get the size you need.

Adjusting the finished bust size

For sweaters that you work in horizontal rows, adjusting the bust size is fairly simple. Suppose that the pattern for a cardigan offers finished bust measurements of 36, 40, and 44 inches, but you need a 48-inch finished bust. To get the extra 4 inches you need, adjust the directions for the largest size by adding 2 inches to the back width and 1 inch to each of the two front pieces (or 2 inches to the front width if you're working the front as one piece). You work the armholes and the length in the same manner as in the size-44 pattern.

Now check the gauge (refer to Chapter 3) for the pattern stitch and calculate approximately how many extra stitches you need to add to the back and the front to get your 4 extra inches. For example, if the pattern has just one stitch, such as single crochet, and the gauge is 9 stitches = 2 inches, you need to add approximately 9 stitches to the back width and approximately 5 stitches to each front piece of the cardigan.

But if you have a stitch pattern that repeats across the body of the sweater, you need to increase your stitch count in multiples of the stitch repeat. For example, if the pattern for the body of the sweater is • (double crochet, chain 1, double crochet) in next stitch, skip next 2 stitches •, then the multiple (or repeated part of the pattern) is 3 stitches, and any adjusting you do has to be in a multiple of 3 stitches. For the back, you can easily add 9 stitches, which is a multiple of 3 stitches. But, for the front, 5 stitches isn't divisible by 3, so you need to add the next multiple of 3, which is 6 stitches. (Refer to Chapter 5 for more on multiples and repeated patterns.)

This method works well with fairly simple patterns, but for patterns with large repeats, adjusting the size and maintaining the original pattern isn't always possible. Sometimes, changing to a larger crochet hook and working the largest size offered creates a sweater that's a size larger. Crochet a gauge swatch (refer to Chapter 3) with the next larger size hook and calculate how big the sweater would be if you used that hook size. If this isn't large enough, try the next larger hook. Make sure that the looser gauge produces a comfortable fabric that isn't too sloppy looking or so holey that you can see through it.

Lengthening the sweater and sleeves

If you want to adjust the sweater or sleeve length, you can usually just increase or reduce the number of rows you work. Adjust the length of the sweater by adding or deleting rows at the bottom edge (so you don't mess up the shaping around the arm holes). Alter the sleeve length either above or below the shaping, depending on how it's made. Just make sure that you've added all the stitches to ensure a comfortable fit around the upper arm and shoulder.

Simple Sweater Project

The pullover sweater design in this project (pictured in the color photo section in this book) has minimal shaping and only a few simple stitches but creates a beautiful sweater you can wear for years to come. It features drop shoulders and a crew neck finished with simple rounds of single crochet. The yarn for this pattern is a heavy worsted-weight wool blend that allows you to crochet the sweater in a relatively short amount of time.

Size

Directions are for size Small (4–6). Changes for Medium (8–10), Large (12–14), and X-Large (16–18) are in parentheses. Finished bust: 36 (40, 44, 48) in. Back length: 26 (26, 27, 28) in. Sleeve length: 21 in. Use the sweater schematic in Figure 10-8 to determine which size to make.

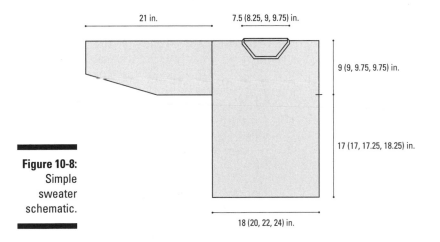

21 in.   7.5 (8.25, 9, 9.75) in.

9 (9, 9.75, 9.75) in.

17 (17, 17.25, 18.25) in.

18 (20, 22, 24) in.

Figure 10-8:
Simple
sweater
schematic.

Materials

- ✓ **Yarn:** Fiesta Yarns "Kokopelli," heavy worsted-weight yarn (60% mohair/ 40% wool) (4 oz. [113 *gm*], 130 yds. each hank): 8 (9, 9, 10) hanks of #K20 Indian Paintbrush

- ✓ **Hook:** Crochet hook size K-10½ U.S. or size needed to obtain gauge (refer to Chapter 3 for more on gauge)

- ✓ **Yarn needle**

Vital statistics

✔ **Gauge:** 8 sts = 3 in.; 10 rows in pat = 5 in.

✔ **Stitches used:** Chain stitch (ch), slip stitch (sl st), single crochet (sc), half double crochet (hdc), double crochet (dc), triple crochet (tr). **Crossed dc:** • Skip next st, dc in next st, working behind dc just made, dc in last skipped st •. (For more information on the crossed double crochet stitch in this design, see Chapter 12.) **Dec 1 hdc:** • (Insert hook in next st, yo, draw yarn through st) 2 times, yo, draw yarn through 3 loops on hook •. Figure 10-9 shows a reduced sample of the stitch pattern for Rows 1–12. See the Cheat Sheet at the front of the book to decipher all the symbols used.

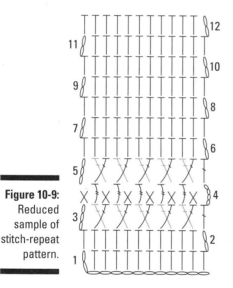

Figure 10-9: Reduced sample of stitch-repeat pattern.

Directions

We give you the row-by-row instructions for this sweater as you'd see them in any crochet publication. If they seem like Greek to you, head on over to Chapter 5 for information on reading crochet patterns.

Back

Chain 47 (53, 59, 65) + 2 (first hdc).

Row 1 (wrong side): Hdc in third ch from hook, hdc in each ch across (48 [54, 60, 66] hdc), *turn*.

Row 2 (right side): Ch 2 (first hdc), hdc in each hdc across, hdc in top of turning ch (48 [54, 60, 66] hdc), *turn*.

Row 3: Ch 3 (first dc), • skip next hdc, dc in next hdc, working behind dc just made, dc in skipped hdc (crossed dc made) •, rep from • to • across to within turning ch, dc in top of turning ch (48 [54, 60, 66] dc), *turn*.

Row 4: Ch 4 (first tr), • sc in next dc, tr in next dc •, rep from • to • across to within turning ch, sc in top of turning ch (48 [54, 60, 66] sts), *turn*.

Row 5: Ch 3 (first dc), • skip next tr, dc in next sc, working behind dc just made, dc in last skipped tr (crossed dc made) •, rep from • to • across to within turning ch, dc in turning ch (48 [54, 60, 66] dc), *turn*.

Rows 6–12: Ch 2 (first hdc), hdc in each st across, hdc in turning ch (48 [54, 60, 66] hdc), *turn*.

Rows 13–52: Rep Rows 3–12 (4 times). Fasten off sizes Small and Medium.

For sizes Large and X-Large only: Rows 53–54 (53–56): Rep Row 2 (2 [4] times). Fasten off.

Front

Work same as back through Row 46 (46, 48, 50).

Shape Right Neck: Row 47 (47, 49, 51): Ch 2 (first hdc), hdc in each of next 17 (19, 21, 23) hdc (18 [20, 22, 24] hdc), *turn*.

Row 48 (48, 50, 52): Ch 2 (first hdc), dec 1 hdc in next 2 sts, hdc in each hdc across, hdc in top of turning ch (17 [19, 21, 23] hdc), *turn*.

Row 49 (49, 51, 53): Ch 2 (first hdc), hdc in each hdc across to within last 2 sts, dec 1 hdc in last 2 sts (16 [18, 20, 22] hdc), *turn*.

Rows 50–51 (50–51, 52–53, 54–55): Rep Rows 48–49 (48–49, 50–51, 52–53) 1 time (14 [16, 18, 20] hdc at end of last row), *turn*.

Row 52 (52, 54, 56): Ch 2 (first hdc), hdc in each st across (14 [16, 18, 20] hdc). Fasten off.

Shape Left Neck: Row 47 (47, 49, 51): With wrong side facing, skip 12 (14, 16, 18) hdc to the left of last hdc made in first row of Right Neck Shaping, join yarn in next st, ch 2 (first hdc), hdc in each hdc across, hdc in top of turning ch (18 [20, 22, 24] hdc), *turn.*

Row 48 (48, 50, 52): Ch 2 (first hdc), hdc in each hdc across to within last 2 sts, dec 1 hdc in last 2 sts (17 [19, 21, 23] hdc), *turn.*

Row 49 (49, 51, 53): Ch 2 (first hdc), dec 1 hdc in next 2 sts, hdc in each hdc across, hdc in top of turning ch (16 [18, 20, 22] hdc), *turn.*

Rows 50–51 (50–51, 52–53, 54–55): Rep Rows 48–49 (48–49, 50–51, 52–53) 1 time (14 [16, 18, 20] hdc at end of last row), *turn.*

Row 52 (52, 54, 56): Ch 2 (first hdc), hdc in each st across (14 [16, 18, 20] hdc). Fasten off.

Sleeves

Make 2: Ch 23 (23, 27, 27) + 2 (first hdc).

Row 1 (wrong side): Hdc in third ch from hook, hdc in each ch across (24 [24, 28, 28] hdc), *turn.*

Row 2 (right side): Ch 2 (first hdc), hdc in each hdc across, hdc in top of turning ch (24 [24, 28, 28] hdc), *turn.*

Row 3: Ch 3 (first dc), • skip next hdc, dc in next hdc, working behind dc just made, dc in skipped hdc (crossed dc made) •, rep from • to • across to within turning ch, dc in top of turning ch (24 [24, 28, 28] dc), *turn.*

Row 4: Ch 4 (first tr), • sc in next dc, tr in next dc •, rep from • to • across, to within turning ch, sc in top of turning ch (24 [24, 28, 28] sts), *turn.*

Row 5: Ch 3 (first dc), • skip next tr, dc in next sc, working behind dc just made, dc in last skipped tr (crossed dc made)•, rep from • to • across to within turning ch, dc in top of turning ch (24 [24, 28, 28] dc), *turn.*

Row 6: Ch 2 (first hdc), hdc in first dc (inc made), hdc in each st across to within turning ch, 2 hdc in top of turning ch (inc made) (26 [26, 30, 30] hdc), *turn.*

Row 7: Ch 2 (first hdc), hdc in each hdc across, hdc in top of turning ch (26 [26, 30, 30] hdc), *turn.*

Row 8: Ch 2 (first hdc), hdc in first dc (inc made), hdc in each st across to within turning ch, 2 hdc in top of turning ch (inc made) (28 [28, 32, 32] hdc), *turn*.

Row 9: Ch 2 (first hdc), hdc in each hdc across, hdc in top of turning ch (28 [28, 32, 32] hdc), *turn*.

Row 10: Ch 2 (first hdc), hdc in first dc (inc made), hdc in each st across to within turning ch, 2 hdc in top of turning ch (inc made) (30 [30, 34, 34] hdc), *turn*.

Row 11: Ch 2 (first hdc), hdc in each hdc across, hdc in top of turning ch (30 [30, 34, 34] hdc), *turn*.

Row 12: Ch 2 (first hdc), hdc in first dc (inc made), hdc in each st across to within turning ch, 2 hdc in top of turning ch (inc made) (32 [32, 36, 36] hdc), *turn*.

Rows 13–32: Rep Rows 3–12 (twice) (48 [48, 52, 52] sts at end of last row).

Rows 33–35: Rep Rows 3–5 (once).

Rows 36–42: Ch 2 (first hdc), hdc in each st across, hdc in top of turning ch (48 [48, 52, 52] hdc), *turn*. Fasten off.

Assembly

With right sides of front and back facing each other, take a yarn needle and yarn and follow these steps:

1. **Sew front to back across shoulders.**

   (See Chapter 15 for more on sewing.)

2. **With the right side of the fabric facing in, fold sleeves in half lengthwise.**

3. **Matching the center fold to the shoulder seam, sew each sleeve in place.**

4. **Beginning at lower edge of side, match stitches across side edges and sew side and underarm seams.**

Use the schematic in Figure 10-8 to check your finished pieces for accuracy in sizing.

Finishing

The neck edging is just your basic single crochet stitch.

Rnd 1: With right side facing, join yarn in one shoulder seam, ch 1, sc evenly around entire neck edge, sl st in first sc to join.

Rnds 2–3: Ch 1, sc in each sc around, sl st in first sc to join. Fasten off.

Chapter 11

Fancy Stitches That Steal the Show

*O*ne of the qualities of crochet that makes it so unique is its flexibility — you can fashion an almost endless array of patterns and textures based on a few simple stitches. Chapters 4 and 6 show you how to create these basic stitches. This chapter shows you how to combine them to make pattern stitches like shells and clusters, and textured stitches like popcorns, bobbles, and loops. And along with illustrations of the completed stitches, we give you the International Crochet Symbol for each stitch so you're prepared for reading stitch diagrams (see Chapter 5 for more). The pillow top sampler project at the end of the chapter incorporates many of these stitches, so you can practice them while creating nifty home decor.

Adding Some Spice: Pattern Stitches

The versatile V-stitch, crossed double crochet, shell, picot, cluster, and reverse single crochet stitches can create stitch designs that are open and lacy or tight and compact. As you become familiar with these stitches, you'll recognize them in many, many patterns — anywhere from home decor to fashion.

As you branch out in the crocheting world, you'll probably come across variations of the pattern stitches in this section. So don't assume that you always work a cluster stitch exactly as we define it here. But no worries — pattern instructions usually tell you specifically how to work a pattern stitch, so be sure to carefully read the notes at the beginning.

Showing the V: The V-stitch

The *V-stitch* (abbreviated *V-st*) combination is so called because it resembles (guess what?) a *V*.

To create a V-stitch, work 1 double crochet stitch, chain 1, and then work another double crochet stitch all in the same stitch (see Figure 11-1a for a completed stitch). In crochet-speak, that's (Dc, ch 1, dc) in the same stitch. Figure 11-1b shows the V-stitch symbol.

This V-stitch is one of the most common stitches, but as always, you can find variations.

Figure 11-1:
Common
V-stitch.

a.   b.

XXX: The crossed double crochet stitch

For the *crossed double crochet stitch* (abbreviated *crossed dc*), you work two double crochet stitches on an angle, producing a pattern that looks like an *X*. To make a crossed double crochet stitch, follow these steps:

1. **Skip the next stitch in the row.**

2. **Work 1 double crochet (dc) in the next stitch.**

3. **Working behind the double crochet that you just made, work 1 double crochet in the stitch that you skipped. (See Figure 11-2a.)**

   Figure 11-2b shows the completed stitch, and Figure 11-2c shows the stitch symbol.

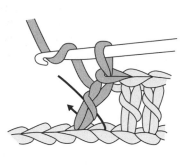

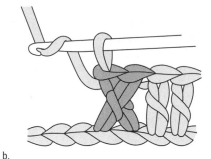

Figure 11-2:
Working a
crossed
double
crochet.

To continue working crossed double crochet stitches across the row, repeat Steps 1 through 3.

Fanning out: The shell stitch

The *shell stitch* (abbreviated *shell*) is very versatile, and you can find it just about anywhere. The variation we describe here is one common version of this adaptable stitch. To make a shell stitch, work 4 double crochet stitches in the same stitch (see Figure 11-3a for the completed stitch and Figure 11-3b for the stitch symbol).

Figure 11-3:
One
complete
4-double-
crochet
shell stitch.

Little knobbies: The picot stitch

Picots (no abbreviation) are pretty little round-shaped stitches that add a decorative touch to an edging or fill an empty space in a mesh design. You see them quite often in thread crochet, but you can also make them with yarn. To make a picot, follow these steps:

1. **Chain (ch) 3.**

2. **Insert your hook in the third chain from the hook. (See Figure 11-4a.)**

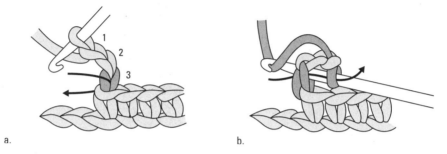

Figure 11-4: Making a picot stitch.

a.   b.

3. **Yarn over (yo).**

4. **Draw the yarn through the stitch and through the loop on the hook. (Refer to Figure 11-4b.)**

   One picot is complete, as shown in Figure 11-5a. Check out the stitch symbol in Figure 11-5b.

Figure 11-5: Finished picot stitch.

a.   b.

Pythagorean delight: The cluster stitch

A *cluster* (no abbreviation) is a set of stitches that you work across an equal number of stitches and join together at the top, forming a triangle shape that resembles an upside-down shell stitch. Many crocheters use this stitch combination in conjunction with shells. To make a cluster of 4 double crochet stitches, work through these steps:

1. **Yarn over (yo), insert the hook into the next stitch, yarn over, draw the yarn through the stitch, yarn over, draw the yarn through 2 loops on the hook (2 loops remain on the hook).**

   One half-closed double crochet is complete. A *half-closed stitch* is one that's only worked partway, and then finished at the end of the combination.

2. **Repeat Step 1 three times (see Figure 11-6a).**

   You should end up with 5 loops on the hook.

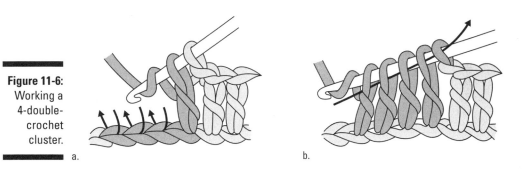

Figure 11-6: Working a 4-double-crochet cluster.

a.   b.

3. **Yarn over and draw the yarn through all 5 loops on the hook. (Refer to Figure 11-6b.)**

   One 4-double-crochet (4-dc) cluster is complete. See Figure 11-7a for the completed cluster and Figure 11-7b for the symbol.

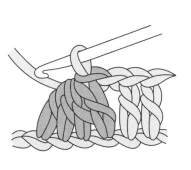

Figure 11-7: Finished 4-double-crochet cluster stitch.

a.   b.

Getting crabby: The reverse single crochet stitch

The *reverse single crochet* stitch (abbreviated *reverse sc*) is sometimes called the crab stitch. The actual mechanics are the same as for a regular single crochet — except in reverse. Instead of working from right to left, you work from left to right. It creates a somewhat twisted, rounded edge that's good for making a simple finished edge for your work. You usually don't work stitches into the tops of the reverse single crochet, so you won't find this stitch in the middle of a project. To work reverse single crochet, follow these steps:

1. **With the right side of your work facing you, insert the hook, from front to back, in the next stitch to the right. (See Figure 11-8a.)**

2. **Yarn over (yo) and draw the yarn through the stitch. (See Figure 11-8b.)**

Figure 11-8:
Working
a reverse
single
crochet.

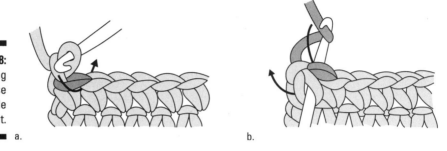

a.   b.

3. **Yarn over and draw the yarn through the 2 loops on the hook. (See Figure 11-9a.)**

   One reverse single crochet is complete.

4. **Repeat Steps 1 through 3 in each stitch across the row.**

   Figure 11-9b shows several completed reverse single crochet stitches, and Figure 11-9c shows the stitch symbol.

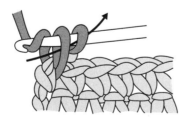

a.

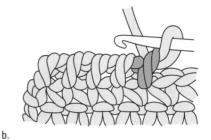

b.

Figure 11-9:
Finishing
the reverse
single
crochet.

c.

It's beginner's luck — I mean talent! With just basic skills you can make these colorful placemats and coasters. Make them each a different color for a rainbow effect or choose one color to match your decor (see pattern in Chapter 4).

These floral motifs make great package toppers. Or sew them on a jean jacket or a crocheted hat. You can use the same pattern with a fine cotton thread for a more delicate flower or with a heavier yarn for a chunky look (see Chapter 8 for the pattern).

This sassy scarf combines all the basic crochet stitches from the chain stitch to the double triple crochet stitch. The pattern may be simple to do, but the result is a smashing accent for your wardrobe (see Chapter 6 for the pattern).

These two colorful bandanas hone your stitch increasing and decreasing skills. Crochet both for twice the fun (see Chapter 7 for the pattern).

This cloche hat introduces the technique of crocheting in rounds. A pretty variegated yarn turns basic stitches into a charming fashion accessory (see Chapter 8 for the pattern).

This attractive floral motif vest demonstrates the versatility of cotton thread. Available in a wide range of thread and yarn weights, this soft and comfortable fiber is not just for doilies anymore (see the vest pattern in Chapter 15).

The basic shaping on this simple sweater combined with the comfortable, heavy-weight yarn makes crocheting your first sweater a breeze (see Chapter 10 for the pattern).

Create the pretty strawberry design on this colorful pillow cover by working with more than one yarn color at a time (see Chapter 9 for the pattern).

Combine basic crochet stitches to create fancy shapes and textures. This pillow-top sampler uses many of these fancy combination stitches to produce a lacy covering for an accent pillow (see the pattern in Chapter 11).

These three scarves for all seasons illustrate different stitch placement techniques. The basketweave scarf (left) uses post stitches. The feathery scarf (center) demonstrates working in the spaces or loops. And the textured scarf (right) utilizes front loop and back loop crocheting (see patterns in Chapter 12).

This decorative potholder introduces you to Afghan stitch, a popular crochet technique that resembles knitting. These squarish stitches lend themselves to working colored designs as well as cross-stitch patterns (see pattern in Chapter 13).

You can join crocheted pieces together in many ways. This motif Afghan illustrates one method of joining motifs. The yarn used to make it produces a soft, cuddly accent that's quick and easy to make (see pattern in Chapter 15).

This country cardigan demonstrates many of the embellishments used to accent sweaters. Patch pockets and contrasting edgings give this versatile sweater its country charm (see Chapter 16).

This beautiful butterfly runner, created using filet crochet, is also lovely framed on a solid color background or sewn onto a pillow front. (Chapter 14 reveals how to make this runner.)

Moving into the Third Dimension: Texture Stitches

If you want to add even more pizzazz to your crocheting, these three-dimensional stitch combinations create great textures in your crocheted fabric. You can interchange the first three because they all look like different versions of a bumpy oval. The last one, the loop stitch, creates long, fun loops that come in handy when making toys, sweaters, slippers, and wallhangings.

Because stitches aren't standardized in any way, you may come across many different names for them. For example, *puff stitches* are sometimes referred to as *bobbles,* even though they're created in completely different ways. So always read the specifics for each stitch before beginning your work.

Not a magic dragon: The puff stitch

The *puff stitch* (abbreviated *puff st*) is aptly named because it gently puffs up into an oval shape. Making a puff stitch is similar to making a cluster in that you half-close several stitches worked in the same stitch and then join them together to finish the stitch. To make a 3-double-crochet puff stitch, follow the yellow brick road:

1. **Yarn over (yo), insert the hook in the stitch, yarn over, draw the yarn through the stitch, yarn over, and draw the yarn through the 2 loops on the hook.**

   One half-closed double crochet is complete, and 2 loops remain on the hook, as Figure 11-10a shows.

2. **In the same stitch, repeat Step 1 twice.**

   You should have 4 loops on your hook.

Figure 11-10:
Creating a
puff stitch.

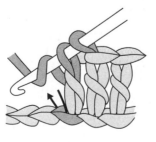

a.

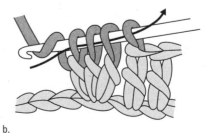

b.

3. **Yarn over and draw the yarn through all 4 loops on the hook. (Refer to Figure 11-10b.)**

   One 3-double-crochet puff stitch is complete. (See Figure 11-11a for the completed stitch and Figure 11-11b for the symbol.)

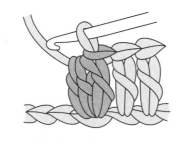

Figure 11-11:
Completed
puff stitch.

a.   b.

Forget the butter: The popcorn stitch

This stitch really pops! The *popcorn stitch* (abbreviated *pop* or *pc*) is a nicely rounded, compact oval that stands out from the fabric. It takes a bit more time to make than other raised stitches, but it's well worth the effort. For even more fun, you can work popcorn stitches so that they "pop" to the front or the back of the fabric, depending on where you want them to stand out. The following steps show how to work a 5-double-crochet popcorn stitch both ways.

To pop to the front of your design:

1. **Work 5 double crochet (dc) stitches in the same stitch.**

2. **Drop the loop from your hook.**

3. **Insert your hook from front to back under the top 2 loops of the first double crochet of the group.**

4. **Grab the dropped loop with your hook and pull it through the stitch. (See Figure 11-12a.)**

   One front-popping popcorn is complete. (See Figure 11-12b.) Note that the stitch symbol shown in Figure 11-12c is the same for a back or front popcorn.

To pop to the back of the work:

1. **Work 5 double crochet (dc) stitches in the same stitch.**

2. **Drop the loop from your hook.**

3. **Insert your hook from back to front under the top 2 loops of the first double crochet of the group.**

4. **Grab the dropped loop with your hook and pull it through the stitch. (See Figure 11-13a.)**

   One back-popping popcorn is complete. (See Figure 11-13b.)

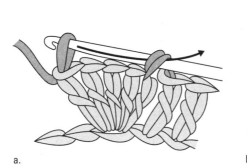

a.

b.

Figure 11-12: Completing a front popcorn stitch.

c.

Figure 11-13: Completing a back popcorn stitch.

a.

b.

Gently bumping along: The bobble stitch

A *bobble stitch* (no abbreviation) differs slightly from the other raised stitches because you make it with a series of loops, rather than stitches. This stitch creates a smooth, oval bump and works well with a heavier-weight yarn. To make a bobble, follow these steps:

1. **Yarn over (yo) and insert the hook in the stitch. (See Figure 11-14a.)**

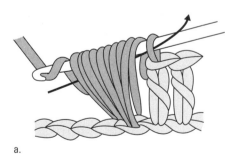

Figure 11-14:
Fashioning
a bobble
stitch.

a.   b.

2. **Yarn over and draw the yarn through the stitch, bringing the loop up to the height of the previous stitch.**

   You should have 3 loops on the hook. (Refer to Figure 11-14b.)

3. **Working in the same stitch, repeat Steps 1 through 2 four times.**

   You should have 11 loops on the hook.

4. **Yarn over and draw the yarn through all 11 loops on the hook. (See Figure 11-15a.)**

   One bobble is complete. (See Figure 11-15b for the completed stitch and Figure 11-15c for the stitch symbol.)

a.   b.

Figure 11-15:
Finishing
the bobble
stitch.

c.

Bobbles, along with puff and popcorn stitches, sometimes need an extra chain stitch at the top of the stitch to close them securely. If this is the case, the pattern usually tells you to do so.

Feeling loopy: The loop stitch

The *loop stitch* (no abbreviation) gets its name from the long, loose loops it leaves behind. Getting the loops all the same length takes some practice, but when you get the hang of it, the loop stitch adds a lot of interest to garments. It also works great to make a beard for Santa when worked in several consecutive rows.

To make a loop stitch, work through these steps:

1. **Wrap the yarn from front to back over the index finger of your yarn hand.**

   The length of the loop depends on how loose or tight you wrap the yarn in this step.

2. **Insert the hook in the next stitch.**

3. **With the hook, grab the strand of yarn from behind your index finger.**

4. **Draw the yarn through the stitch. (See Figure 11-16a.)**

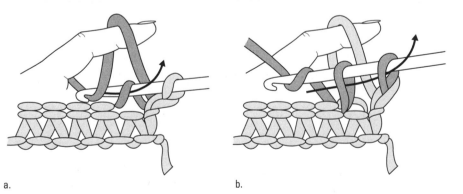

Figure 11-16: Making a loop stitch.

a.   b.

5. **With the yarn loop still on your index finger, yarn over (yo) the hook and draw the yarn through the 2 loops on your hook. (Refer to Figure 11-16b.)**

   One loop stitch is complete. (See Figure 11-17a for the completed stitch and Figure 11-17b for the symbol.)

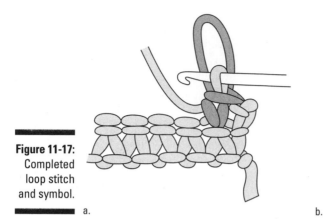

Figure 11-17:
Completed
loop stitch
and symbol.

a.　　　　　　　　　　　b.

Make sure that all the loops are the same length in order to achieve a finished look.

After working an area of loop stitch, you can cut all the loops to create a shaggy dog look.

Pillow Top Sampler Project

This pillow topper (which you can see in all its glory in the color section of this book) lets you practice most of the stitches in this chapter and show off your crochet skills while turning a plain, inexpensive pillow into an attractive home decor accent. Although the pillow looks fancy, the technique is actually quite easy because you're just working one new stitch per row. As always, feel free to experiment with your own color combinations.

Materials

- ✔ **Yarn:** J. & P. Coats "LusterSheen" sport-weight yarn (100% acrylic), Article A95 (1¾ oz. [*50 gm*], 150 yds. each ball): 2 balls of #129 Lilac
- ✔ **Hook:** Crochet hook size F-5 U.S. or size needed to obtain gauge (refer to Chapter 3 for info on gauge)
- ✔ **Sewing needle and clear nylon sewing thread**
- ✔ **Pillow:** 17 in. x 17 in.

Vital statistics

- ✔ **Measurements:** 14 in. x 14 in.

- ✔ **Gauge:** 10 sts in shell pat = 2 in.; 6 rows in pat = 2½ in.

- ✔ **Stitches used:** Chain stitch (ch), single crochet (sc), double crochet (dc). **V-st:** • (Dc, ch 1, dc) in same st or space •. **Shell:** • 5 dc in same st or space •. **Puff st:** • 5 dc (half closed and joined tog) worked in same st •. **Bobble:** • (Yo, insert hook in st, yo, draw through st) 5 times in same st, yo, draw yarn through 11 loops on hook •. **Popcorn (pop):** Work 5 dc in same st, drop loop from hook, insert hook from back to front in top of first dc of group, pull dropped loop through st •. **Picot:** • Ch 3, sl st in 3rd ch from hook •.

Directions

You work this project in three parts so that the stitches run in the same direction. After you complete the first half, simply turn the crocheted piece so that the foundation chain is facing up and work the five rows of the center strip design off the foundation chain. You then complete the second half (which is identical to the first half) by working off the center strip. Crocheter's use this method quite frequently to create a symmetrical design. See Figure 11-18 for the stitch diagram.

We give you the following steps as you'd see them in a regular crochet publication. If you need to refresh your memory a bit, flip back to Chapter 5.

First half

Ch 69 + 3 (first dc) + 1 (first space).

Row 1 (wrong side): V-st in 6th ch from hook, • ch 3, skip next 4 ch, V-st in next ch •, rep from • to • across to within last 2 ch, ch 1, skip next ch, dc in last ch (14 V-sts), *turn.*

Row 2: Ch 3 (first dc), shell in ch-1 space of each V-st across, skipping each ch-3 loop between V-sts, dc in top of turning ch (14 shells), *turn.*

Row 3: Ch 3 (first dc), ch 1, skip next 2 dc, V-st in next dc • ch 3, skip next 4 dc, V-st in next dc •, rep from • to • across to within 3 dc, ch 1, skip next 2 dc, dc in top of turning ch (14 V-sts), *turn.*

Row 4: Rep Row 2.

Row 5: Rep Row 3.

Row 6: Ch 3 (first dc), ch 2, • puff st in next V-st, ch 3, skip next ch-3 loop •, rep from • to • across to within last V-st, puff st in last V-st, ch 2, dc in top of turning ch (14 puff sts), *turn.*

Row 7: Ch 3 (first dc), ch 1, V-st in top of next puff st, • ch 3, V-st in top of next puff st •, rep from • to • across, ch 1, dc in top of turning ch (14 V-sts), *turn.*

Row 8: Ch 3 (first dc), ch 2, • bobble in next V-st, ch 3, skip next ch-3 loop •, rep from • to • across to within last V-st, bobble in last V-st, ch 2, dc in top of turning ch (14 bobbles), *turn.*

Row 9: Ch 3 (first dc), ch 1, V-st in top of next bobble, • ch 3, V-st in top of next bobble •, rep from • to • across, ch 1, dc in top of turning ch (14 V-sts), *turn.*

Row 10: Rep Row 6.

Row 11: Rep Row 7.

Row 12: Rep Row 2.

Row 13: Rep Row 3. Fasten off.

Center

Row 1: With wrong side facing, working across opposite side of foundation ch, join yarn in first ch, ch 1, sc in each ch across (70 sc), *turn.*

Row 2: Ch 3 (first dc), • skip next sc, dc in next sc, working behind dc just made, dc in skipped sc (crossed dc made) •, rep from • to • across to within last sc, dc in last sc (34 crossed dc), *turn.*

Row 3: Ch 3 (first dc), ch 1, skip next dc, • pop in next dc, ch 1, skip next dc, dc in next dc, ch 1, skip next dc •, rep from • to • across to within last 4 dc, pop in next dc, ch 1, skip next dc, dc in next dc, dc in top of turning ch (70 sts), *turn.*

Row 4: Ch 3 (first dc), • skip next st, dc in next st, working behind dc just made, dc in skipped st (crossed dc made) •, rep from • to • across to within last st, dc in top of turning ch (34 crossed dc), *turn.*

Row 5: Ch 1, sc in each st across (70 sc), *turn.*

Second half

Row 1: Ch 3 (first dc), ch 1, skip next sc, V-st in next sc, • ch 3, skip next 4 sc, V-st in next sc •, rep from • to • across to within last 2 sc, ch 1, skip next sc, dc in last sc (14 V-sts), *turn.*

Rows 2–13: Rep Rows 2–13 of First Half. *Do not turn. Do not* fasten off.

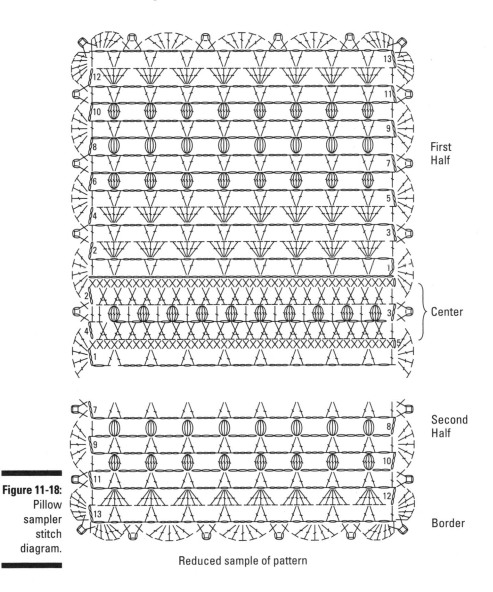

First
Half

Center

Second
Half

Figure 11-18:
Pillow
sampler
stitch
diagram.

Border

Reduced sample of pattern

Border

Rnd 1: Ch 1, (sc, picot, sc, shell) in first row-end dc, working in row-end sts across side edge, ••• • skip next row-end st, (sc, picot, sc) in next row-end st, skip next row-end st, shell in next row-end st •, rep from • to • twice, skip next 2 row-end sts, (sc, picot, sc) in next row-end st, skip next 2 row-end sts, shell in next row-end st, rep from • to • twice, skip next row-end st, (sc, picot, sc) in next row-end st, skip next row-end st, (shell, sc, picot, sc, shell) in next corner space, working across bottom edge, •• skip next V-st, (sc, picot, sc) in next ch-3 space, skip next V-st, shell in next ch-3 space •, rep from •• to •• across to within last 2 spaces, (sc, picot, sc) in next ch-3 space, skip next V-st, (shell, sc, picot, sc, shell) in next corner space •••, rep from ••• to ••• around, ending with shell in last corner space, sl st in first sc to join. Fasten off.

Assembly

If your piece seems a bit uneven, you can block your design to achieve the square dimensions of the finished crochet piece (see Chapter 18). Center your crocheted top on the front of the pillow. Using your sewing needle and nylon thread, sew the pillow topper to the pillow.

Chapter 12

Getting Creative: Working Stitches in Places You Never Thought Of

Crocheting can be addictive when you get going, and like any addict, you crave ever-new forms of — stitches. Until now, you've been content making typical crochet stitches with their tops, bottoms, and loops in between, by inserting your hook through the top loops of the stitches in the previous row, over and over again. But now it's time to get a little crazy — instead of working a new stitch in the top loops, insert your hook in the bottom loops or around the middle loops! This deviant behavior creates a variety of new textures and designs in your fabric.

This chapter details the anatomy of a stitch and shows you a few of the numerous places where you can work new stitches. The scarf projects at the end of the chapter give you a chance to practice these new techniques.

As you get funky with your hook placement, keep in mind that a stitch is a stitch is a stitch. . . . Regardless of where you insert your hook to begin it, you always work the stitch the same way.

Switching Up Your Stitch Placement

Depending on the type of look you're trying to achieve, you can work a stitch pretty much anywhere you can fit your hook — nothing is off-limits. For example, you can work single crochet stitches in the back loops of previous stitches to make ribbing for sweaters. This section gives you the lowdown on all the parts of a stitch and what you can do with them.

The anatomy of a stitch

Before you can go switching things around, you need to know the different parts of a stitch. Don't worry. A stitch's anatomy isn't nearly as complicated as the frog you dissected in high school. Check out the following parts list and Figure 12-1, which illustrates each one:

- ✔ **Top:** The two loops you see at the top of the stitch when you complete it. Referred to in pattern instructions as the *top two loops.*

- ✔ **Front loop:** The top loop closest to you.

- ✔ **Back loop:** The top loop farthest from you or behind the front loop.

- ✔ **Base:** The two loops at the bottom of the stitch. The base of a new stitch is the top of the stitch below it. The base is the most stable part of a stitch to work into when working a border or sewing pieces together.

- ✔ **Post:** The body of the stitch, located between the top two loops and the base. It varies in height depending on the stitch. Also referred to as the *stem.* The post is also considered the side of a stitch when located at the end of a row and is worked in when adding a border or edging to your work.

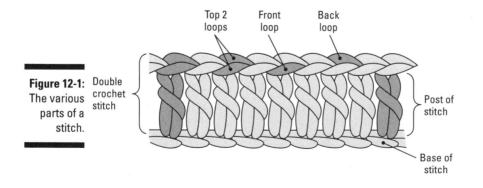

Top 2 loops   Front loop   Back loop

Figure 12-1: The various parts of a stitch.

Double crochet stitch

Post of stitch

Base of stitch

Working up top

You have three different ways you can work a stitch into the top of another that each create different effects in your finished fabric. The resulting look can be either smooth or textured, depending on whether you insert your hook in both top loops, just the front, or just the back loop (see Figure 12-2a; Figure 12-2b shows the symbols):

- **Crocheting under both loops:** Working under both top loops is the typical way to crochet a stitch and is the method presented in the earlier chapters. It creates a smooth, flat fabric.

- **Crocheting in the front loop only:** Working under the front loop creates a ridge on the opposite side of the fabric. This is great for making a rib at the bottom edge and cuffs of a sweater. Another reason to leave the back loop free is so that you can work a stitch in a later row into it.

- **Crocheting in the back loop only:** Like front-loop-only stitching, working new stitches in the back loop creates a rib, just on the opposite side of the fabric. You may also work in just the back loops when joining two pieces of crocheted fabric together. Leaving the front loops free when joining pieces together creates a decorative raised seam on the front of your work.

Figure 12-2: Working in the different loops at the top of a stitch and the relevant stitch symbols.

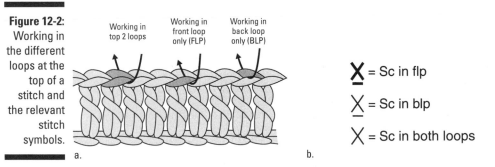

Working in top 2 loops   Working in front loop only (FLP)   Working in back loop only (BLP)

X̲ = Sc in flp

X̣ = Sc in blp

X = Sc in both loops

a.   b.

Working in just one loop at the top of a stitch also adds flexibility — a bit of stretch that working in both top loops doesn't offer. This comes in handy when working with a yarn that doesn't offer much elasticity, such as cotton, or when making a rib around the bottom or cuff edges of a sweater where you want the fabric to have some stretch.

Working in the front or back loop of a stitch doesn't necessarily designate the design's front or back. After you turn your work at the end of a row, the front loop on the previous row becomes the back loop.

Stitching up the sides

You often work around the side of a stitch when you're adding a border to a crocheted item, smoothing out an edge, or joining two pieces of fabric. Only the stitches that are at the end of a row come into play, which is why most pattern instructions refer to working in the side of a stitch as working in *row-end* stitches. These row-end stitches serve as the base for the stitches used to create a border or edging (see the section "The anatomy of a stitch").

When working across row-end stitches, especially if the stitches are longer than a single crochet, be careful to insert your hook properly along each stitch so that you get a nice even edging without many gaps. This also holds true when sewing pieces of crocheted fabric together, which we discuss in Chapter 15. Figure 12-3 shows the proper placement of the hook in the side of a stitch. To avoid gaping holes across the edges, insert your hook where two stitches join together, whether at the base or the top of the stitches or both. You work the new stitch the same whether you're working into a complete row-end stitch or a turning chain.

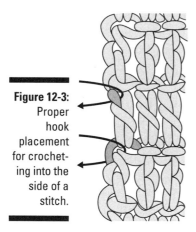

Figure 12-3:
Proper hook placement for crocheting into the side of a stitch.

Working Outside the Stitch: Spaces and Posts

Who says you have to work in a stitch at all? You can create some nice stitch effects by going outside the box. This section shows you how to work stitches into the spaces between stitches or those created by chain loops and how to work a stitch around the middle or post of another.

Squeezing into spaces

Unlike the tight weave of knitted fabric, crocheted fabric has spaces between the stitches because they're not linked on the sides, which opens a whole new world of opportunity in which to create new stitches. Even though the spaces between stitches aren't always obvious, trust us, they're there. Chain loops are also another great place to work new stitches into and are often used to create open lacy patterns.

Working between stitches

Because crocheted stitches aren't linked at the sides, you can work your stitches in between other stitches (see Figure 12-4). When you work in between stitches, you lower the base of the new stitch, altering the alignment of the row. You can use this technique to create a zigzag effect: Just work one stitch in between stitches and the next one in the top of the row. Or create a brick pattern by alternating every four stitches, for example, rather than every other one.

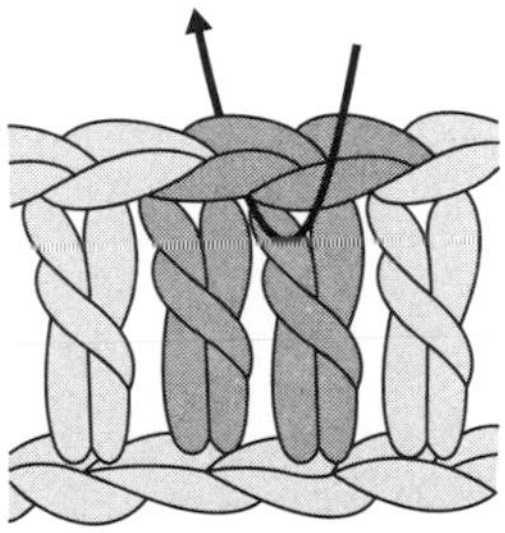

Figure 12-4:
Crocheting between the stitches.

Working in between stitches is a great help when you're using novelty yarns. Because highly textured yarns can make individual stitches hard to see, working between them keeps your design untangled and keeps you out of the loony bin. You can make a whole design without ever working into the top of another stitch.

Working in the loop or space

Many lacy patterns, such as filet crochet (see Chapter 14), use chain loops and spaces in their designs in order to achieve a loose, airy look. Although spaces and loops may look fancy and complicated, working a stitch into them is a piece of cake because you don't have to be too particular about where you stick your hook. As long as it lands somewhere within the loop or space, you're good to go. Figure 12-5 shows you where to put your hook.

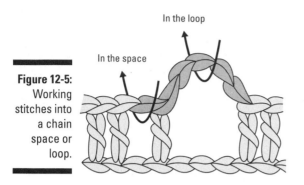

In the loop

In the space

Figure 12-5:
Working
stitches into
a chain
space or
loop.

Going round the middle: Post stitches

You can insert your hook around the post of a stitch that's one or more rows below the current row to make — you guessed it — a *post stitch.* Post stitches create raised patterns, such as ribbing and cables. The way you insert your hook around the post determines whether you're creating a *front post* or *back post.* This section shows you how to make both.

Note: You generally work around the post with longer stitches, such as double crochet and triple crochet.

Front post stitches

Front post stitches are raised on the surface of the fabric facing you. To create a front post double crochet (abbreviated *FP dc*), follow these steps:

1. **Work a row of normal double crochet (dc) for the first row and turn.**

2. **Chain (ch) 2 for your first double crochet.**

   Because a post stitch is shorter than a normal stitch, you make the turning chain with one chain stitch less than the normal turning chain requires.

3. **Yarn over (yo) and insert your hook from front to back between the posts of the first and second double crochet of the row below and then from back to front again between the posts of the second and third stitches. (See Figure 12-6a.)**

   The hook should now be positioned horizontally behind the double crochet that you're working around. (See Figure 12-6b.)

4. **Yarn over and draw the yarn around the post of the stitch.**

   You now have 3 loops on the hook.

5. Yarn over and draw the yarn through the 2 loops on the hook, twice. (See Figure 12-7a.)

One front post double crochet (FP dc) is complete. (See Figure 12-7b for the completed stitch and Figure 12-7c for the stitch symbol.)

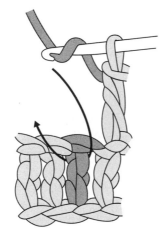

Figure 12-6:
Inserting the hook for the front post double crochet.

a.

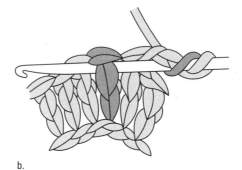

b.

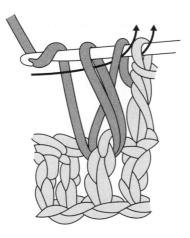

a.

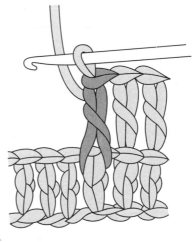

b.

Figure 12-7:
Finishing a front post double crochet.

c.

$$\text{\textsf{∫}} = \text{FP dc}$$

Back post stitches

Back post stitches appear to recede on the side of the fabric facing you. To create a back post double crochet (abbreviated *BP dc*), follow these steps:

1. **Work a row of normal double crochet (dc) for the first row and turn.**

2. **Chain (ch) 2 for the first double crochet.**

    Because a post stitch is shorter than a normal stitch, you make the turning chain with one chain stitch less than the turning chain normally requires.

3. **Yarn over (yo) and insert your hook from back to front between the posts of the first and second double crochet in the row below and then from front to back again between the posts of the second and third stitches. (See Figure 12-8a.)**

    The hook should now be positioned horizontally in front of the double crochet that you're working around. (See Figure 12-8b.)

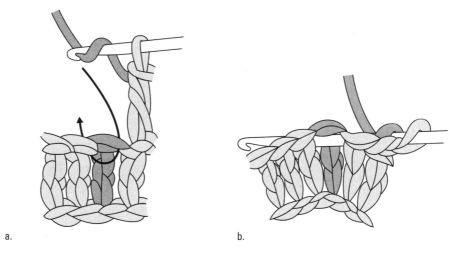

Figure 12-8: Inserting the hook for the back post double crochet.

a.   b.

4. **Yarn over and draw the yarn around the post of the stitch.**

    You now have 3 loops on the hook.

5. **Yarn over and draw the yarn through the 2 loops on the hook, twice. (See Figure 12-9a.)**

    Figure 12-9b shows one complete back post double crochet (BP dc), and Figure 12-9c shows the stitch symbol.

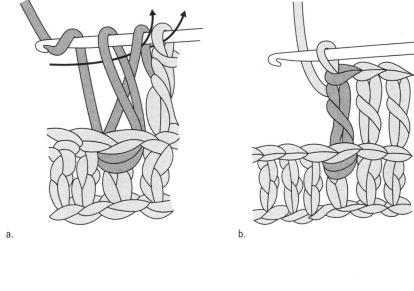

a.

b.

Figure 12-9:
Finishing a
back post
double
crochet.

$\updownarrow$ = BP dc

c.

Spiking into previous rows

Long stitches (also known as *spikes*) are usually single crochet stitches that you work into either the tops of stitches or spaces between stitches one or more rows below the current row, creating a vertical spike of yarn that extends over several rows of stitches. Long stitches produce a spike on both sides of the fabric, so they're well suited for a design that's reversible, such as an Afghan. They're also particularly striking in a contrasting color. To create a long single crochet stitch:

1. **Insert the hook from front to back under the top two loops of the designated stitch one or more rows below. (See Figure 12-10.)**

2. **Draw the yarn through the stitch and up to the current level of work.**

3. **Yarn over (yo) and draw the yarn through the 2 loops on your hook.**

   Figure 12-11a shows you a complete long single crochet stitch (although the length varies depending on where you stick the hook, of course). Figure 12-11b shows a few long-single-crochet stitch symbols.

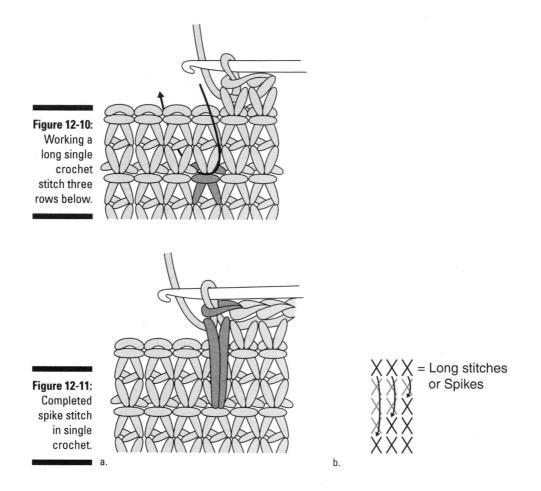

Figure 12-10: Working a long single crochet stitch three rows below.

Figure 12-11: Completed spike stitch in single crochet.

a.

b.

X X X = Long stitches
 X X X   or Spikes

To make other types of long stitches, such as a long double crochet, you follow the same steps as for the single crochet. Just remember to yarn over as necessary and then make the stitch the same way you always do. You just stick the hook in a different place.

Putting It into Practice: Three Scarf Projects

The three beautiful scarves in this section give you some practice with the techniques in this chapter. Feel free to change the yarn colors or to try something new. But if you do make your own changes, be sure to check your gauge (see Chapter 3 for a refresher on how gauge affects your project).

REMEMBER

If the directions in these projects look a little bit like Chinese to you, flip over to Chapter 5 for the lowdown on reading crochetese.

Basketweave scarf project

Crocheting this scarf provides an opportunity to work with post stitches and see the texture that they create. Take your time on the first couple of rows and you'll breeze through the rest. Figure 12-12 shows a reduced sample of this stitch pattern. The yarn in this design is a wonderfully soft, flexible acrylic that's available in most craft stores. If the beige color shown in the color photo section isn't your style, go ahead and get another color. This stitch pattern shows up beautifully in any solid color.

Materials

✔ **Yarn:** Lion Brand Yarn "Microspun" sport-weight yarn, (100% microfiber acrylic), Article #910 (2.5 oz. [*70 gm*], 168 yds. each skein): 4 skeins of #124 Mocha

✔ **Hook:** Crochet hook size H-8 U.S. or size needed to obtain gauge (see Chapter 3 for more on gauge)

Vital statistics

✔ **Measurements:** 8 in. x 60 in.

✔ **Gauge:** 8 sts in pat = 2 in.; 8 rows in pat = 2¾ in.

✔ **Stitches used:** Chain stitch (ch), double crochet (dc), front post double crochet (FP dc), back post double crochet (BP dc)

Directions

Chain 33 + 3 (first dc).

Row 1: Dc in 4th ch from hook, dc in each ch across (34 dc counting the turning chain as 1 dc), *turn.*

Rows 2–5: Ch 2 (first post dc), • FP dc around the post of each of next 4 dc, BP dc around the post of each of next 4 dc •, rep from • to • across to within last dc, dc in last dc (34 sts), *turn.*

Rows 6–9: Ch 2 (first post dc), • BP dc around the post of each of next 4 dc, FP dc around the post of each of next 4 dc •, rep from • to • across to within last dc, dc in last dc (34 sts), *turn.*

Rep Rows 2–9 for pat until scarf measures 60 in. long or desired length, ending with Row 5 or Row 9 of pat. Fasten off.

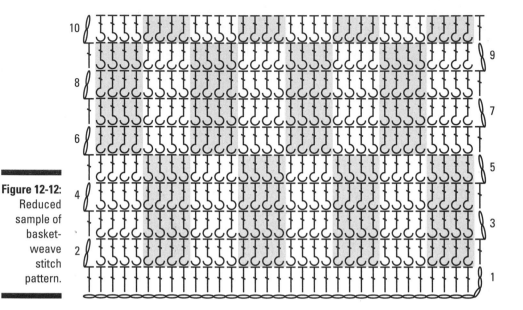

Figure 12-12:
Reduced
sample of
basket-
weave
stitch
pattern.

Feathery scarf project

You create this scarf design by working V-stitches into chain loops (see Chapter 11 for more on V-stitches) with a fun, fringy eyelash yarn. Keeping your stitches loose is key to crocheting with eyelash yarn. If you want an even looser design, use a larger hook. The *eyelashes* on the yarn fill in any open spaces. If you prefer not to work with this type of yarn, this stitch pattern is also pretty with a worsted-weight chenille or even a bulky wool yarn. Figure 12-13 shows the reduced stitch diagram.

Materials

- **Yarn:** Muench — GGH Yarns "Fee," eyelash yarn (80% nylon/15% rayon/5% polyester), Article #G137 (1.75 oz. [*50 gm*], 82 yds. each ball): 3 balls of #3 Brown/Gold

- **Hook:** Crochet hook size J-10 U.S. or size needed to obtain gauge (see Chapter 3 for more on gauge)

Vital statistics

- **Measurements:** 9 in. x 63 in.

- **Gauge:** 3 V-sts = 3 in.; 4 rows in pat = 3 in.

- **Stitches used:** Chain stitch (ch), single crochet (sc), double crochet (dc). **V-st:** • (Dc, ch 2, dc) in same st or space •.

Directions

Ch 22 for foundation chain.

Row 1: Sc in 2nd ch from hook, sc in each ch across (21 sc), *turn.*

Row 2: Ch 3 (first dc), skip next sc, • V-st in next sc, skip next sc •, rep from • to • across to within last sc, dc in last sc (9 V-sts), *turn.*

Row 3: Ch 3 (first dc), V-st in each ch-2 space across, dc in top of turning ch (9 V-sts), *turn.*

Rep Row 3 until scarf measures 62½ inches from beginning.

Last Row: Ch 1, work 21 sc evenly spaced across. Fasten off.

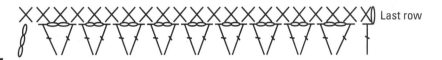

Last row

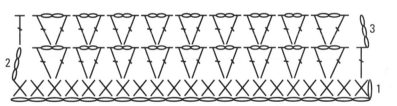

Figure 12-13: Reduced sample of stitch pattern for feathery scarf.

Textured scarf project

You get the textured fabric in this scarf by alternating between working stitches in the back top loop and the front top loop. (See the photo in the color section of this book.) Worked in single crochet with a slightly larger hook than you normally use for a worsted-weight yarn, the back loop/front loop pattern creates a nubby effect, and the fringe at each end finishes the design off nicely. The scarf is a perfect accessory for a cool fall afternoon, and you can find the yarn in a wide variety of colors to match your wardrobe. The stitch diagram for this pattern is shown in Figure 12-14.

Materials

- ✔ **Yarn:** Coats & Clark Red Heart "Fiesta" 4-ply worsted-weight yarn, (73% acrylic/27% nylon), Article #E704 (6 oz. [*170 gm*], 330 yds. each skein): 2 skeins of #6013 Wheat

- ✔ **Hook:** Crochet hook size I-9 U.S. or size needed to obtain gauge (see Chapter 3 for more on gauge)

Vital statistics

- ✔ **Measurements:** 6½ in. x 60 in.
- ✔ **Gauge:** 6 sts and 6 rows sc = 2 in.
- ✔ **Stitches used:** Chain stitch (ch), single crochet (sc)

Directions

Chain 21 for foundation chain.

Row 1: Sc in 2nd ch from hook, sc in each ch across (20 sc), *turn.*

Row 2: Ch 1, sc in blp of first sc, sc in flp of next sc, • sc in blp of next sc, sc in flp of next sc •, rep from • to • across (20 sc), *turn.*

Row 3: Ch 1, sc in flp of first sc, sc in blp of next sc, • sc in flp of next sc, sc in blp of next sc •, rep from • to • across (20 sc), *turn.*

Rep Rows 2–3 for pat until scarf measures 60 in. long, or to desired length.

Last Row: Ch 1, sc in both loops of each sc across (20 sc). Fasten off.

Fringe: Cut yarn into 11-in. lengths. Using 2 lengths for each fringe, single knot 1 fringe in each st across each short edge of scarf. Trim ends even. For more on how to make fringe, see Chapter 17.

Figure 12-14:
Stitch diagram of single crochet in front loop/back loop pattern.

Chapter 13

A Stitch in Time: The Afghan Stitch

The Afghan stitch, despite its name, isn't used just for Afghans, nor are Afghans made with just this stitch. You can crochet with the Afghan stitch to make anything from home decor items, such as Afghans, place mats, and rugs, to sweaters, coats, and accessories. It produces a rather solid fabric that closely resembles knitted fabric, although it uses much more yarn and therefore produces a heavier fabric than knitting. When making clothing, use a lighter weight yarn, such as a sport weight. Worsted-weight yarn is more suitable for Afghans, and rugs work up beautifully using bulky-weight yarn. The stitches themselves are squarish, which makes the fabric perfect for working multicolored designs or as a base for cross-stitch designs.

The Afghan stitch has many variations that look quite different from each other, but in this chapter we tell you how to work three of the most common ones: the basic Afghan stitch and the knit and purl variations. This stitch is distinguished from standard crochet stitches in that each row is worked in two separate halves: The first half adds the loops to your hook, and the second half takes them off. We also show you what special hooks you need, how to increase and decrease stitches, and how to work from a chart for designs with color changes as well as for cross-stitch designs. After you master the basic Afghan stitch technique, try out the colorful potholder project at the end of this chapter.

Note: The Afghan stitch has many names attached to it. So if you come across any of the following names, you know they're referring to the Afghan: *Tunisian crochet, tricot crochet, shepherd's knitting, hook knitting,* and *railroad knitting.*

Timeout for Tools

The Afghan stitch is a unique form of crochet that calls for a unique hook. Unlike standard crochet where you work each stitch off to one loop before going on to the next, with the Afghan stitch, you pick up a whole row of stitches on the hook before you work off the loops on a second pass. To accommodate all these stitches, you need a hook with a cap or a stopper on the end to hold the stitches. Afghan hooks are longer, too, coming in a variety of lengths and sizes:

- ✔ The 10-inch hook comes in U.S. sizes G-6 through J-10.
- ✔ The 14-inch hook comes in sizes G-6 through K-10½.
- ✔ The 22-inch flexible hook comes in sizes G, H, and J.
- ✔ The 40-inch, flexible, double-ended hook comes in sizes G through K.

The longer-length hooks are ideal for making large Afghans. A sampling of Afghan crochet hooks is pictured in Figure 13-1.

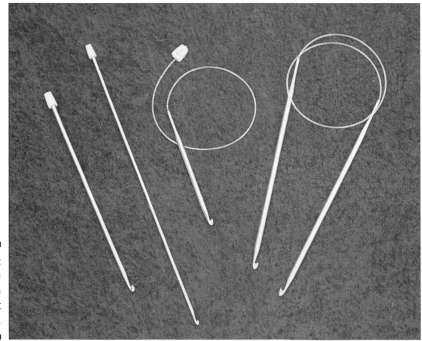

Figure 13-1:
A sample
of Afghan
crochet
hooks.

The best way to determine what hook length best suits your purpose is to refer to the beginning of the pattern instructions. If the materials list doesn't mention a specific length, then take a look at the measurements of the pieces you'll be working. For example, if each piece is 13 inches wide, use a 14-inch hook. If you work an Afghan in one piece that measures 40 inches wide, then the 22-inch flexible hook or the 40-inch double-ended hook is appropriate.

Use the hook that fits the size of the piece that you're making. The longer hooks can be cumbersome if you don't need the extra length.

You can also use a standard crochet hook to crochet small pieces with Afghan stitches (or to just try out the technique). Simply wrap a rubber band several times around the base of the hook to keep the stitches from falling off the end. If you want to try crocheting Afghan stitches with finer yarn or cotton thread, use a smaller crochet hook.

Working in Basic Afghan Stitch

If a pattern calls for the Afghan stitch, it's usually referring to the *basic Afghan stitch*. Basic Afghan stitches are shaped like little squares with two horizontal strands of yarn and a vertical bar on top of them. (See Figure 13-2.)

You make rows of Afghan stitches in two halves:

- ✔ **First half:** Picking up the loops.
- ✔ **Second half:** Working off the loops, without turning your work between rows.

Figure 13-2: Swatch of basic Afghan stitch.

You start out with a foundation row that you work the same for all variations of the Afghan stitch. The second row establishes the pattern, in this case the basic Afghan stitch. Check out the section "Varying Your Afghan Stitch" for instructions on the knit stitch and purl stitch variations. You usually work the second half of each row (which involves working off the stitches) in the same way for all variations of the Afghan stitch.

To practice working the basic Afghan stitch, use a worsted-weight yarn and a 10-inch size H-8 Afghan crochet hook.

Starting out with a foundation row

Because Afghan stitches require you to pull loops up through existing stitches, you need to start with a foundation row, which is actually the first row of the design. Chain 16 stitches for your foundation chain, and you're ready to begin the first half of your foundation row of Afghan stitch.

Working the first half of your foundation row

Follow these steps to work the first half of the foundation row, drawing up the loops of Afghan stitch on your foundation row:

1. **Insert your hook in the second chain (ch) from the hook.**

    (See Chapter 4 for more on counting chain stitches.)

2. **Yarn over (yo) the hook.**

3. **Draw your yarn through the chain stitch. (See Figure 13-3a.)**

    You should have two loops on your hook.

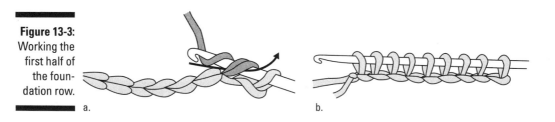

Figure 13-3: Working the first half of the foundation row.

a.

b.

4. **Insert your hook in the next chain and repeat Steps 2 and 3 in each chain across the foundation chain.**

    Your hook is now loaded up with loops, as Figure 13-3b shows. This is known as *drawing up the loops.* You should have 16 loops — one for each chain stitch in your foundation chain. The first half of your foundation row of Afghan stitch is complete.

Working the second half of your foundation row

To work the second half of the row, work the loops off the hook:

1. **Yarn over (yo) the hook.**

2. **Draw your yarn through 1 loop on the hook. (See Figure 13-4a.)**

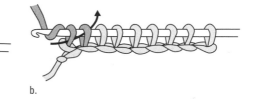

Figure 13-4:
The second half: working off the loops.

a.   b.

3. **Yarn over the hook.**

4. **Draw your yarn through the next 2 loops on the hook. (Refer to Figure 13-4b.)**

5. **Repeat Steps 3 and 4 across the row until 1 loop remains on the hook.**

   You have successfully worked the Afghan stitch across your foundation row. One loop remains on your hook and counts as the first stitch of the next row. (See Figure 13-5.)

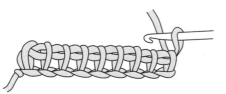

Figure 13-5:
Completed foundation row.

Continuing on to the second row

You place your hook differently for the stitches in the second row of Afghan, but otherwise, you work them across the row in the same manner as for the foundation row. You then work each successive row the same way as the second row.

Working the first half of the second row

To begin the first half of your next row of basic Afghan stitch:

1. **Insert your hook behind the next vertical bar in the row below.**

   Don't work into the vertical bar directly below the loop on your hook.

2. **Yarn over (yo) the hook.**

3. **Draw the yarn through the stitch. (See Figure 13-6a.)**

Figure 13-6:
Working
the first
half of your
second row.

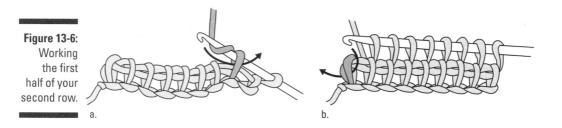

a.   b.

4. **Repeat Steps 1 through 3 in each vertical bar across the row until you reach the next-to-last stitch.**

5. **Insert your hook under the last 2 vertical bars at the end of the row. (Refer to Figure 13-6b.)**

6. **Yarn over the hook.**

7. **Draw your yarn through both vertical bars.**

   You should have 16 loops on your hook. The first half of this row is complete.

Working the second half of the second row

To work the second half of this row, repeat Steps 1 through 5 from the section, "Working the second half of your foundation row." Continue working rows of basic Afghan stitch until you feel comfortable with this technique (a good length for a practice swatch is 4 inches).

Ending a good thing: Binding off

When you finish your last row of basic Afghan stitch, you can't just fasten off your yarn like you do with other standard crochet stitches. You need to *bind off* the top edge of your last row of Afghan stitch with a row of slip stitches. (See Chapter 4 for info on slip stitches.) If you don't bind off the last row, the stitches have gaps in them and don't look like the rest of the piece. So, using the same hook, work a slip stitch under each vertical bar across the last row.

The different variations of Afghan stitch may call for a different binding-off stitch. Some call for a row of single crochet, for example. The specific pattern that you're following indicates what stitch to use when binding off, so make sure you check.

At the end of the last row, after you finish binding off, the pattern may ask you to begin working a border or it may instruct you to fasten off the yarn, depending on the pattern.

Shaping the Basic Afghan Stitch: Increasing and Decreasing

Sometimes, you may need to shape your work when working in Afghan stitch, particularly when making sweaters. The great thing about Afghan stitches is that you increase and decrease the same way whether you do it at the beginning or the end of a row. And the same general technique applies to all variations of Afghan stitch — you do all your increasing and decreasing on the first half of a row.

Increasing in basic Afghan stitch

You always make increases in the first half of a row of basic Afghan stitch, creating the extra loops on your hook; then you work off all the loops in the second half as usual.

To practice making increases, grab the swatch you made in the section "Working in Basic Afghan Stitch" or head back there to make one. To increase 1 stitch, work the first half of the row as follows:

1. **With 1 loop on your hook from the previous row, insert your hook between the first and second stitch (not in the vertical bar). (See Figure 13-7a.)**

2. **Yarn over (yo).**

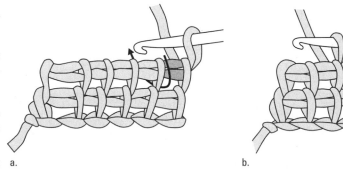

Figure 13-7: Increasing at the beginning of the first half of a row.

a.   b.

3. **Draw the yarn through the stitch.**

   One increase at the beginning of the row is complete.

4. **Work in basic Afghan stitch, starting in the next vertical bar across the rest of the row.**

   You should have 17 loops on your hook. (Remember, you added one.) (Refer to Figure 13-7b.)

To work the second half of the increase row, repeat Steps 1 through 5 from the "Working the second half of your foundation row" section. Working the second half of a row is pretty standard, whether you're working the foundation row or row 12 of Afghan stitch.

Decreasing in basic Afghan stitch

Making a decrease is pretty similar to the increase: You decrease in the first half of a row of basic Afghan stitch, subtracting loops from your hook; then you work off all the loops in the second half as usual.

To practice making decreases, you can use the swatch you just made the increase on (if you're following the book in order) or head back to the section, "Working in Basic Afghan Stitch," to make a swatch. To decrease 1 stitch, work the first half of the row as follows:

1. **With 1 loop on your hook from the previous row, insert your hook behind the first and second vertical bars in the row below. (See Figure 13-8a.)**

2. **Yarn over (yo).**

3. **Draw the yarn through both stitches.**

   One decrease at the beginning of the row is complete.

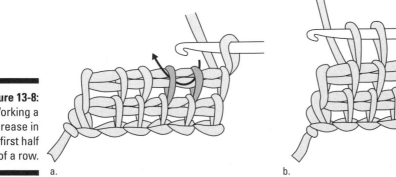

Figure 13-8:
Working a
decrease in
the first half
of a row.

a.   b.

4. **Work in basic Afghan stitch across the rest of the row.**

   You should have 15 loops on your hook. (Remember, you decreased 1 stitch.) (Refer to Figure 13-8b.)

To work the second half of the decrease row, repeat Steps 1 through 5 of the "Working the second half of your foundation row" section, earlier in this chapter. Working the second half of a row is pretty standard, whether you're working the foundation row or row 12 of Afghan stitch.

Varying Your Afghan Stitch

Two of the most common variations of the basic Afghan stitch are the *Tunisian stockinette (knit) stitch* and the *Tunisian purl stitch,* which, not surprisingly, resemble the knitting stitches that they're named after — *knit* and *purl.* The crocheted fabric is thicker than the knitted, however, and you can see a noticeable ridge on the back of the work.

Addressing the curling problem

Fabric made of Afghan stitches tends to curl up along the bottom edge. This is normal and happens because more yarn is on the back of the work than on the front. If you're having problems with curling, try working your Afghan stitch in one of the following ways:

✔ Work the foundation row in only the *top loop* (the one at the top when the right side is facing you) of the foundation chain. (Refer to Chapter 4 for more on foundation chains.)

✔ Work the foundation row in the top two loops (the part of each chain stitch that forms a *V*) of the foundation chain.

✔ Work the foundation row in the back loop of the foundation chain. To do this, turn your foundation chain over, and you notice one little raised-up loop on the backside of each stitch. Work your foundation row in these loops.

✔ After working the foundation row, purl the first row or two. Because purl stitch tends to have just as much yarn in the front of the work as it does on the back, it doesn't curl much. Working a few rows of purl stitch before beginning the pattern may solve your curling problem. (See the section "Tunisian purl stitch," earlier in this chapter, for more on purl stitch.)

If your work still curls after trying these methods, don't despair. You can remedy the curling problem with one of the following methods:

✔ Block your design while working on it or after you finish the design. (See Chapter 18 for blocking directions.)

✔ Place a heavy object (such as a large book) on the edge of your work for a few days to flatten it out.

✔ Work a border around the design, especially a heavy border with lots of stitches.

When working any variation of Afghan stitch, begin the pattern on the second row of your piece — after the foundation row of basic Afghan stitch. You always work the foundation row the same way.

Tunisian stockinette stitch

Tunisian stockinette stitch (also known as *knit stitch*) looks like rows of *V*s nesting in the row below. (See Figure 13-9.) You can use it for Afghans, as well as home decor and fashion items. Like working with any kind of Afghan stitch, you begin with a foundation row made up of basic Afghan stitch. For the purposes of this exercise, work a foundation row of 16 stitches. (See the section "Starting out with a foundation row," earlier in this chapter, to find out how.)

Figure 13-9:
Swatch of
Tunisian
stockinette
stitch (knit
stitch).

To begin the first row of Tunisian stockinette stitch, follow these steps:

1. **Insert your hook, from front to back, between the front and back strands of the next vertical stitch.**

2. **Yarn over (yo).**

3. **Draw the yarn through the stitch. (See Figure 13-10a.)**

4. **Repeat Steps 1 through 3 across the row to the next-to-last stitch.**

5. **Insert your hook under the last 2 vertical bars at the end of the row. (See Figure 13-10b.)**

6. **Yarn over.**

7. **Draw the yarn through the stitch.**

    You should have 16 loops on your hook.

Figure 13-10:
Working the first half of the Tunisian stockinette row.

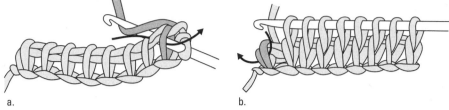

a.   b.

To work the second half of the row, repeat Steps 1 through 5 of the "Working the second half of your foundation row" section across the row. The first row of Tunisian stockinette stitch is now complete. (See Figure 13-11.)

Figure 13-11:
First row of Tunisian stockinette stitch (knit stitch) is complete.

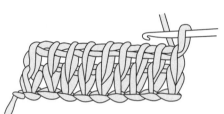

For each additional row of Tunisian stockinette stitch, repeat the steps above. Work this stitch until you feel comfortable with this technique.

Tunisian purl stitch

Tunisian purl stitch (also known as *purl stitch*) looks like rows of rounded bumps (see Figure 13-12) and is useful by itself or in combination with other Afghan stitches to produce textured patterns. The following sections tell you how to work in Tunisian purl stitch. Like working any other type of Afghan stitch, you need to build from a foundation row. To get started, work a 16-stitch foundation row (See the "Starting out with a foundation row" section, earlier in this chapter.)

People tend to tighten up their stitches when working in purl stitch. Be very conscious of tension and be sure to double-check your gauge when working this stitch. If you feel that you can't loosen up with the hook that a pattern suggests, change to a larger hook in order to get the desired gauge. (For more on gauge, refer to Chapter 3.)

Figure 13-12:
Swatch of
Tunisian
purl stitch.

To begin the first half of your first row of purl stitch, follow these steps:

1. **With the index finger of your yarn hand, bring the working yarn to the front of your work; insert your hook under the next vertical stitch, but behind the strand of working yarn.**

   Figure 13-13a shows this action, as well as how to work Steps 2 and 3 that follow.

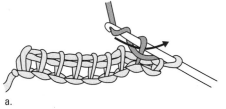

Figure 13-13:
Working the
first half of
the Tunisian
purl stitch.

a.   b.

2. **Yarn over (yo).**

3. **Draw the yarn through the stitch.**

4. **Repeat Steps 1 through 3 across the row until you reach the next-to-last stitch.**

5. **Insert your hook under the last 2 vertical bars at the end of the row. (Refer to Figure 13-13b.)**

6. **Yarn over.**

7. **Draw the yarn through the stitch.**

   You should have 16 loops on your hook.

To work the second half of the row, repeat Steps 1 through 5 of the "Working the second half of your foundation row" section, earlier in this chapter.

For each additional row of purl stitch, repeat the steps above. Figure 13-14 shows a finished row of purl stitch. Work in purl stitch until you feel comfortable working this technique.

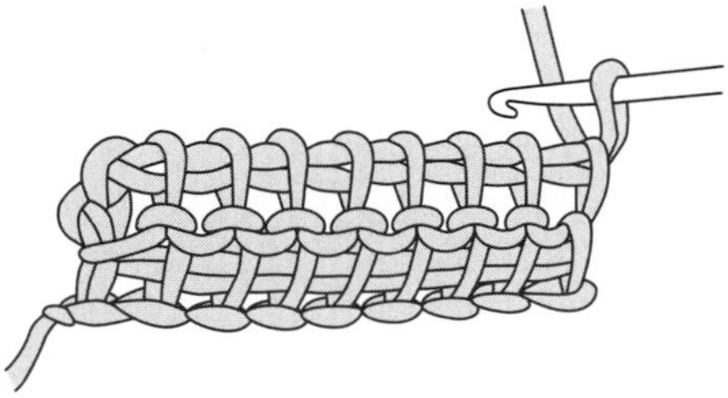

Figure 13-14:
A completed
row of
purl stitch.

Color It Beautiful

Because the basic Afghan stitch produces a gridlike stitch pattern, it's an excellent medium for creating colored designs. You can work color into the design while you're crocheting, or you can cross-stitch a colored design onto the surface after you've finished crocheting. Either of these techniques works great for Afghans, wallhangings, rugs, place mats, potholders, and even sweaters.

Crocheting with more than one color

Most patterns that call for color changes in Afghan stitch provide a chart to show where you switch colors. If you're going to use a color again in the same row with no more than 3 stitches in between, you can carry the color loosely on the wrong side of the work and pick it up later, as Chapter 9 shows you how to do. However, be aware that the carried strand is visible on the back of your work. So, if you have more than 3 stitches in between, fasten off and rejoin the yarn when you need it.

When working with several different colors and different balls of yarn, alleviate the inevitable tangle on the back of your work by joining small balls of yarn instead of whole skeins of each color. If you're only going to work a few stitches of a certain color, estimate the amount of yarn that you need for a patch of color by counting the number of stitches in the patch and allow 2 inches for each stitch plus 4 more inches at each end. Wind the allotted amount of yarn into a small ball or wrap it around a yarn bobbin. (See Chapter 2 for info on yarn bobbins.)

Figure 13-15 shows you an example of a chart, a chart key, and the end product. To use the color chart, read all the rows from right to left when working the first half of the rows. After you work the second half of the row, you're back at the right side to begin the next row. Each square counts as one complete Afghan stitch.

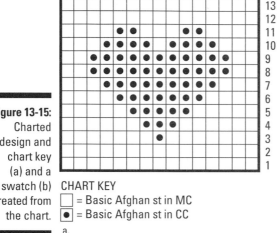

Figure 13-15: Charted design and chart key (a) and a swatch (b) created from the chart.

CHART KEY

☐ = Basic Afghan st in MC

⦿ = Basic Afghan st in CC

a.

b.

Note that the following steps for following a color chart for basic Afghan stitch changes are general and don't correspond with the chart in Figure 13-15:

1. **Draw up the designated number of loops of the first color according to the squares on the chart.**

   Remember, the first loop on the hook counts as the first stitch of the row.

2. **When you need to switch to a new color, drop the first color to the wrong side so that you can pick it up in the second half of the row.**

3. **With the new color behind your work, insert your hook in the next stitch, yarn over (yo) with the new color, and draw that yarn through the stitch.**

4. **Continue by drawing up the designated number of loops of the new color. (See Figure 13-16.)**

5. **Repeat Steps 2 through 4 for each section of a new color across the row of the chart.**

6. **For the second half of the row, work off the loops with the matching color until 1 loop of the current color remains on the hook.**

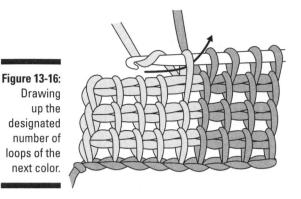

Figure 13-16:
Drawing up the designated number of loops of the next color.

7. **Pick up the next color in sequence from the wrong side of the work, drawing it under the working end of the first color, thus twisting the yarn to prevent holes in the work, and yarn over.**

8. **Draw the new color through 1 loop of previous color and 1 loop of matching color. (See Figure 13-17.)**

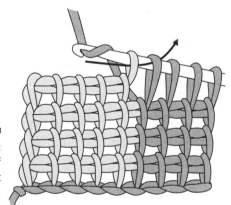

Figure 13-17:
Working off the next color.

9. **Repeat Steps 6 through 8 as needed across the row until 1 loop remains on the hook.**

   Each time you finish changing colors, continue working off the loops as you normally do. Then, repeat Steps 6 through 8 as necessary to change colors. One row of the chart is complete.

10. **Repeat Steps 1 through 9 for each row of the chart.**

Cross-stitching on top of Afghan stitch

Afghan stitch, especially basic Afghan stitch, makes an ideal base for working cross-stitch designs and is often used just for that. You can produce a more delicate color pattern as well as a more elaborate one when cross-stitching on Afghan stitch rather than working color changes within the crochet — and you don't have to deal with changing colors in the middle of the row while crocheting.

You work cross-stitch designs following a chart (see Figure 13-18) so you can see where to place the stitches. Each square on the chart represents 1 stitch in Afghan stitch and one cross-stitch. If you're working a small design on a large piece of crocheted fabric, the instructions tell you where to position the design on your piece. A chart key accompanies the chart, indicating what color the symbols on the chart stand for. Cross-stitch in one color at a time, following the chart from left to right in rows. If you're going to work several stitches in a row with the same color, work the first half of each stitch across the row, and then come back from right to left to work the second half of each stitch.

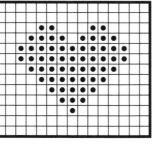

Figure 13-18:
Cross-stitch
chart
and key.

CHART KEY
□ = Background Afghan stitch
● = Cross st

Standard cross-stitch technique, where the needle goes through the fabric to the back, and then up through the fabric to the front, produces a rather sloppy back on your item. To avoid the yarn showing on the back, be careful to slide your needle under the two horizontal strands of the Afghan stitch near the surface of your work. Check the back of your work frequently to make sure nothing is showing.

If you make your cross-stitches too tight, you can ruin your design. The cross-stitches should lay over the Afghan stitch without causing the background to pucker.

To work cross-stitch on basic Afghan stitch, follow these steps to make the first half of a row. The steps reference Figure 13-19:

1. **Thread a length of the designated color yarn onto a yarn needle.**

   Use a length of yarn that's comfortable to work with. An 18-inch length is about average.

2. **Insert the needle from back to front at position A (the bottom left-hand corner of the designated stitch) and draw the needle up, leaving a 4-inch length of yarn on the back (which you'll later weave in).**

3. **Insert the needle at position B (the top right-hand corner of the same stitch), angled vertically down, behind the two horizontal threads.**

4. **Bring the needle out at position C (the bottom right-hand corner of the same stitch) and draw the yarn through until it stretches neatly across the stitch.**

5. **Position C now becomes position A of the next stitch.**

6. **Repeat Steps 3 through 5 across the row in the stitches where the chart calls for cross-stitching.**

   The first half of the row is now complete.

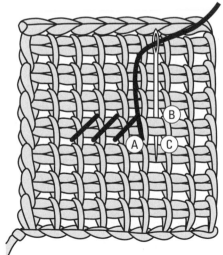

Figure 13-19:
Working the
first half
of a row of
cross-stitch
on Afghan
stitch.

To make the second half of a cross-stitch row, follow these steps. The steps reference Figure 13-20:

1. **Insert your needle at position D (the top left-hand corner of the same stitch you ended the first half with), angled vertically down, behind the 2 horizontal threads.**

   The thread should form an *X* with the already-completed first half of the stitch.

2. **Bring the needle out at position E (the bottom left-hand corner of the same stitch) and draw the yarn through until it stretches neatly across the stitch.**

3. **Repeat Steps 1 and 2 across the row, completing each cross-stitch.**

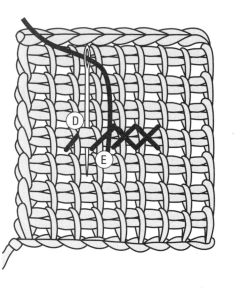

Figure 13-20:
Working the second half of a row of cross-stitch on Afghan stitch.

When you're finished working cross-stitches with a particular color, weave the ends through the Afghan stitch background for several inches to hide the strands, and then clip off the excess yarn.

Figure 13-21 shows a finished cross-stitch design.

Always work cross-stitches with the thread crossing on top in the same direction. And don't tie knots in the yarn at the beginning or the end of your work. Simply weave in the ends to secure them and then clip off the excess.

Figure 13-21:
A swatch of cross-stitch on Afghan stitch.

Decorative Potholder Project

This project uses basic Afghan stitch to make a decorative potholder that you can create in any two contrasting colors. If you want to try cross-stitching on Afghan stitch, make two solid-color pieces and cross-stitch the design on the front.

Materials

- **Yarn:** Coats & Clark Red Heart(r) Classic(r) 4-ply worsted-weight yarn (100% acrylic), Article E2670 (3.5 oz. [*99 gm*], 198 yds. each skein for solids; 3 oz. [*85 gm*], 174 yds. each skein for multis): 1 skein each of #759 Cameo Rose (MC) and #972 Wedgewood (CC).

- **Afghan hook:** 10-in. Afghan crochet hook, size H-8 U.S. or size needed to obtain gauge (refer to Chapter 3 for information on gauge).

- **Hook:** Standard crochet hook size H-8 U.S. or size needed to obtain gauge. This hook is for adding the edging to the piece.

- **Yarn needle.**

Vital statistics

- **Measurements:** 7½ in. x 7½ in.

- **Gauge:** Working in basic Afghan stitch with Afghan crochet hook, 4 sts and 4 rows = 1 in.

- **Stitches used:** Chain st (ch), slip st (sl st), single crochet (sc), double crochet (dc), reverse single crochet (reverse sc), basic Afghan stitch

Directions

You work the back of this potholder in basic Afghan stitch following the chart in Figure 13-22, which we provide at the end of the instructions. Read all rows from right to left. Refer to the section, "Crocheting with more than one color," for the techniques for working with more than one color.

Making the foundation row

With Afghan crochet hook and main color (MC), ch 25. The following steps explain in detail how to work your foundation row for this project: Insert hook in 2nd ch from hook, yo, draw yarn through st, • insert hook in next st, yo, draw yarn through st •, rep from • to • across, keeping all loops on hook (25 loops — first half of foundation row complete), beg 2nd half of row, yo, draw yarn through 1 loop on hook, •• yo, draw yarn through 2 loops on hook ••, rep from •• to •• across (1 loop remains and counts as first st of next row).

Working the rest of the pattern

Follow the next series of steps to complete the backside of your potholder:

1. **Rows 1–23: Work in basic Afghan stitch across all 25 stitches, following the chart in Figure 13-22 for color changes.**

2. **Last row: With MC, sl st in each vertical st across. Fasten off both colors.**

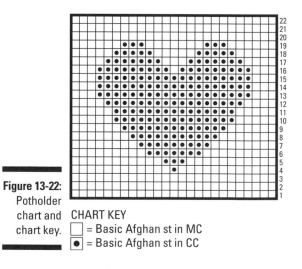

Figure 13-22: Potholder chart and chart key.

CHART KEY
☐ = Basic Afghan st in MC
⦿ = Basic Afghan st in CC

Working the edging

With standard crochet hook, ch 1, working across side edge of back, • sc in each row-end st across side edge to next corner, work 3 sc in next corner st, sc in each st across bottom edge to next corner, work 3 sc in next corner st •, rep from • to • around, sl st in 1st sc to join. Fasten off both colors.

Working the front

Front: Work same as back. Don't fasten off MC at end of last row.

Adding a border

This section shows how to join the front and back sections together and add a decorative border and hanging loop.

Border (joining rnd): Rnd 1 (right side): With wrong sides of front and back facing each other and top edges aligned, ch 1, working through double thickness, • sc in each st across to next corner, work 3 sc in next corner st •, rep from • to • around, sl st in first sc to join. Fasten off MC.

Rnd 2: With right side facing you, join CC in top right-hand corner sc, ch 1, working from left to right, reverse sc in each sc around, sl st in first reverse sc to join. (See Chapter 11 for more on the reverse single crochet.)

Hanging loop: Ch 12, sl st in corner st forming a loop, sl st in ch-12 loop just made, ch 1, work 16 sc in ch-12 loop, sl st in corner st of border. Fasten off.

Chapter 14

Filet Crochet: Creating a New Style

*N*ot to be confused with filet mignon or filet of sole, *filet crochet* (also known as *net stitch*) is a technique that imitates a 17th-century form of lace worked on mesh netting stretched across a frame. Over the years, the technique evolved into what it is today — a series of blocks and spaces that form a design. Because of the uniformity of the designs, the directions are shown in a chart, with each square of the chart representing specific stitches.

This chapter gives you the lowdown on filet crochet — how to create the blocks and spaces, how to read filet crochet charts, and how to increase and decrease when you work a filet crochet design.

Filet Crochet for Newbies

You've probably seen filet crochet many times and not known it. Its distinct mesh-like designs, usually worked in white cotton thread, are often used for tablecloths, runners, curtains, and wallhangings and are especially elegant against a dark wood surface or brightly colored cloth background. Filet crochet is much simpler than it looks, so it's great for beginners. The project at the end of this chapter, a butterfly runner that you can see in the color photo section, is a typical example of the filet crochet technique.

What is filet crochet?

Perhaps you've seen a drawing or painting made of small dots or squares. Looking at the drawing from a distance, you see only the design or picture, but as you come closer, you can see the tiny squares that make up the larger picture. Similar to the tiny squares in the drawing, filet crochet is a grid of blocks and spaces that make up a design: The spaces form the background, and the blocks create the design. Patterns for these designs are given as charts (see the next section, "Following a chart"). Because of its detail, filet crochet is commonly used for lettering. The earliest known text depicted with filet crochet is *The Lord's Prayer*.

Each space and block is made up of 3 stitches:

- ✔ **Spaces** begin with a double crochet stitch, followed by a space of 2 chain stitches.

- ✔ **Blocks** are made up of 3 double crochet stitches, which you can work in the stitches or spaces of the previous row.

To make sure your design is clear, work filet crochet patterns with cotton thread. Start with size 10 thread and a size 7 steel hook, and after you have some experience with this technique, move on to a smaller size 20 or size 30 thread and a size 12 or 14 steel hook to create a much more delicate and elegant design.

Following a chart

Because of the repetitive nature of filet crochet, the instructions are usually depicted in chart form. Not only would written instructions be really lengthy, but also you'd probably lose your place and become cross-eyed in no time at all. After you understand how to follow a chart, you'll find it's much easier to follow than written instructions.

Filet crochet charts look somewhat like graph paper. They're made up of plenty of squares, some of which are empty (spaces), and some of which are filled in (blocks). Each pattern also provides you with a chart key that explains what each square means and whether you work each space or block with 3 stitches or with another number of stitches that the designer may have chosen. Long empty spaces are bars, and the small, curved lines — the ones that look kind of like *V*s — are the lacets (see the section "Spacin' Out with Lacets and Bars" for the lowdown on these two stitches). Figure 14-1a shows a sample chart, and Figure 14-1b shows a sample chart key.

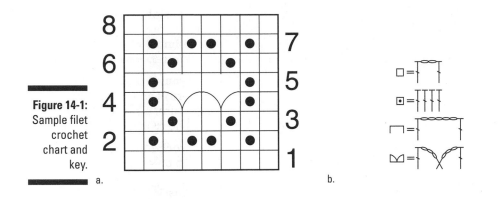

Figure 14-1: Sample filet crochet chart and key.

Each row of the chart has a number, beginning with Row 1 at the bottom of the chart and ending with the last row at the top of the chart. The instructions normally tell you the number of chains that you need to make for the foundation chain and they may or may not write out the first row's instructions. When crocheting, you work from right to left, so you read the chart in the same direction that you work: Read all odd-numbered rows from right to left. You read all even-numbered rows from left to right because you actually work the second row from the left-hand side of the piece to the right side. (Although because you turn your work, it seems like you're going right to left.)

Sometimes, large patterns that repeat a series of rows over and over again show you the repeated rows only once in the chart. The instructions tell you to work the chart from Row 1 to the last row, and then repeat the chart, beginning at Row 1 again, a designated number of times to complete the project. This is often the case when making a table runner, tablecloth, or curtains.

TIP

If the chart is for a large piece, the squares may be small and hard to read. Make a copy of the chart and enlarge it for easier reading instead of working directly from the original instructions. With a copy, you can also mark the chart without destroying the original. Sometimes, highlighting the row you're working on is helpful, or you can place a mark next to the last row that you worked when you have to put your work down for a while.

Chaining the foundation

You need to do a little bit of math in order to make your foundation chain. Each block or space in a filet chart is actually three stitches. This means that each row of filet crochet has a multiple of 3 stitches plus 1 double crochet at the end to complete the last space or block. To create a foundation chain for a sample design that calls for 5 spaces across the first row, you have to

1. **Multiply the number of spaces (or blocks) in the row by 3.**

   5 x 3 = 15 chain stitches

2. **Add 3 more chain (ch) stitches for the turning chain of the next row's first double crochet (dc) stitch. (Refer to Chapter 4 for more on turning chains.)**

   15 + 3 (first double crochet) = 18 chain stitches

Getting the tension just right for your foundation chain is important. If your foundation chain is too tight, your design can pucker or be misshapen. If it's too loose, you'll have a lot of droopy loops hanging off the edge. The stitches in your foundation chain should be the same size and just big enough to fit your hook comfortably into. Most people have a tendency to chain too tightly. If you fall in this category, go to the next larger hook size to work the foundation chain. If you chain too loosely, try the next size down.

Nothing is more frustrating than getting to the end of your first row in a large design and finding out that you don't have enough stitches. If you're working on a large filet crochet design, chances are that the foundation chain is several hundred stitches long. To avoid a miscount, crochet your foundation chain with a separate ball of thread. When you think you have the right number of chain stitches, attach a new ball of thread in the first chain stitch that you created, working your first row from there. If you miscounted, you can easily add (or subtract) chain stitches at the end of the foundation row with the first ball of thread that you used. Fasten off the first ball of thread when you complete the first row and weave in the end to keep it from unraveling.

Creating spaces

Using the foundation chain from the last section, you start the first row. To work a first row of spaces:

1. **Chain (ch) 2 to create the top of the first space.**

   Remember that you already chained the turning chain for the first stitch in the last section.

2. **Double crochet (dc) in the eighth chain from your hook to make the first space.**

   (Refer to Chapter 6 to find out how to make a double crochet stitch.)

3. **Chain 2.**

4. **Skip the next 2 chain stitches.**

5. **Double crochet in the next chain to make the second space.**

6. **Repeat Steps 3 through 5 across the row.**

   You work your last double crochet in the last chain of the foundation chain, and you should have 5 spaces at the end of the row, as Figure 14-2 shows.

Figure 14-2:
First row of filet crochet spaces.

To work a second row of spaces:

1. **Turn your work.**

   (Refer to Chapter 4 for information on turning your work.)

2. **Chain (ch) 3 for the turning chain for your first double crochet (dc).**

3. **Chain 2 to make the first space.**

4. **Skip the next 2 chain stitches.**

5. **Double crochet in the next double crochet stitch to make the first space of the second row.**

6. **Repeat Steps 3 through 5 across the row.**

   You should have 5 spaces at the end of the second row.

Work each successive row the same way as the second row until you're comfortable with the technique. Take care to notice the way that the spaces form squares and that they line up one on top of another. Filet crochet is a symmetrical design technique, and if the squares are skewed, then your whole piece will look out of kilter. If you find that you've made a mistake, tear out your work to that spot, and rework your design from there. You can't hide mistakes in filet crochet.

Building blocks

Blocks are what create the actual substance of a design. Some designs also start with a row of blocks for the first row to create a border. Using the foundation chain of 15 chain stitches plus 3 for the turning chain (see the section "Chaining the foundation"), work a first row of blocks:

1. **Double crochet (dc) in the fourth chain (ch) from the hook.**

2. **Double crochet in each of the next 2 chain stitches to complete the first block.**

3. **Double crochet in each of the next 3 chain stitches to complete the second block.**

4. **Repeat Step 3 across the row.**

   You should have 5 blocks at the end of the row (or 15 double crochet stitches plus the turning chain), as Figure 14-3 shows. You always have 1 more stitch than the multiple of 3.

Figure 14-3:
First row of filet crochet blocks.

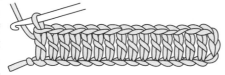

To work the second row of blocks:

1. **Turn your work.**

   (Refer to Chapter 4 for information on turning your work).

2. **Chain (ch) 3 for the turning chain for your first double crochet (dc).**

3. **Double crochet in each of the next 3 double crochet stitches to make the first block.**

4. **Double crochet in each of the next 3 double crochet stitches to complete the second block.**

5. **Repeat Step 4 across the row.**

   You should have 5 blocks at the end of the second row.

Combining spaces and blocks

To create the design that you want, you have to combine spaces and blocks, which is easy to do because both techniques are based on three stitches.

Make sure that the blocks and spaces line up with all the vertical and horizontal lines laying at right angles. The double crochet stitches that form the beginning and ending of each block or space must line up one on top of the other to create the gridlike appearance.

To work a space in the next row over a block:

1. **Work the first double crochet (dc).**

2. **Chain (ch) 2.**

3. **Skip the next 2 double crochet stitches.**

   The double crochet that closes the space is actually considered the first stitch of the next space or block in the row.

To work a block over a space:

1. **Double crochet (dc) in the first double crochet stitch of the space below.**

2. **Work 2 double crochet stitches in the chain-2 space or in the 2 chain (ch) stitches in the row below.**

   You can either work your stitches in the chain space or directly into the chain stitches — try it both ways to see which you prefer. (Flip back to Chapter 12 for the lowdown on working in chain-2 spaces.) Most crocheters find working in the space easier and neater. Don't worry if the stitches look a bit skewed. After you finish the design, you can pin it out and starch it (see Chapter 18 for more on this process, called blocking), to straighten out the stitches. Figure 14-4 shows a swatch of filet crochet.

Figure 14-4:
Swatch of filet crochet combining both spaces and blocks.

Diving into Deeper Waters: Shaping Your Design

You're not limited to straight-edged, rectangular pieces in filet crochet. You can add interest to corners and edges by increasing or decreasing the number of spaces and blocks in a row to make inset corners and steplike edges.

Increasing spaces and blocks

Increasing the number of spaces and blocks at the end of a row shapes the edges of the design. Because most filet crochet designs are symmetrical, if you increase at the beginning of a row, you need to increase at the end of the row, too. However, the process is a little different for each end.

Increasing one space at the beginning of a row

In order to increase one space at the beginning of a row, you must chain enough stitches to make up a space. To work a 1-space increase at the beginning of a row, follow these steps:

1. **At the end of the row that precedes the row you're going to increase, turn your work, and then chain (ch) 2 to create the base of the first increase space.**

2. **Chain 3 more for the turning chain of the space's first double crochet (dc).**

3. **Chain 2 more to complete the top of the first space.**

4. **Double crochet in the last double crochet stitch of the previous row. (See Figure 14-5a.)**

   One increase is complete, which you can see in Figure 14-5b. Continue across the row with blocks or spaces, as detailed earlier in this chapter.

Increasing more than one space at the beginning of a row

Increasing more than one space at the beginning of a row works the same way as increasing one space; you just have to know how many additional chain stitches to make for each additional space.

When increasing spaces, chain 2 for the first space increase, and then chain 3 more for each additional space required. The first double crochet of a row is always a chain 3.

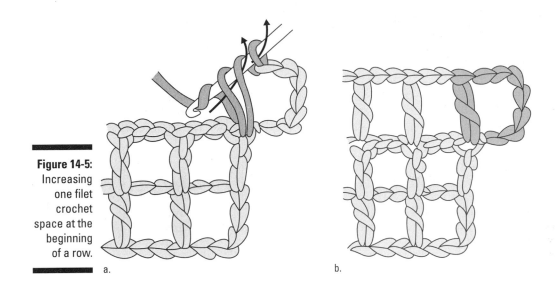

Figure 14-5:
Increasing
one filet
crochet
space at the
beginning
of a row.

a.   b.

To increase more than one space, follow these steps:

1. **When you reach the end of the row that precedes the row you're going to increase, turn your work, and then chain (ch) 2 for the base of the first increase space.**

2. **Chain 3 more for each additional space required.**

   The example in these steps adds one more space for a total of two increases.

3. **Chain 3 more for the turning chain of the row's first double crochet (dc) stitch.**

4. **Chain 2 more for the top of the first space.**

5. **Double crochet in the eighth chain from the hook. (See Figure 14-6a.)**

6. **Chain 2 for the top of the second increase space.**

7. **Skip the next 2 chain stitches.**

8. **Double crochet in the next chain stitch.**

   You have now increased the row by two spaces.

9. **Chain 2 to make the top of the next space.**

10. **Skip the next 2 stitches.**

11. **Double crochet in the next double crochet stitch to make the next space of the row.**

12. **Repeat Steps 9 through 11 across the row to complete a row of spaces. (See Figure 14-6b.)**

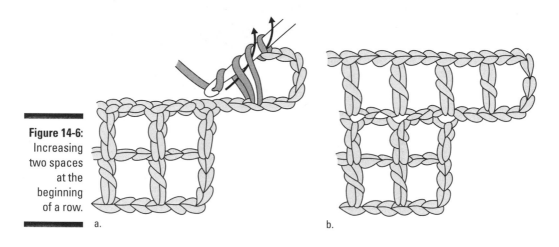

Figure 14-6: Increasing two spaces at the beginning of a row.

a.   b.

Increasing one or more blocks at the beginning of a row

Increasing one block at the beginning of a row is similar to increasing one space, but you replace the two chain stitches you make for the top of the space with two double crochet stitches. To increase one block at the beginning of a row:

1. **At the end of the row that precedes the row you're going to increase, turn your work, and then chain (ch) 2 to make the base of the first increase block.**

2. **Chain 3 more to complete the turning chain of the block's first double crochet (dc) stitch.**

3. **Double crochet in the fourth chain from the hook to complete the second double crochet stitch of the block. See Figure 14-7a.**

4. **Double crochet in each of the next 2 chain stitches to complete the block.**

   The first block increase is complete. (See Figure 14-7b.) Continue making blocks or spaces across the row.

To increase additional blocks, you follow the same steps as for one block. The only difference is how many additional chain stitches you make for the additional blocks. Here's the simple math: Chain 2 for your first increase block, chain 3 more for each additional block, and then chain 3 for the turning chain of the row's first double crochet. So if you want to increase 2 blocks at the beginning of a row, you chain 2 for the first block, 3 for the second block, and 3 more for the turning chain, which is 11 chain stitches total. After you chain the required number of stitches, follow Steps 3 and 4 in the previous list to make the first block and then work another set of 3 double crochet stitches for the other increase block (see Figure 14-8).

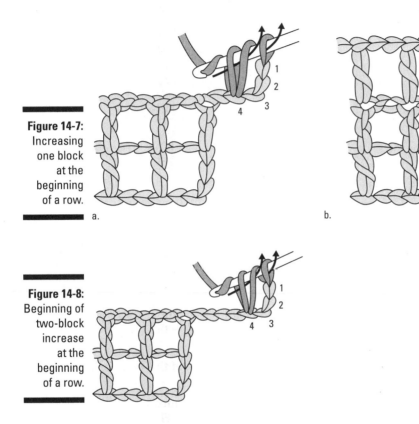

Figure 14-7:
Increasing
one block
at the
beginning
of a row.

a.

b.

Figure 14-8:
Beginning of
two-block
increase
at the
beginning
of a row.

Increasing one or more spaces at the end of a row

When you need to increase a space at the end of a row, you start at the *top* of the last double crochet in the row just prior to the increase. In order to create the extra space(s), you work a chain-2 space followed by a stitch called a *triple triple crochet* (trtr), which is one step taller than a *double triple crochet* (refer to Chapter 6). By working a triple triple crochet stitch, you create a length equivalent to 5 chain stitches, which is what you need to make one filet space — 2 chain stitches for the width of the space plus 3 chain stitches for the height of one double crochet.

To increase one space at the end of a row:

1. **Chain (ch) 2 to create the top of the first space.**

2. **Yarn over the hook (yo) 4 times.**

3. **Insert your hook in the same stitch as the last double crochet (dc) stitch that you worked. (See Figure 14-9a.)**

4. **Yarn over and draw the yarn through the stitch.**

5. **Yarn over and draw the yarn through 2 loops on the hook.**

6. **Repeat Step 5 three times until you have 1 loop on the hook, completing 1 triple triple (trtr) crochet.**

This completes one space increase, as shown in Figure 14-9b.

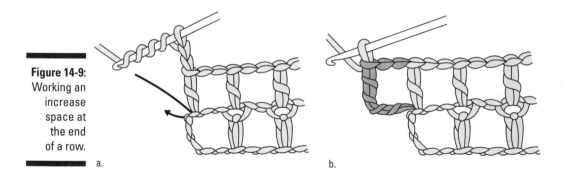

Figure 14-9: Working an increase space at the end of a row.

a.   b.

To increase more than one space at the end of a row, you just repeat the steps for increasing one space. The only difference is that in Step 3, you insert the hook in the middle of the post (refer to Chapter 12 for stitch parts) of the triple triple (trtr) crochet that you made for the first space increase. See Figure 14-10.

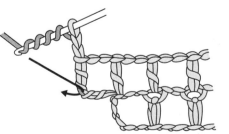

Figure 14-10: Working additional spaces at the end of a row.

Increasing one or more blocks at the end of a row

Increasing a block at the end of a row is a bit tricky but still relatively simple. The trick is to make sure that you don't tighten up too much on your stitches.

When increasing blocks, you use a triple crochet stitch instead of a double crochet. The extra length compensates for not having a row of chain stitches to serve as the base.

To increase one block at the end of a row:

1. **Yarn over (yo) twice.**

2. **Insert your hook in the top of the last stitch of the previous row, which is where you just worked the last double crochet (dc) of the current row. (See Figure 14-11a.)**

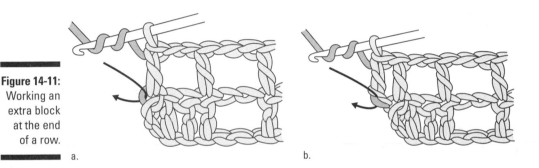

Figure 14-11:
Working an extra block at the end of a row.

a.   b.

3. **Yarn over and draw the yarn through the stitch.**

4. **Yarn over and draw the yarn through 2 loops on the hook.**

5. **Repeat Step 4 twice.**

   You have 1 loop remaining on the hook and have completed 1 triple crochet (tr) and the second stitch of the block.

6. **Yarn over twice.**

7. **Insert your hook near the bottom of the post of the last triple crochet (tr) that you made. (Refer to Figure 14-11b.)**

8. **Yarn over and draw the yarn through 2 loops on the hook.**

9. **Repeat Step 8 twice until you have 1 loop on the hook (completing one triple crochet).**

10. **Repeat Steps 7 through 9 (completing the third stitch of the block). (See Figure 14-12.)**

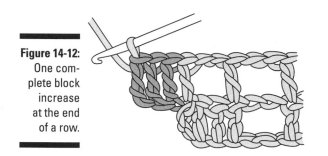

Figure 14-12:
One complete block increase at the end of a row.

After you master increasing one block, increasing more than one is easy. You just repeat Steps 7 through 9 three times for each additional block that you want.

Decreasing spaces and blocks

Fortunately, the method for decreasing both spaces and blocks is the same and is simply a matter of counting.

Decreasing spaces or blocks at the beginning of a row

To decrease one space or block at the beginning of a row, you simply slip stitch across to where you want to begin the first space or block. Follow these steps:

1. **At the end of the row preceding the row you're decreasing, turn your work.**

2. **Slip stitch (sl st) across 3 stitches for each space or block that you're decreasing.**

   If you're decreasing 1 space or block, then slip stitch across 3 stitches; if you're decreasing 2 spaces or blocks, slip stitch across 6 stitches.

3. **Slip stitch in the next stitch.**

   This brings your hook into the correct stitch to begin your first space or block of the row.

4. **Chain (ch) 3 for the turning chain of the row's first double crochet (dc). (See Figure 14-13.)**

5. **Work across the row with either blocks or spaces.**

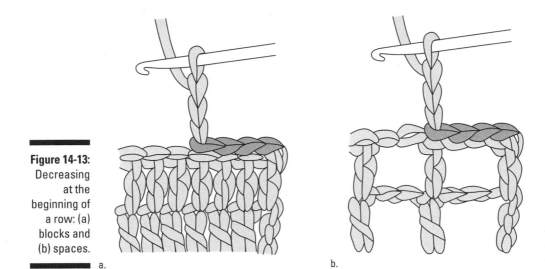

Figure 14-13: Decreasing at the beginning of a row: (a) blocks and (b) spaces.

a.

b.

Decreasing spaces or blocks at the end of a row

The method for decreasing spaces or blocks at the end of a row is the same regardless of how many you need to decrease. You work across the row following the chart, stop crocheting at the point where you want to make the decrease, and then turn your work to begin the next row. Keep in mind that the decrease must end with a double crochet stitch or a complete space or block. Figure 14-14 shows the decrease at the end of a row after you've turned and are ready to begin the next row.

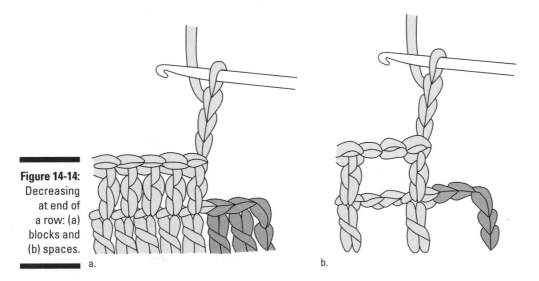

Figure 14-14: Decreasing at end of a row: (a) blocks and (b) spaces.

a.

b.

Spacin' Out with Lacets and Bars

Lacets and bars are two more filet crochet stitches that create an elegant, lacy look. Despite their fancy names, you work them with just double crochet, chain, and single crochet stitches, but the spacing is different. Instead of being worked across 3 stitches, they are worked in 5 stitches or 2 spaces. (Remember, the last stitch that completes the block is really the first stitch of the next space or block.) Not all filet crochet designs incorporate these fancy schmancy stitches, but they can add interest to a design.

Getting fancy with lacets

A *lacet,* which is sometimes called a *fancy stitch,* looks somewhat like a *V* and is worked across five stitches or the width of two spaces. To make a lacet:

1. **Work the first double crochet (dc) as you would to begin a regular block or space.**

   See the section "Creating spaces," earlier in the chapter.

2. **Chain (ch) 3.**

3. **Skip the next 2 stitches.**

4. **Single crochet (sc) in the next stitch.**

   If you're working the lacet over a bar, you can work the single crochet in the center chain stitch or in the chain loop, whichever you prefer. If it's being worked over two separate spaces or blocks, then you work the single crochet in the center double crochet between the first and second space or block.

5. **Chain 3.**

6. **Skip the next 2 stitches.**

7. **Double crochet in the next double crochet to complete 1 lacet. (See Figure 14-15.)**

Figure 14-15: A finished lacet over two spaces.

Bridging the gap with bars

Bars, sometimes referred to as *double spaces,* are long spaces that cross over the two blocks or spaces or the one lacet below them. Generally, they're worked over a lacet. To make a bar:

1. **Work the first double crochet (dc) as you would to begin a regular block or space.**

   See the section "Creating spaces," earlier in the chapter.

2. **Chain (ch) 5.**

3. **Skip the next 5 stitches or 2 spaces.**

4. **Double crochet in the next double crochet stitch to complete 1 bar. (See Figure 14-16.)**

Figure 14-16: Bar worked over a lacet.

Figure 14-17 shows a swatch of filet crochet worked with all four stitches: blocks, spaces, lacets, and bars.

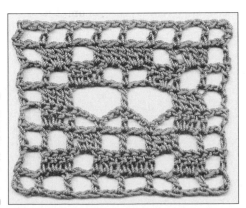

Figure 14-17: Finished swatch of filet crochet with all four stitches.

Butterfly Runner Project

This beautiful filet crochet runner is a simple rectangle that uses spaces, blocks, bars, and lacets. We made the sample in the color photo section by using size 20 thread with a size 12 steel hook, but if you'd feel more comfortable, go ahead and make it using the larger size 10 thread with a size 7 steel hook. This results in a larger finished design but is just as pretty.

If you're feeling pretty confident and want to spice up the runner a little bit, you can shape the corners of the runner by using the increasing and decreasing technique. The runner shown in the color photo section of this book has this corner variation. We include another chart and directions for this change.

For complete information on reading crochet instructions, refer to Chapter 5.

Materials

- **Cotton thread:** DMC "Cebelia", size 20 crochet cotton (100% mercerized cotton), Article #167 (*50 gm*, 405 yds. each ball): 1 ball of White

- **Hook:** Steel crochet hook size 12 U.S. or size needed to obtain gauge (refer to Chapter 6 to find out about gauge)

Vital statistics

- **Measurements:** 10 in. x 12½ in.

- **Gauge:** 7 spaces = 2 in.; 9 rows dc = 2 in.

- **Stitches used:** Chain stitch (ch), slip stitch (sl st), single crochet (sc), double crochet (dc). **Filet st:** • Dc in dc, ch 2, skip next 2 sts •, 1 space made. • Dc in dc, dc in each of next 2 sts •, 1 block made. • Dc in dc, ch 3, skip next 2 sts, sc in next st, ch 3, skip next 2 sts •, 1 lacet made. • Dc in dc, ch 5, skip next 5 sts, or 2 spaces •, 1 bar made.

- **Additional stitches for corner option: To dec one space at beg of row:** Sl st to designated dc, ch 3 (first dc) to beg row. **To dec one space at end of row:** Work to designated dc, then *turn* to beg next row.

Directions

Ch 180 + 3 (first dc) + 2 (first space).

Row 1: Dc in 8th ch from hook, (ch 2, skip next 2 ch, dc in next ch) 5 times, •
dc in each of next 6 ch, rep from (ch 2, skip next 2 ch, dc in next ch) 4 times,
ch 2, skip next 2 ch, dc in last ch (first row of chart complete — 60 spaces
and blocks), *turn.*

Rows 2–48: Work in blocks, spaces, bars, and lacets foll chart (see Figure
14-18). Read all odd-numbered rows from right to left, all even-numbered
rows from left to right. Fasten off at end of last row.

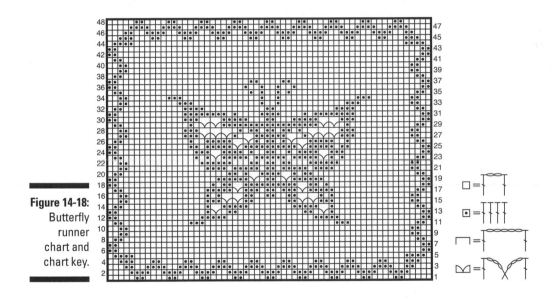

Figure 14-18:
Butterfly
runner
chart and
chart key.

Optional directions for corner variation

Ch 150 + 3 (first dc).

Row 1: Dc in 4th ch from hook, dc in each of next 5 ch, • (ch 2, skip next 2 ch,
dc in next ch) 4 times, dc in each of next 6 ch •, rep from • to • across (first
row of chart complete — 50 spaces and blocks), *turn.*

Rows 2–48: Work in blocks, spaces, bars, and lacets foll chart (see Figure 14-19). Read all odd-numbered rows from right to left, all even-numbered rows from left to right. Fasten off at end of last row.

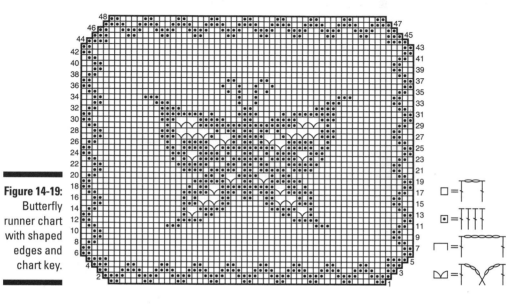

Figure 14-19:
Butterfly
runner chart
with shaped
edges and
chart key.

Finishing

Using liquid starch, block the finished piece. (See Chapter 18 for detailed blocking instructions.)

Part IV
Putting It All Together

The 5th Wave   By Rich Tennant

BERNICE CROCHETS AN AFGHAN

In this part . . .

A crocheted project is rarely complete when you fasten off the last row or round. Certain finishing techniques help to complement and enhance your project.

This part presents several methods for neatly joining projects made in pieces and shows you how to add the finishing touches and embellishments to your projects. Finally, we offer tips on caring for your valuable crocheted handiwork so that it looks its best and can withstand the test of time. All these finishing methods can help enhance the beauty of your projects so that you get the most satisfaction from all your hard work.

Chapter 15

When the Plan Comes Together: Joining Seams

*W*hether you're working with the seams of a garment, the individual motifs of an Afghan, or the long panels of a shawl, the techniques for joining crocheted pieces are many and varied. Do you want a visible or an invisible seam? Is the seam an integral part of the overall design or is it purely functional? Should you crochet the seam or do you feel more comfortable sewing it?

If you're crocheting a design pattern, the instructions usually tell you how to put the pieces together. However, if you don't care for the method or want to try another, feel free to experiment. This chapter details the various methods, so you can choose which joining method is best for you. The two great projects at the end of the chapter give you an opportunity to try out a couple of the joining methods we give you.

Yarn and Needle: Sewing Pieces Together

When the seams of a piece are functional, rather than decorative, sewing them together is probably your best bet. A sewn seam is flexible, nearly invisible, and doesn't add any additional bulk. You don't need a sewing machine or many special tools, just grab a yarn needle or tapestry needle, whichever works with the material you're using, and the leftover yarn or cotton that you used to crochet your design. (See Chapter 2 for the info on needles.)

All you really need to know to sew crocheted pieces together is two simple stitches: the whipstitch and the blanket stitch.

If the design that you're sewing together has a striped pattern, leave a yarn tail at least 6 inches long at the beginning and ending of each stripe. When it comes time to sew the pieces together, you have the correct yarn colors available and positioned right where you need them. Just slip your yarn needle onto the tail and sew the corresponding color stripes together. This saves you a lot of time when you're finishing up your project.

Whipping up the whipstitch

The *whipstitch* is best for joining rows made up of the shorter stitches, such as single crochet, half double crochet, and double crochet. You join the pieces by sewing the row-ends together (when sewing the side seams of a garment) or you may work in the tops of the stitches (when you're sewing shoulder seams or motifs). The key to joining seams together successfully is to match up the crocheted stitches on each side of the seam, using straight, even stitches, without pulling too tightly.

The whipstitch can also create a decorative seam, especially when you're sewing motifs together. With the wrong sides of the motifs facing and their stitches matched across each edge, sew the motifs together through the back loop of the stitches only. This creates a raised ridge on the right side of the work. The floral motif vest at the end of this chapter uses this method.

To make a whipstitch:

1. **Position the pieces with right sides (or wrong sides) facing each other. Match the stitches across each side edge.**

2. **Using a yarn needle and matching yarn, weave the yarn back and forth through several stitches on one of the pieces to secure the end.**

   You can tie a small knot at the beginning of the seam if you want to secure it better.

3. **Insert the needle and pull the yarn through the inside loops of the first 2 corresponding stitches of the 2 pieces to be joined.**

4. **Draw the needle up and over the 2 loops of the first stitch.**

   Pull the yarn tight enough so that the pieces of fabric rest fairly snug against each other, but not so tightly that the stitches become distorted.

5. **Repeat Steps 3 and 4 across the edges to be joined. (See Figure 15-1.)**

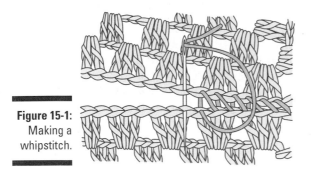

Figure 15-1:
Making a
whipstitch.

6. **At the end of the seam, weave the yarn back through several stitches to secure.**

   Figure 15-2 shows a completed whipstitch seam.

Figure 15-2:
Completed
whipstitch
seam.

Covering the blanket stitch

The *blanket stitch* is a good choice when you're joining pieces with longer stitches, such as triple crochet and taller. This stitch adds some stability to the backside of the seam and reduces the seam's tendency to gap. Remember to always join the taller stitches at the top and at the base, which is how the stitches are joined to each other within the fabric.

To make a blanket stitch:

1. **With the correct sides facing each other (right side/wrong side, depending on pattern), lay the pieces of fabric on a flat, smooth surface and align the edges and stitches.**

2. **Using a yarn needle and matching yarn, thread the yarn through the base of the first few corresponding stitches, leaving a yarn length to weave in later to secure the seam.**

3. **Lay the working end of the yarn against the fabric in the direction of the stitches. (See Figure 15-3.)**

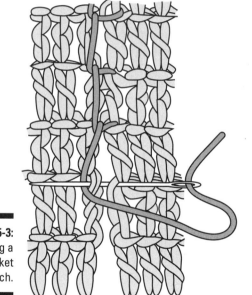

Figure 15-3:
Making a
blanket
stitch.

4. **Thread your yarn through the base of the next 2 corresponding stitches, making sure that the working end of the yarn is underneath the needle.**

5. **Repeat Steps 3 and 4 across the edges to be joined.**

6. **At the end of the seam, weave the yarn back through several stitches to secure.**

Figure 15-4 shows a complete blanket stitch seam.

Figure 15-4:
Completed
blanket
stitch seam.

Crocheting Pieces Together

Sometimes the pattern asks you to crochet your seams, whether for functional or decorative purposes. A crocheted seam is strong and comes in handy when joining pieces that are going to be put through a lot of wear and tear, such as motifs in an Afghan.

Crocheted seams can also become a part of your design. If worked on the right side of the fabric, a crocheted seam becomes part of the pattern in addition to holding the pieces together.

If the wrong sides of the pieces are facing each other when you join a seam, then the seam appears on the right side. If the right sides are facing, then the seam appears on the wrong side. Take a few seconds to make sure that your pieces are facing in the correct direction based on where you want your seam to appear before joining them. It's pretty frustrating to have to rip out a seam.

Slip stitching a seam

A slip stitch seam is very secure, but a little inflexible. When you work it on the wrong side of the fabric, this seam is great for items that take a beating, like a purse or tote bag. If worked on the right side of the fabric, the seam looks like an embroidered chain stitch. You can join pieces with the slip stitch to create two different looks: a ridged seam or a flat seam.

TIP

Crocheting seamlessly

If you hate to sew just as much as you love to crochet, you may find yourself with lots of crocheted pieces and no finished garments. Work around your sew-phobia by making it your mission to find interesting and attractive sweaters in styles with few, if any, seams. Here are a few ideas:

✔ Search out a raglan-style sweater — you can work it without a single seam from the neck down, all in one piece.

✔ Work a cardigan in one piece across the fronts and the back to the armholes, and then work the fronts and backs off of the body. The only sewing you have to do is the shoulder seams.

✔ Work the sleeves in rounds and directly off of the armholes, thus eliminating the underarm and shoulder seams.

✔ Trim cuffs and bottom edges in post double crochet ribbing right off of the edges of the sweater (see Chapter 16 for more on ribbing).

If you choose to create a ridge along your seam, you can either hide it (on the wrong side of the fabric) or make it part of the design (on the right side). To slip stitch a ridged seam, follow these steps:

1. **Position the two pieces together with right sides facing (for a wrong side seam) or wrong sides together (for a right side seam).**

   Make sure that the stitches across each edge match.

2. **Working through the double thickness of both pieces and using the same size crochet hook that you used in the design, insert your hook through the back 2 loops of the first 2 stitches, leaving a yarn tail about 6 inches long.**

3. **Yarn over (yo). (See Figure 15-5.)**

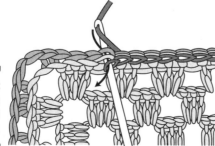

Figure 15-5:
Slip stitching
pieces laid
together.

4. **Pull the yarn through and repeat Steps 2 and 3 in each stitch across. Fasten off and weave in the ends.**

Figure 15-6 shows a completed slip stitch seam.

Figure 15-6:
Two pieces joined with a ridged slip stitch seam.

The second way to slip stitch two pieces together creates a flat seam. To slip stitch a seam in this fashion:

1. **Lay the two pieces on a flat surface side by side, with right sides facing (for a wrong side seam) or wrong sides together (for a right side seam).**

   Make sure that the stitches across each edge match.

2. **Working in the top loops of the stitches only and using the same size crochet hook you used in the design, insert your hook through the loops of the first 2 stitches, leaving a yarn tail several inches long.**

3. **Yarn over (yo).**

4. **Pull the yarn through the loops and repeat Steps 2 and 3 in each stitch across. Fasten off and weave in the ends.**

Joining with single crochet

When you join two pieces with single crochet stitches, you create a sturdy seam that's more flexible than one created with slip stitches. A seam made with single crochet creates a raised ridge that looks like a decorative chain. If you work it in a matching or contrasting color, it can become an integral part of your design.

Using single crochet stitches to join the seam in a garment has both positive and negative sides. Used to join seams that have no decorative value, the seam can cause uncomfortable lumpiness if it's on the inside. However, used on the right, or outside of the work, it can add wonderful texture and another design element to your creation.

To work a seam using single crochet stitches:

1. **Position the pieces with the right sides (or wrong sides) together. Match the stitches across each side edge.**

2. **Working through the double thickness of both pieces and using the same size crochet hook that you used in creating the design, insert your hook through the top 2 loops of the first 2 corresponding stitches.**

3. **Yarn over (yo).**

4. **Pull the yarn through both stitches. (See Figure 15-7.)**

Figure 15-7:
Single crocheting two pieces together.

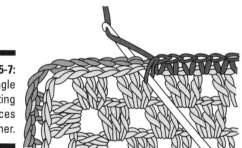

5. **Yarn over, and pull the yarn through the 2 loops on your hook.**

6. **Insert the hook through the top 2 loops of the next 2 corresponding stitches, and then repeat Steps 3 through 5 in each stitch across.**

   Figure 15-8 shows a completed single crochet seam.

Joining with a row of stitches

Joining two pieces with another row of stitches creates a different look from the other seams. Rather than working through the double thickness of two crocheted pieces, you work back and forth between them, usually on the right side of the piece. The row between the two pieces can be as narrow as a single stitch or it can be wide and lacy. You can use this method to join motifs when making a shawl, to add interest to the side seams of a garment, or to join panels when crocheting an Afghan.

Figure 15-8:
A decorative single crochet seam on the right side of the work.

To crochet a joining row that's a chain-2 space wide:

1. **Lay the pieces side by side on a flat surface, matching stitches across the adjacent edges that you're going to join.**

2. **Insert your hook under the top two loops in the designated stitch on the first piece, chain (ch) 1, single crochet (sc) in same stitch, and then 2 stitches for the joining row.**

3. **Insert your hook under the top two loops of the designated corresponding stitch on the second piece, yarn over (yo), and pull the yarn through the stitch. (See Figure 15-9.)**

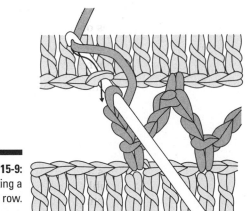

Figure 15-9:
Crocheting a joining row.

4. **Yarn over, and then draw the yarn through the 2 loops on your hook. Single crochet (sc) stitch complete.**

5. Chain 2, and then insert your hook under the top 2 loops of the designated stitch on the first piece, yarn over, and pull the yarn through the stitch.

6. Yarn over, and then draw the yarn through the 2 loops on your hook.

7. Chain 2, and then repeat Steps 3 through 6 across the row to the designated ending point.

Floral Motif Vest Project

You can make this beautiful motif vest in the three different colors shown in the color photo section to create the impression of a daisy garden, or you can pick your own colors. If you like a simple look (and don't like changing colors), you can make the motifs all one color. The cotton yarn suggested is wonderfully soft and easy to work with. After you finish making the motifs, you join them together with the whipstitch. For information on color changes, flip back to Chapter 9.

Materials

✔ **Yarn:** Paton's "Grace" 4-ply fingering-weight yarn (100% cotton), Article #246060 (1.75 oz. [*50 gm*], 136 yds. each ball):

- 1 skein of #60603 Apricot (A)

- 2 (3) skeins of #60005 Snow (B)

- 2 (3) skeins of #60027 Ginger (C)

✔ **Hook:** Crochet hook size G-6 U.S. or size needed to obtain gauge (refer to Chapter 3 for more on gauge)

✔ **Yarn needle**

Size

Directions are for child's size 6–8. Changes for adult sizes 8–12 are in parentheses. Finished bust = 28 (35) in. Back length = 18½ (21) in.

Figure 15-10 is a schematic showing the finished measurements of the child and adult vests. For detailed information on sweater sizing and reading the sweater schematic, see Chapter 10.

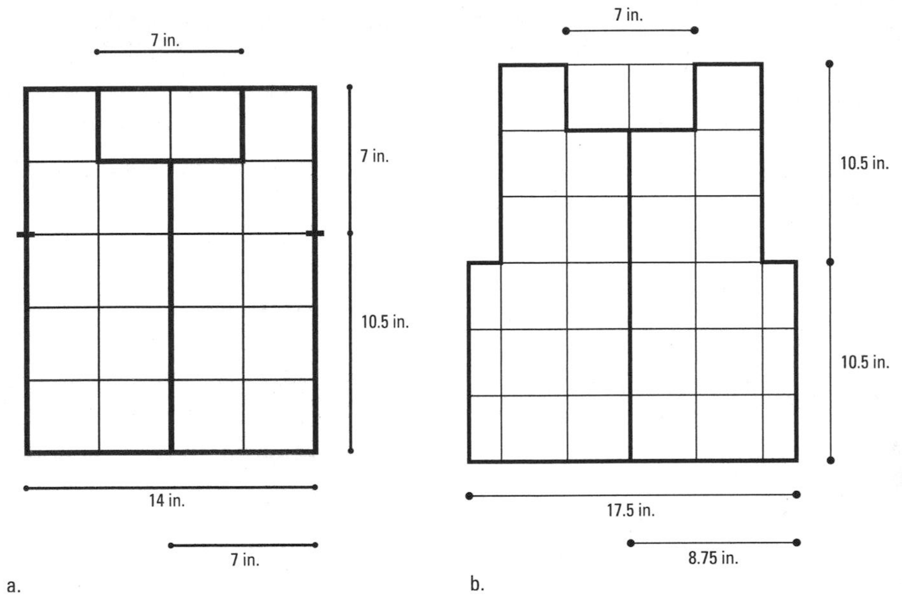

Figure 15-10:
Vest
schematics
showing
measure-
ments: (a)
a child's and
(b) an
adult's.

a.

b.

Vital statistics

- **Gauge:** First rnd of motif = 1¼ in.; motif = 3½ in. x 3½ in.

- **Stitches used:** Chain stitch (ch), slip stitch (sl st), single crochet (sc), double crochet (dc), triple crochet (tr)

Directions

The first step is making the motifs. You make them all exactly the same, but you make 38 motifs for the child size and 52 for the adult. Figure 15-11 shows a stitch diagram of the motif, which you can use along with the written instructions to fully see the stitch placement.

For the lowdown on reading patterns, refer to Chapter 5.

Center ring: With color A, ch 6 and close into a ring with 1 sl st in first ch.

Rnd 1: Ch 3 (first dc), work 11 dc in ring, sl st in top of ch-3 to join (12 dc). Fasten off color A, join color B in top of first ch-3 of rnd.

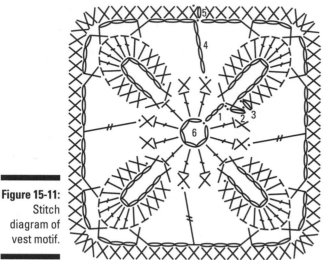

Figure 15-11:
Stitch
diagram of
vest motif.

Rnd 2: With color B, ch 1, (sc, ch 9, sc) in top of first ch-3, sc in each of next 2 dc, • (sc, ch 9, sc) in next dc, sc in each of next 2 dc •, rep from • to • around (4 ch-9 loops), sl st in first sc to join.

Rnd 3: Sl st in first ch-9 loop, ch 1, (3 sc, 2 hdc, 5 dc, 2 hdc, 3 sc) in ch-9 loop, skip next sc, sl st in next sc, skip next 2 sc, • sl st in next ch-9 loop, (3 sc, 2 hdc, 5 dc, 2 hdc, 3 sc) in ch-9 loop, skip next sc, sl st in next sc, skip next 2 sc •, rep from • to • around to within last sc, sl st in last sc (4 petals made). Fasten off color B.

Rnd 4: With right side of motif facing, join color C in sl st bet any 2 petals, ch 4 (first tr) in sl st bet petals, ch 3, skip first 4 sts on next petal, sc in next hdc, ch 3, skip next 2 dc on petal, sc in next dc at center top of petal, ch 3, skip next 2 dc on petal, sc in next hdc, ch 3, skip next 4 sts on petal, • tr in sl st bet next 2 petals, ch 3, skip first 4 sts on next petal, sc in next hdc, ch 3, skip next 2 dc on petal, sc in next dc at center top of petal, ch 3, skip next 2 dc on petal, sc in next hdc, ch 3, skip next 4 sts on petal •, rep from • to • around, sl st in top of first ch-4 to join (16 ch-3 loops).

Rnd 5: Ch 1, sc in top of ch-4, • 3 sc in next ch-3 loop, sc in next sc, 3 sc in next ch-3 loop, 3 sc in next sc, 3 sc in next ch-3 loop, sc in next sc, 3 sc in next ch-3 loop, sc in next tr •, rep from • to • around omitting last sc from last rep, sl st in first sc to join. Fasten off color C.

Assembly

After you complete all the required motifs, you sew them together with the whipstitch. Here's how:

1. **With a yarn needle, weave in all loose ends for each motif.**

2. **Block all motifs.**

   See Chapter 18 for blocking instructions.

3. **Using a yarn needle and color C, sew motifs together with the whip-stitch, matching stitches from corner to corner, working through back loops of the stitches in Round 5 of the motifs.**

   Follow the construction chart in Figure 15-12 for the appropriate size.

4. **Sew fronts to back across the shoulders.**

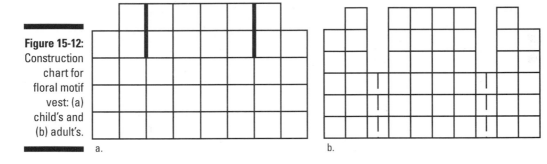

Figure 15-12: Construction chart for floral motif vest: (a) child's and (b) adult's.

a.

b.

Finishing

Now you add the finishing touches by crocheting the edgings and then adding the ties and tassels. For more details on making tassels, see Chapter 17.

- **Vest edging:** With right side of vest facing you, join color C in center back top of vest at neck edge, ch 1, sc evenly around outside edge of vest, sl st in first sc to join. Fasten off.

- **Armhole edging:** With right side of vest facing you, join color C in lower edge of armhole, ch 1, sc evenly around entire armhole, sl st in first sc to join. Fasten off. Repeat armhole edging around other armhole.

- **Front tie:** With right side of vest facing you, join color C in outside corner at top of front, ch 50 (75). Fasten off. Repeat on the other side of front.

- **Tassels:** Cut three 5-inch lengths each of colors A, B, and C. Holding all lengths together as one, fold in half. Cut two more 6-inch lengths of color C. Using one 6-inch length of yarn, tie the bundle securely together around the center fold, leaving equal lengths on each side. With bundle folded in half, wrap the second length of yarn several times around folded bundle approximately ¾ inch below folded end. Tie tightly to secure. Using remaining ends of yarn from first tie at center top of tassel, tie to end of front tie. (Repeat the process from the beginning to make a second tassel for the other front tie.)

Motif Afghan Project

You make this beautifully soft and textured Afghan by joining motifs together with a single crochet seam. If the colors that are shown in the color photo section of this book don't rev your engine, go ahead and change them. Whatever you choose, this Afghan is a wonderful take-along project that you'll wrap yourself up in for years to come.

To make this project even simpler, crochet each motif in one solid color, instead of changing between the three suggested colors. So when the directions tell you to change colors, just ignore them and continue on with the next round of stitches. You can make all the motifs the same color for a solid Afghan or make one-third of the motifs one color, one-third another color, and one-third another for a colorblock effect. Or you can let your fancy run free and use whatever color combinations your heart desires.

Materials

- **Yarn:** Coats & Clark Red Heart "Light & Lofty" bulky-weight yarn (100% acrylic), Article E708 (6 oz. [*170 gm*], 148 yds. for solids; 4.5 oz. [*127 gm*], 110 yds. each skein for multis):
    - 4 skeins of #9372 Antique Rose (A)
    - 3 skeins of #9631 Sage (B)
    - 5 skeins of #9978 Country Club (C)
- **Hook:** Crochet hook size M-13 U.S. or size needed to obtain gauge (refer to Chapter 3 for info on gauge)

Vital statistics

- **Measurements:** Motif = 10¼ in. x 10¼ in. Afghan = 54 in. x 64 in.
- **Gauge:** First 2 rnds of motif = 5¼ in.
- **Stitches used:** Chain stitch (ch), slip stitch (sl st), single crochet (sc), double crochet (dc), reverse single crochet (reverse sc). **Puff st:** • 2 tr (half closed and joined tog) worked in same st •. (See Chapter 11 for more on special stitches.)

Directions

The directions here tell you how to make one motif. We give them to you in standard crochet language, but if they seem like a bunch of gibberish, refer to Chapter 5 for info on reading patterns. The stitch diagram in Figure 15-13 also shows you where to make your stitches. Make 20 motifs to complete the Afghan or, if you want to make it larger, make 30 motifs, but be sure to buy one and a half times the yarn given in the materials list.

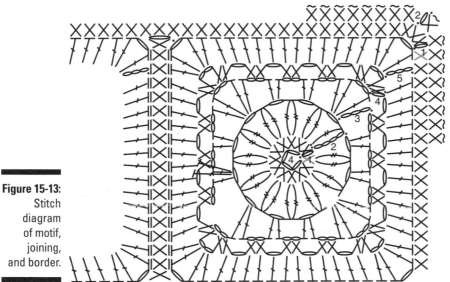

Figure 15-13: Stitch diagram of motif, joining, and border.

Motif (make 20): With A, ch 4 and close into a ring with 1 sl st in first ch.

Rnd 1 (right side): Ch 1, work 12 sc in ring, sl st in first sc to join. Fasten off A, join C.

Rnd 2: With C, ch 4 (first tr), tr in same sc, ch 1, • puff st in next sc, ch 1 •, rep from • to • around, sl st in turning ch to join. Fasten off C.

Rnd 3: With right side facing you, join A in any ch-1 space, ch 3 (first dc), (dc, ch 2, 2 dc) in same ch-1 space, • (ch 2, 2 dc in next ch-1 space) twice, ch 2, (2 dc, ch 2, 2 dc) in next ch-1 space for corner •, rep from • to • twice, (ch 2, 2 dc in next ch-1 space) twice, ch 2, sl st in top of turning ch to join. Fasten off A.

Rnd 4: With right side facing you, join C in any ch-2 corner space, ch 1, •
(2 sc, ch 2, 2 sc) in ch-2 space, (ch 1, 2 sc in next ch-2 space) 3 times, ch 1 •,
rep from • to • around, sl st in first sc to join. Fasten off C.

Rnd 5: With right side facing you, join B in any ch-2 corner space, ch 3 (first
dc), (dc, ch 1, 2 dc) in same space, • skip next sc, dc in each of next 12 sts,
skip next sc, (2 dc, ch 1, 2 dc) in next ch-2 corner space •, rep from • to • twice,
skip next sc, dc in each of next 12 sts, skip next sc, sl st in top of turning ch to
join. Fasten off B.

Assembly

With the wrong sides of two motifs facing each other, stitches matched from
corner to corner, and working through double thickness, join C in corner ch-1
space, ch 1, sc in blp of each sc across. (Refer back to Figure 15-13.) Continue
joining each motif in the same manner, 5 motifs wide by 6 motifs long.

Border

After you've joined all the motifs, make a border of single crochet and reverse
single crochet (refer back to Figure 15-13):

Rnd 1: With right side of Afghan facing you, join C in first dc to the left of
corner ch-1 space in top right-hand corner, ch 1, sc evenly around entire
Afghan, working 3 sc in each corner space, sl st in first sc to join. Fasten off C.

Rnd 2: With right side facing you, join A in center sc in top left-hand corner,
ch 1, working from left to right, reverse sc in each sc around, sl st in first
reverse sc to join. Fasten off A.

Chapter 16

Finishing Functionally: Borders, Buttons, and Pockets

. . . .

In This Chapter

▶ Finishing off the edges

▶ Buttoning up and tying it together

▶ Working pretty pockets

▶ Sporting a classic cardigan

. . . .

*Y*ou've conquered crochet and completed the body of a great new sweater or cardigan. But something's missing. How are you going to keep those wide-open sleeves from dragging without a cuff? Or how is that cardigan going to keep you warm if you can't fasten it shut? This chapter shows you how to make your new garments functional with important finishing touches like borders, cuffs, collars, buttonholes, and pockets. And the best part is that creating these finishing touches is easy. Try out the country cardigan project at the end of the chapter for a beautiful garment — and a little practice making ribbing, buttonholes, and pockets.

If you just want to practice your buttonholes or collars before trying them in another pattern, grab a few of the practice swatches that you made when practicing new stitches and add a buttonhole or collar to them.

Adding Trims: Edgings, Borders, and Collars

If you're thinking that you can make only the most basic of sweaters — two squares hung on your shoulders — forget it. This section shows you how to add simple edgings, ribbed borders, and elegant collars that bring your projects to life without a lot of work.

Outlining your design with edging

Crocheting a basic edging of one or two rows or rounds on the outer edges of a design can smooth out the rough spots and add a finished, professional look to your crocheted items. You can even add crocheted edgings to other materials. Here are a few options:

- ✔ Crochet a round of single crochet stitches around the bottom edge, neck edge, and cuffs of a sweater, especially one that you worked in a heavier weight yarn.

- ✔ When making a patchwork Afghan or sweater, edge each panel or motif with a row of stitches to create a smoother edge for joining.

- ✔ Crochet decorative strips of some of the fancier stitches, such as shells, clusters and chain loops, with cotton thread and sew these edgings on pillowcases, sheets, handkerchiefs, and towels — or down the seam of your jeans!

Although it's helpful to know how to do a simple edging on your own, any pattern that includes an edging to finish off the design will tell you in detail how to complete it.

Bordering your masterpiece with ribbing

Borders can be quite elaborate and may consist of a number of rows or rounds that are a design unto themselves. If intricate borders tickle your fancy, check out a few of the many publications available to find dozens of intricate border designs. (See Chapter 19 for a list of some of the best publications.) In this section, however, we show you how to make two of the most common borders used on garments: single crochet ribbing and post stitch ribbing.

Single crochet ribbing

Single crochet ribbing is a long strip of very short vertical single crochet rows. Because these rib rows will lay perpendicular to the rows in the body of the finished sweater, you normally make the ribbing first and then work the body of the sweater off the row-end stitches along the long edge of the rib.

Typically, you want the ribbing to cinch in a little around the bottom of the sweater and at the cuffs but still be flexible enough to stretch. You accomplish this by first making the rib with a hook one size smaller than the one you use for the rest of the sweater and then by working in only the back loops of each single crochet stitch across the row. You can make a wider border by increasing the stitches in each row (and make it narrower by working fewer stitches). A typical bottom rib is 1 to 3 inches wide, or about 4 to 10 stitches. To make ribbing that's approximately 2 inches wide, using worsted-weight yarn and a size H-8 U.S. hook, follow these steps:

1. **Chain (ch) 9.**

2. **Single crochet (sc) in the second chain from the hook, and then single crochet in each chain across, *turn*.**

   You now have 8 single crochet stitches.

3. **Chain 1 and then single crochet in the back loop of each single crochet across the row, *turn*. (See Figure 16-1.)**

Figure 16-1: Working single crochet ribbing.

4. **Repeat Step 3 until the rib reaches the desired length.**

   Typically, you make the rib an inch or two shorter than the width or diameter of the part of the sweater that you are crocheting. The amount of "cinching in" that you want to achieve, as well as the elasticity of the yarn you're working with, are both determining factors in deciding the length of the strip.

Figure 16-2a shows how a standard single crochet ribbing should appear, and Figure 16-2b shows the stitch diagram.

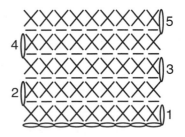

Figure 16-2: Swatch of single crochet ribbing and its stitch diagram.

a.

b.

You can add single crochet ribbing after you've crocheted the body of a sweater, but it takes more time, and its appearance may not be as neat as if you worked the ribbing first. However, if the pattern you're working asks you to do this, it will provide instructions.

Single crochet ribbing works better with some yarns than with others. If the yarn you're using is soft and has little elasticity, it may not be suitable for single crochet ribbing. If your ribbing looks flat, try working with a smaller hook to tighten it up. As a last resort, you can tighten up your flat ribbing by weaving elastic thread in several places around the bottom rib of a sweater to cinch it in. If that doesn't do the trick, you may want to opt for the post stitch ribbing discussed in the next section.

Post stitch ribbing

Post stitch ribbing, which is typically double crochet stitches worked around the posts of previous stitches, isn't as elastic as single crochet ribbing but it creates a more rounded style of ribbing that always maintains its ribbed appearance. Because you work post stitch ribbing in horizontal rows, you can either make the ribbing first, and then work the body across the top edge of the ribbing, or you can make the body first, and then work the ribbing off the bottom edge of the garment, which is normally how it's done. To make a typical post stitch ribbing across the bottom edge of a sweater:

1. **Work 1 row of double crochet (dc) across the bottom edge,** *turn.*

2. **Chain 2 (ch 2; counts as the first post stitch).**

3. **Work 1 front post double crochet (FP dc) around the post of the next double crochet. (See Figure 16-3a.)**

   See Chapter 12 for info on working post stitches.

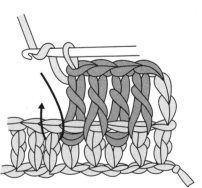
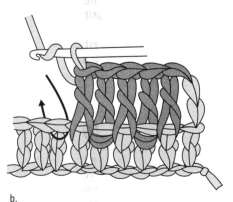

Figure 16-3:
Working post stitch ribbing.

a.

b.

4. **Work 1 back post double crochet (BP dc) around the post of the next double crochet. (Refer to Figure 16-3b.)**

5. **Repeat Steps 3 and 4 until you reach the last stitch.**

6. **Work 1 half double crochet (hdc) in the last stitch, *turn*.**

7. **Repeat Steps 2 through 6 until the rib measures the desired depth.**

   Figure 16-4a shows a post stitch ribbing swatch, and Figure 16-4b shows the stitch diagram.

Figure 16-4:
Double crochet post stitch ribbing swatch and stitch diagram.

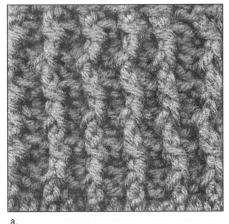

a.

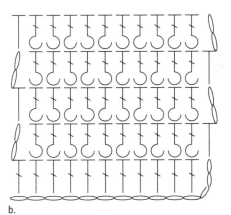

b.

When making post stitch ribbing, always make sure that the post stitches are raised to the same side in each successive row or round. Keep an eye on the ribs and remember: If the stitch you're working is raised to the front, work a front post stitch; if the stitch is raised to the back, work a back post stitch.

Post stitch ribbing is much thicker and tighter than single crochet ribbing. If you're using a heavier yarn, it can be pretty stiff and inflexible. Using a larger crochet hook gets you a softer, more flexible feel.

Gracing your neck with collars

Collars are a broad subject, with variations too numerous to explain in detail. However, if you can make basic crochet stitches, you can fashion almost any style collar you can think of. Among the myriad collar options are soft, draping shawl collars, stiff mandarin-style collars, turtlenecks, and the traditional flared collar. In this section, we show you how to make two basic collars. But any pattern that you work will give you detailed instructions for the collar called for.

To make a simple single crochet rib turtleneck collar, follow these steps:

1. **With the hook you used to make the body of your sweater, join the yarn with a slip stitch in one shoulder seam.**

2. **Chain (ch) 1 and single crochet (sc) evenly around the neck opening. Slip stitch (sl st) in the first single crochet to join.**

   This first round of single crochet stitches creates a solid base from which to work the rib.

3. **Change to the next smaller size hook than the one you used for the body of the sweater, and chain 41.**

   The length of the chain determines the depth of the collar. For a mock turtleneck, try using a foundation chain of only 15 stitches.

4. **Single crochet in the second chain from the hook and then single crochet in each chain stitch across (40 single crochet stitches).**

5. **Slip stitch in the next free single crochet stitch on the neck edge, *turn*.**

6. **Working across the single crochet stitches just made, single crochet in the back loop of each single crochet across (40 single crochet stitches), *turn*.**

7. **Chain 1 and then single crochet in the back loop of each single crochet stitch across.**

8. **Repeat Steps 5 through 7 around the neck edge.**

9. **Fasten off your yarn, leaving a sewing length.**

   The sewing length should be long enough to join the two edges of the collar.

10. **Using a yarn or tapestry needle and the sewing length, sew the last row of the rib to the first row of the rib. Fold the top edge of the rib down toward the right side of the sweater to form the turtleneck.**

A second common collar is the traditional flared collar, which features pointed ends like a standard shirt collar. This collar is typically used on cardigans, pullovers with crew necks, or polo-style sweaters with front openings and plackets. To work a flared collar, follow these steps:

1. **With the right side of the sweater facing you, join the yarn with a slip stitch in the top right-hand corner of the right front neck edge. Chain (ch) 1.**

2. **Single crochet (sc) evenly from the right front neck edge around to the top left-hand corner stitch of the left front neck edge, *turn*.**

3. **Chain 1 and then work 2 single crochets in the first single crochet stitch. Single crochet in each stitch across, ending with 2 single crochets in the last stitch, *turn*.**

   Work the extra stitch at both edges of the collar to add the flare to it.

4. **Repeat Step 3 until the collar reaches 3 inches deep or your desired depth.**

5. **Fasten off at the end of the last row.**

Holding Things Together: Buttonholes, Ties, and Drawstrings

When you button up your shirt in the morning, do you ever stop to think about which side the buttons are on and which side the holes are on? Or about how much space is between them? How about the ties on that cute new cover-up? Is the tie flat or round? Does it have tassels or beads at the end, or is it just finished with a knot? This section shows you all you need to know to keep your new clothes on — with buttons, ties, and drawstrings, that is.

Making room for buttons: Buttonholes

The design of the garment you're crocheting determines whether you work buttonholes horizontally or vertically, although both appear as vertical slits when finished. If the garment has front *plackets* (those narrow bands that run up the inside edges of the front of a shirt or sweater opening), you create the buttonhole horizontally right into the placket. If the design doesn't have front plackets, you work buttonholes vertically into the garment itself.

Remember which side you're on! On a woman's shirt, the buttonholes are on the right side of the shirt when you're wearing it; on men's shirts, buttonholes are on the left. Of course, you can't have buttonholes without buttons: Check out Chapter 17 for info on making your own buttons.

Working buttonholes in front plackets

Making buttonholes in front plackets is easy. All you do is skip enough stitches in the designated row of the placket to accommodate the button size wherever you want a buttonhole. The buttonhole is usually created in a row close to the center of the placket, with a row or two following to add strength. To make a standard buttonhole using this method, follow these steps:

1. **Place markers across the front edge of the placket to mark the beginning and the end of each desired buttonhole position.**

2. **Crochet across the row to the first marker, chain (ch) 2 (or required number for the button size), skip the next 2 stitches (same number of stitches as chain stitches), and then continue crocheting across to the next marker. (See Figure 16-5a.)**

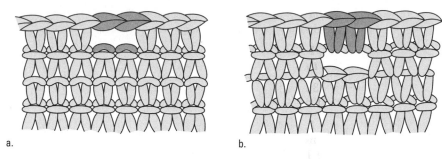

Figure 16-5:
Working a
buttonhole
horizontally.

a.

b.

3. **Repeat Step 2 for each marker until you reach the end of the row,** *turn.*

4. **Crochet evenly across the previous row, working an equal number of stitches into the chain space as it has chain stitches.**

   Refer to Figure 16-5b to see the completed buttonhole.

The number of stitches that you skip, and therefore chain, depends on the size of the button. Have your buttons on hand before crocheting this part — better to fit the hole to the button than have to find a button to fit the hole.

Working buttonholes in the garment body

If your design doesn't have front plackets, you work the buttonholes right into the body of the sweater by working across the row to the point where the buttonhole will appear and then turning your work, leaving several stitches unworked. You then fasten off your work and rejoin the yarn in the stitch on the other side of the buttonhole, skipping a stitch to create the buttonhole, and then working in the few stitches that you left unworked in previous rows to create the other side of the buttonhole. This means you have to plan ahead and determine the buttonhole positions before you work the body of the sweater. To crochet a vertical buttonhole like the one illustrated in Figure 16-6 on a single crochet sweater, follow these steps:

1. **When you're ready to begin the designated row for the bottom of the buttonhole, chain (ch) 1 to start the new row. Single crochet (sc) in each of first 3 stitches, and then turn, leaving the remaining stitches of the row unworked.**

2. **Chain 1 and then single crochet in each stitch across the first half of the buttonhole,** *turn.* **(See Figure 16-6a.)**

3. **Repeat Step 2.**

4. **Fasten off the yarn and, with the right side facing you, skip 1 single crochet and rejoin the yarn on the other side to begin making the second side of the buttonhole.**

   Remember to rejoin the yarn so that you work in the same direction as the other side; otherwise, you end up with a different stitch pattern. If the first row of the buttonhole row is worked with the right side of your work facing you, make sure that when you rejoin your yarn to work the second side, the right side of your work is also facing you.

5. **Chain 1 and single crochet in each stitch across the remainder of the front,** *turn.*

6. **Work 3 more rows of single crochet across, ending with a wrong side row at the top of the buttonhole.**

7. **Chain 1, skip the space for the buttonhole, and single crochet in each of the next 3 single crochets on the first side of the buttonhole. (See Figure 16-6b.)**

8. **Repeat Steps 1 through 7 for each buttonhole.**

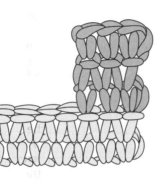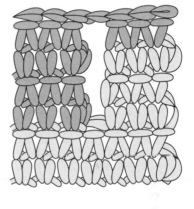

Figure 16-6:
Working a buttonhole vertically.

a.   b.

Working button loops

Button loops are nice alternatives to buttonholes. You can use them in a lightweight garment where you don't need a tight closure to the front or as a simple one-button closure at the top of the neckline. You work these loops into the final rows of an edging of a garment: If you're using a lightweight yarn, work the loop in the last two rows to give it more strength. If you're using a heavier yarn, a loop worked in the last row is sufficient. To make a button loop on the last two rows of an edging, follow these steps:

1. **On the next-to-last row of the edging, mark positions across the front edge where you want the beginning of your loops to be positioned.**

2. **Crochet across the row until you reach a marked position.**

3. **Make a chain just long enough to make a loop that the button can slip through.**

4. **Without skipping any stitches, continue crocheting until you reach the marker for the next loop.**

5. **Repeat Steps 2 through 4 across the row,** *turn.*

6. **For the last row, crochet evenly across, crocheting into each chain stitch in each loop. (See Figure 16-7 for a sample single crochet button loop.)**

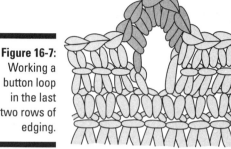

Figure 16-7:
Working a button loop in the last two rows of edging.

To make a button loop on the last row of an edging:

1. **Before you begin the last row, mark positions across the front edge where you want to place your loops, marking both the beginning and ending of each loop.**

2. **Crochet across the row until you reach the second marker for the first loop,** *turn.* **(See Figure 16-8a.)**

3. **Make a chain large enough to slip the button through.**

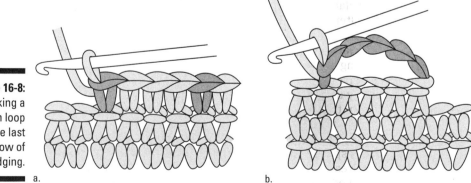

Figure 16-8:
Working a button loop in the last row of edging.

a.

b.

4. **Slip stitch (sl st) the chain to the edge at the first marker of the first loop,** *turn.* **(Refer to Figure 16-8b; note that the work shown hasn't been turned yet.)**

5. **Work a single crochet (sc) stitch into each chain (ch) of the chain loop and continue across the row.**

6. **Repeat Steps 2 through 5 for each button loop.**

   Figure 16-9 shows a completed button loop.

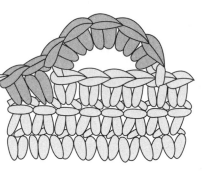

Figure 16-9: Completed button loop on the edge of a work.

Keeping your clothes on (or just spicing them up): Ties and drawstrings

Ties and drawstrings make fun and easy closures for the front (or back) of a garment. They can be as simple as a single tie attached to each side of the front or as elaborate as a threaded drawstring criss-crossing the back of a summer halter top.

You usually attach ties to the top of the fronts close to the neck opening or at the beginning of the front neck shaping, centered over the chest. You can also place ties in a row down the entire front of a sweater. Ties are attached to the garments by using the excess lengths of yarn left from the beginning of the tie to "tie" them to the correct position on the garment.

Drawstrings, which you weave through a *beading round* (a round created with spaces specifically used for weaving ties through) crocheted into the body of a sweater or sleeve (see Chapter 17), often adorn the neckline, waistline, bottom edges, and cuff edges. You can also place drawstrings in the center back, weaving them back and forth between the open edges of a halter top to draw the sides together.

The following list gives you a few options for making a tie or drawstring:

- **Make a simple chain:** Chain the required length for the tie or the drawstring. (You may use one or more strands of yarn.)

- **Make a round cord:** Chain 5 (or the required number for the thickness of the cord) and slip stitch in the first chain to join. Single crochet in each chain around. Then, working in a spiral, continue to single crochet in each single crochet around until the cord reaches the length you desire.

- **Single crochet or slip stitch a cord:** Chain the required length, turn, and slip stitch or single crochet in the back bump loop of each chain across.

The previous list shows you but a few of the many techniques for making cords. To spice them up, add tassels or beads (see Chapter 17 for tips on embellishments) or just tie each end in a simple knot to finish off the cords.

Purely Pockets

If you're like most people, you like a place to stuff things — especially your hands. This section briefly describes three common types of pockets and gives you the basics on how to work them into a garment.

Patch pockets: Tacked onto the front

Patch pockets are by far the simplest form of pocket to create. You simply crochet two squares or rectangles, usually in the same stitch pattern as the body of the sweater, and then sew them onto the front, usually closer to the side seams than to the front edge. If the sweater has a contrasting color yarn for the ribbing, you can outline the top of the pockets with an edging in the same color for a nice touch. (See Figure 16-10.)

Figure 16-10: Several pocket styles.

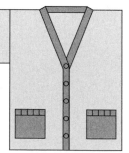
Patch Pockets

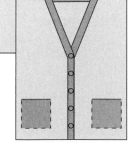
Slashed Pockets

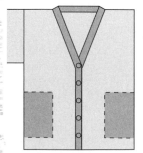
Inseam Pockets

Slashed pockets: Slotted in the front

A slashed pocket is similar to a patch pocket in shape and position. However, instead of sewing the pocket to the outside of the sweater, you make a lining, generally in single crochet, and then attach it to the wrong side (the inside) of the front. A little more planning is involved here because when you're crocheting the front, you have to allow for the opening. You work the first row above the pocket opening across the top of the pocket lining (which you've already crocheted) and then skip the appropriate number of stitches across the front of the sweater to create the opening. Your lining is now attached to the body of the sweater. Sew the lining to the wrong side of the sweater around three sides directly below the opening (see Figure 16-10). For a decorative touch, crochet the top edge of the pocket opening on the front of the sweater in a contrasting color.

Inseam pockets: Hand warmers at your sides

Inseam pockets are openings in the side seams of a garment, as shown in Figure 16-10. To make inseam pockets, you first have to create a solid fabric pocket. This means that you have three layers of crochet at the point where you place the pockets. Keep this in mind if you're working with a heavier weight yarn, as crocheted fabric tends to be thick.

Make the inseam pockets with a lighter weight yarn that matches your sweater and a smaller hook to reduce bulk.

To make a double-sided pocket to be sewn into the inseam, follow these steps:

1. **Chain (ch) the number of chain stitches needed to create the width of the pocket.**

2. **Single crochet (sc) in the second chain from the hook and then single crochet in each chain across, *turn.***

3. **Chain 1, single crochet in each single crochet across.**

4. **Repeat Step 3 until the pocket reaches the desired depth.**

5. **Fasten off the yarn.**

6. **Repeat Steps 1 through 5 to make the second side of the pocket.**

After you make both sides of a pocket and sew them along three sides, either sew or crochet the pocket into the side seam of the garment. Join one side of the pocket opening to the front side seam and the other side of the pocket opening to the back side seam. You close the rest of the side seam however the pattern instructs you to do so.

Country Cardigan Project

The beauty of this cardigan (check it out in the color photo section of this book) comes from its simple design elements. You don't have to be an expert or crochet many fancy stitches to create a garment that you'll love to wear and show off for years to come. The tweed coloration of the yarn gives it a classic country feel, and the stitch pattern, commonly known as *seed stitch,* adds a slight texture to the fabric. (The seed stitch pattern is simply single crochet and double crochet stitches alternated in every other stitch — nothing new here.) Patch pockets, cuffed sleeves, and a V-neck all add up to a versatile, wear-everywhere sweater.

Materials

- **Yarn:** Tahki Yarns "New Tweed" by Tahki/Stacy Charles, worsted-weight yarn (70% merino wool/15% silk/11% cotton/4% viscose) (1.75 oz. [*50 gm*], 103 yds. each ball): 14 (15, 15, 16) balls of #025 brown/white tweed (MC) and 3 balls of #05 dark brown tweed (CC)

- **Hook:** Crochet hook sizes G-6 and H-8 U.S. or sizes needed to obtain gauge (refer to Chapter 3 for information on gauge)

- **Yarn needle**

- **Five buttons:** ¾ in.

- **Sewing needle and sewing thread to match the yarn and buttons**

Size

Directions given are for size Small (8–10). Changes for Medium (12–14), Large (16–18), and X-Large (20–22) are in parentheses. Finished bust: 38 (42, 46, 50) in. Back length: 26 (27, 27, 28) in. Sleeve length: 18 (18, 19, 20) in. The schematic in Figure 16-11 shows the finished measurements.

Vital statistics

- **Gauge:** With smaller hook, 5 sts and 4 rows in sc rib pattern = 1 in. With larger hook, 10 sts and 8 rows in body pat = 3 in.

- **Stitches used:** Chain stitch (ch), slip stitch (sl st), single crochet (sc), double crochet (dc). **Dec 1 sc:** • (Yo, insert hook in next st, yo, draw yarn through st) twice, yo, draw yarn through 3 loops on hook •.

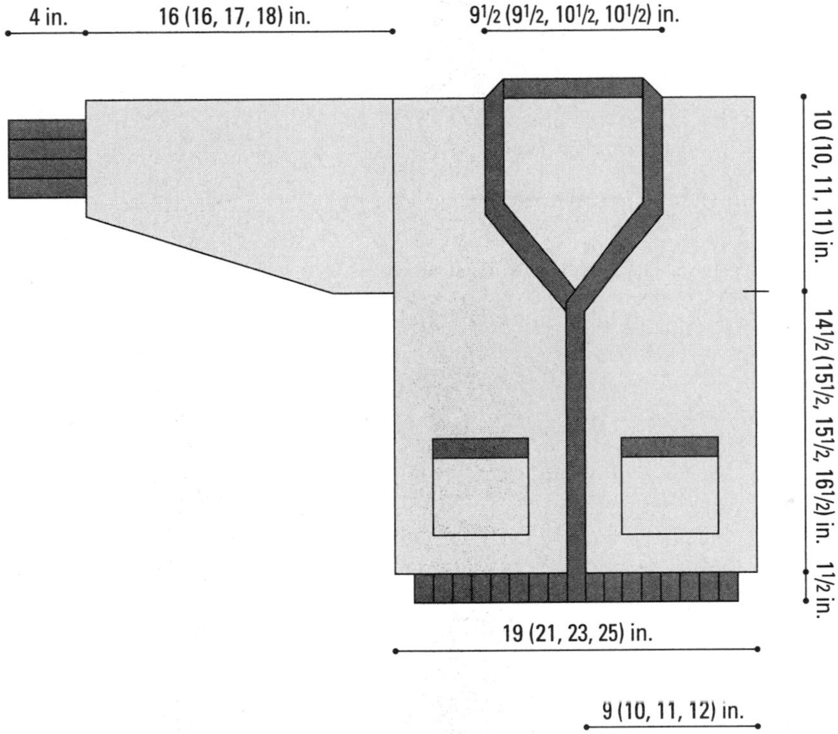

Figure 16-11:
Sweater
schematic.

Directions

You make this garment in one piece, starting at the lower edge and working to the underarm (see Figure 16-11). Work is then divided into front and back by skipping stitches to create the separation between the front and back and the armholes.

Bottom Rib

With smaller hook and CC, ch 9.

Row 1: Sc in 2nd ch from hook, sc in each ch across (8 sc), *turn.*

Row 2: Ch 1, sc in blp of each sc across (8 sc), *turn.*

Rep Row 2 until rib measures 36 (40, 44, 48) in. unstretched. Fasten off.

Body

Row 1: With larger hook, join MC in first row-end st on long edge of rib, ch 1, work 124 (136, 150, 164) sc evenly spaced across long edge of rib, *turn.*

Row 2: Ch 1, sc in first sc, dc in next sc, • sc in next sc, dc in next sc •, rep from • to • across (124 [136, 150, 164] sts), *turn.*

Row 3: Ch 1, sc in first dc, dc in next sc, • sc in next dc, dc in next sc •, rep from • to • across (124 [136, 150, 164] sts), *turn.*

Work even in established pat on 124 (136, 150, 164) sts until body measures 16 (17, 17, 18) in. from beg.

Beg neck shaping: Next row: Dec 1 sc at each end of next row and every row thereafter 4 times (116 [128, 146, 160] sts at end of last row).

First front: Shape armhole: Next row: Ch 1, dec 1 sc in first 2 sts, work in established pat across next 23 (26, 29, 32) sts (24 [27, 30, 33] sts), *turn.*

Work in established pat, dec 1 sc at neck edge on each row until 16 (18, 20, 22) sts rem. Work even in established pat until front measures 26 (27, 27, 28) in. from beg. Fasten off.

Back: Next row: With appropriate side facing, skip 2 sts to the left of last st made in first row of first front. Using larger hook, join MC in next sc, ch 1, sc in same sc, work in established pat across next 63 (69, 77, 83) sts (64 [70, 78, 84] sts), *turn,* leaving rem sts unworked.

Work even in established pat until back measures same as finished first front. Fasten off.

Second front: Next row: With appropriate side facing, skip 2 sts to the left of last st made in first row of back. Using larger hook, join MC in next st, ch 1, sc in same dc, work in established pat across to within last 2 sts, dec 1 sc in last 2 sts (24 [27, 30, 33] sts), *turn.*

Work in established pat, dec 1 sc at neck edge on each row until 16 (18, 20, 22) sts rem.

Work even in established pat on 16 (18, 20, 22) sts until second front measures same as finished back.

Sleeve (make 2)
Rib
With smaller hook and CC, ch 21.

Row 1: Sc in 2nd ch from hook, sc in each ch across (20 sc), *turn.*

Row 2: Ch 1, sc in blp of each sc across (20 sc), *turn.*

Rep Row 2 until rib measures 8 in. in length, unstretched. Fasten off.

Sleeve body

Row 1: With larger hook, join MC in first row-end st on long edge of rib, ch 1, work 34 sc evenly spaced across, *turn*.

Row 2: Ch 1, sc in first sc, dc in next sc, • sc in next sc, dc in next sc •, rep from • to • across (34 sts), *turn*.

Row 3: Ch 1, 2 sc in first dc (inc made), • dc in next sc, sc in next dc •, rep from • to • across to within last 2 sts, 2 dc in last st (inc made) (36 sts), *turn*.

Row 4: Ch 1, sc in each of first 2 dc, • dc in next sc, sc in next dc •, rep from • to • across to within last 2 sc, dc in next sc, sc in last sc(36 sts), *turn*.

Row 5: Ch 1, (sc, dc) in first sc, • sc in next dc, dc in next sc •, rep from • to • across to within last sc, (dc, sc) in last sc (inc made) (38 sts), *turn*.

Rep Rows 2–5 until 68 (68, 74, 74) sts are on work.

Work even in established pat on 68 (68, 74, 74) sts until sleeve measures 20 (20, 21, 22) in. from beg. Fasten off.

Pocket (make 2)

With larger hook and MC, ch 17.

Row 1: Sc in second ch from hook, • dc in next ch, sc in next ch •, rep from • to • across to within last ch, dc in last ch, *turn*.

Row 2: Ch 1, sc in first dc, dc in next sc, • sc in next dc, dc in next sc •, rep from • to • across (16 sts), *turn*.

Work even in established pat until pocket measures 4 in. from beg. Change to CC.

With CC, work even in established pat until pocket measures 5 in. from beg. Fasten off.

Assembly

1. **With the yarn needle and MC, sew the fronts to the back across the shoulders.**

2. **Fold the sleeves in half lengthwise.**

3. **Matching the center fold to the shoulder seam, sew the sleeves in place.**

4. With the yarn needle and matching yarn, sew the underarm seams.

5. Fold the sleeve rib halfway back to the right side to form the cuff.

6. With the yarn needle and matching yarn, sew the pockets to the fronts, positioned 2 inches above the bottom rib and 2 inches in from the side fold.

Finishing

Front edging: Row 1: With right side facing, using smaller hook and CC, join yarn in first st on bottom rib on right front, ch 1, sc evenly across right front edge to neck shaping, sc evenly across neck edge to left front, sc evenly down left front edge to next corner, *turn.*

Row 2: Ch 1, sc in each sc across, *turn.* Mark positions for 5 evenly spaced buttonholes on right front edge, with bottom marker 2 in. above lower edge, top marker ¾ in. below neck shaping, and remaining 3 markers evenly spaced bet.

Row 3: Ch 1, sc in each sc across, working (ch 2, skip next 2 sc) at each marker, *turn.*

Row 4: Ch 1, sc in each sc across, working 2 sc in each ch-2 space, *turn.*

Row 5: Ch 1, sc in each sc across. Fasten off.

With sewing needle and matching sewing thread, sew buttons to left front edge opposite buttonholes.

Chapter 17

It's All in the Details: Embellishing Crochet

In This Chapter

▶ Flirting with fringe

▶ Teasing with tassels

▶ Brightening up with beads

*W*hat is it about your favorite pieces of clothing that strikes your fancy — the color, the style, or maybe a special finishing touch? This chapter shows you how to create those special touches that can turn a so-so piece into one that everybody raves about — from fringes and tassels to beads, ribbons, flowers, and embroidery. And the best part is that creating these finishing touches is very easy. So let your creative side run free.

Hanging Off the Edge: Fringe and Tassels

Fringe and tassels are two of the most common crochet embellishments. Fringe often complements a scarf or Afghan, and tassels sometimes finish off drawstrings or ties on a sweater, the top of a hat, or a filet crochet wall-hanging. (See Chapter 14 for the lowdown on filet crochet.) Simple to make, fringe and tassels don't require any additional materials other than the yarn and hook you use to crochet your piece.

To spice up your look, you can interchange fringe and tassels (meaning that if a design calls for fringe at the ends of the piece, you could add tassels instead, if you prefer the way they look), add beads to individual strands, or even fray the yarn by separating the fibers in a strand to create a fuller, fluffier look.

Tying up fringe

Fringe commonly borders the short edges of a scarf or the ends of an Afghan. It gives a nice finishing touch and also hides those sometimes unsightly end rows. If your design incorporates several colors, you can tie them all together with the fringe. Fringe looks best when it's fluffy and full, so, depending on the type of yarn you use, combine several strands for each fringe or use whatever number your pattern instructions tell you. To make fringe, follow these steps:

1. **Cut the yarn into the required number of equal lengths.**

   For example, if each fringe has 3 strands of yarn, and you have 20 stitches across the edge that you're attaching the fringe to, then you need 60 lengths of yarn, all equal in length.

2. **Fold the strands of yarn for one fringe in half, forming a loop at one end and matching the cut ends of the yarn on the other end.**

3. **Working from the right side of the fabric, take your hook and draw the loop through the stitch that you're attaching the fringe to. (See Figure 17-1a.)**

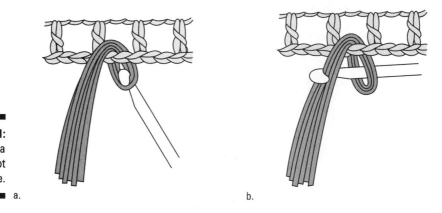

Figure 17-1: Making a single-knot fringe.

a.   b.

4. **Draw the loose ends of the yarn through the loop. (Refer to Figure 17-1b.)**

5. **Holding the top of the fringe in one hand, pull gently on the fringe ends with your other hand to tighten the knot.**

6. **To finish, trim the ends of the fringe so that they're even.**

   You've completed one single-knot fringe. See Figure 17-2.

Figure 17-2:
Finished
fringe
attached to
crochet.

 When making fringe, cut the yarn twice as long as you want the final fringe to be (because you're folding it in half). Err on the safe side and cut them even a little longer to account for the knot. You can always cut the fringe shorter, but you can't make it longer.

Tagging on tassels

You generally use tassels to embellish spots like the points on a shawl, the back of a hat, the ends of drawstrings or ties, or the lower edges of a wall-hanging. Rather than working tassels directly in a stitch as with fringe, you usually make them separately and then tie them on to the design. To make a tassel, follow these steps:

1. **Cut a piece of cardboard the same width as your desired tassel length.**

   If you're following a pattern, the instructions specify what size to cut the cardboard.

2. **Wrap the yarn several times around the piece of cardboard.**

   The more times you wrap the yarn around, the fuller your tassel will be.

3. **Tie the yarn bundle together at one end with a separate length of yarn. (See Figure 17-3.)**

   This separate length of yarn should be at least 6 inches in length, long enough to tie the bundle together and then tie the tassel to the piece when complete. Some instructions may give you an exact length to use.

4. **Slide the bundle of yarn off the cardboard piece.**

5. **Wrap another length of yarn 2 or 3 times around the bundle below the tied end and tie in a knot to secure. (See Figure 17-4.)**

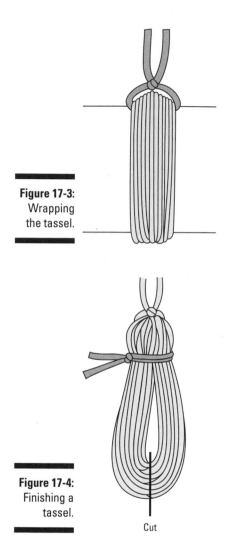

Figure 17-3:
Wrapping
the tassel.

Figure 17-4:
Finishing a
tassel.

Cut

6. **Cut the loops on the opposite end of the bundle from the tied end.**

7. **Trim the ends of the tassel so they're even.**

8. **With the top tie's remaining yarn, attach the tassel to the designated spot.**

Attaching a tassel is the same no matter what you're attaching it to. If it's the back point on a bandana, then the stitch on the very end will hold the knot. If you're attaching tassels across the edges of a scarf, then the instructions will designate which stitches to tie them to (for example, every other stitch or every third stitch).

Getting Serious: Embellishing the Fabric

If you want to embellish your crochet fabric a little bit, you have lots of options. Spice up an otherwise plain cardigan with some pretty buttons. Sew or crochet beads onto a crocheted evening top for a touch of elegance. If you cross-stitch or crewel, the square stitches of the Afghan stitch are the perfect backdrop for your handiwork. Weave a satin ribbon along the edge of a baby blanket. With a minimum of fuss, you can give your crochet design a whole new look.

Brandishing your buttons

If you just can't find the perfect buttons, try making your own by working stitches over a plastic ring. Plastic rings are available in a wide variety of sizes, and you can use them to make buttons with the same yarn that you're using for your design. Crocheting over a ring is similar to working in a chain loop (refer to Chapter 12 to make a chain loop): Instead of inserting your hook into a stitch, you draw your yarn through the center of the ring, thereby working your stitch around the ring. Single or double crochet stitches are best for this. The yarn may be thick enough to fill in the ring with just one round, but sometimes you need to make additional stitches to fill in the hole, which you then draw together and close at the top.

Brightening up with shiny beads

Bead crochet has really gained momentum over the past several years, especially with the ever-expanding selection of beads in craft stores. You can add beads to crochet in two basic ways:

- ✔ Sew them on after you finish crocheting.
- ✔ Crochet them right into the fabric.

If you want only a few larger beads to highlight certain areas, sew them on after you're done crocheting. But if the beads are an integral part of the design, you can easily crochet them in as you work.

Make sure that the weight of the yarn is compatible with the weight of the beads. If you're using a lightweight yarn, don't use heavy, oversized beads. The weight of the beads can cause the stitches to droop and pull, creating an unsightly mess. On the flip side, if you're working with a heavier weight yarn, choose beads that won't get lost in the stitches.

Beading after the fact

Adding beads after you complete your design works well when you're using larger beads or making a design with just a few well-placed beads. If you're using smaller beads, you can sew them on with a regular sewing needle and matching sewing thread or clear nylon thread. If the beads are fairly large, use a yarn or tapestry needle and the yarn used to crochet the piece. To sew the beads to the crocheted fabric:

1. **Using the threaded needle, insert the needle on the wrong side of the fabric in the spot where you want your bead to be positioned and draw it through to the right side, leaving several inches of thread on the wrong side of the fabric.**

   Make sure to insert your needle within the strands of yarn, rather than in the spaces between the stitches.

2. **Thread a bead onto the strand of thread or yarn and slide it down close to the fabric.**

3. **Insert the needle (from the right side to the wrong side) back through the fabric, close to the bead.**

4. **Cut the thread or yarn, leaving several inches at the end.**

5. **Tie the two loose ends of thread or yarn together on the wrong side of the fabric to secure. Weave the remaining ends into the fabric to hide them.**

Crocheting beads into the fabric

If you want to work a lot of fairly small beads into your design, then crocheting them into the design is your best bet. This requires some planning ahead, though, because you have to string all the beads onto the yarn before you make your first stitch. Here's how you start:

1. **String the beads onto the yarn or thread with a needle.**

   The instructions normally tell you how many beads a particular section requires, so you string only the amount of beads that you can easily handle. Control the pre-strung yarn by wrapping it around an empty toilet tissue or paper towel tube. Even though you have beads on the yarn or thread, the yarn slides through them, so you can place each bead exactly where you want it to go by sliding it up close to the hook when you're ready to work with it.

   When working with small beads and fine cotton, you may need a beading needle to string the beads onto the thread. A regular sewing needle may be too fat for the beads to fit over. To figure out which needle will work best, try sliding a bead completely over the needle. If it slips over the eye smoothly, then the needle is the right size.

2. **Begin to crochet according to the pattern (if you're using one) until you reach the first stitch or row where you want to add a bead.**

3. **Insert the hook in the next stitch, draw a bead up close to the hook, yarn over (yo), draw the thread through the stitch, and then complete the stitch as you normally do.**

   The beads show up on the back of the side you're working on, so be sure that the row or round that you add the beads to is a wrong side row. That way the beads show up on the right side. Most designers plan for this when they work out the design.

Beaded single crochet stitches are the most popular, with beaded half double crochet stitches coming in second. You can also add beads to double crochet stitches. With double crochet, the bead appears in the top section of the stitch; with single crochet and half double crochet stitches, the bead appears in the center of the stitch. Figure 17-5 shows beaded double crochet stitches, with a row of regular (non-beaded) single crochet in between.

Figure 17-5:
Beaded
double
crochet
stitches.

Easing into elegant embroidery

Embroidering can be a hoot. Using a needle and thread (or yarn) on the surface of the crocheted fabric gives you the freedom to create unique designs that embellish your work of art. Many relatively plain pieces of crochet are transformed by this method. You can transfer almost any embroidery design onto a piece of crocheted fabric, whether the front of a sweater, the panels of an Afghan, or a crocheted background design. *Crewel* (embroidery worked with yarn instead of thread) and cross-stitch work especially well on crocheting.

Creating crewel work

Traditionally, crewel work requires fine wool yarn, but over the years, it's just come to be a style of embroidery that's worked with any type of yarn, instead of thread. The designs are varied and numerous, and any design that you can embroider with thread, you can work with yarn. Crewel works especially well on plackets, collars, and cuffs, or for creating a large picture on the front or back of a sweater, pillow, or handbag. You can work free-flowing designs in crewel, so let your imagination go. It's a wonderful way to use up all that scrap yarn you have floating around. Check out your local craft store for some crewel designs that you can use.

Enjoying cross-stitch

For those of you who enjoy cross-stitch, adding it to your crochet design is a perfect way to combine your efforts and show off your multi-talented self. An Afghan stitch design (see Chapter 13) just screams to be cross-stitched on. The small squares that are integral to the design make transferring pretty much any cross-stitch pattern to the right side a snap. For more information on the Afghan stitch and adding cross-stitch, refer to Chapter 13.

Weaving and winding your way

Weaving in a length of satin ribbon or a crocheted strip or chain adds interest to a crocheted creation and can also serve a functional purpose.

For example, you can weave

- ✔ Ribbon around the edge of a blanket or Afghan.
- ✔ A drawstring around the neckline of a casual shirt or around the top of a bag or purse for closure.
- ✔ Crocheted strips throughout an entire design, such as an Afghan, coaster, or place mat. (See Figure 17-6.)

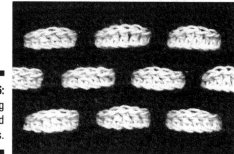

Figure 17-6:
Weaving crocheted strips.

No matter which option you go with, first make sure you have enough room for it. Designs that call for weaving usually have you work a *beading row* or *beading round.* (Don't worry; beads aren't involved.) Making a beading row involves working a row or round of stitches that have spaces in between and are the same height as the width of the material you'll be weaving with. An example of a beading row may be • dc in next sc, ch 1, skip next sc •, rep from • to • around (or across). The ch-1 spaces allow enough room for you to weave the strip through, and the double crochet stitches usually provide enough height. To secure the ends of woven strips, sew them to the fabric using either thread or yarn, whichever is appropriate.

Chapter 18

Neatness Counts: Blocking and Caring for Your Work

In This Chapter

▶ Shaping your pet project with water or starch

▶ Putting some spine into a three-dimensional design

▶ Keeping your design clean and out of trouble

After all your hard work and careful attention to getting the right number of stitches with perfect tension, you may find that your work is a little misshapen or doesn't quite match the dimensions that the pattern gave for the finished item. Don't panic — your project just needs to be *blocked* or pulled into shape with the help of a little water, heat, and starch. Blocking helps to even out those uneven stitches, square off the corners, and make circles out of the rounds. In this chapter, we show you how to block your crocheted items and then how to launder and store them so they last forever (well, almost).

Blocking Your Way into Perfect Shape

To get most crocheted garments, such as sweaters, vests, and jackets, to match the pattern's finished measurements, you block them, which basically means you shape them. *Blocking* is a general term that refers to a process used to shape your crocheted work. It can be as simple as spraying your design with water or completely immersing it in a tub to get it good and wet. Or you may use some heat by applying steam from your steam iron. Some of the necessary tools are depicted in Figure 18-1. Some items, such as cotton doilies or three-dimensional designs, need a little extra shaping help from starch or another stiffening agent.

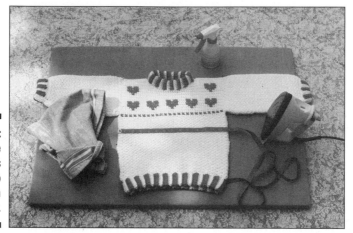

Figure 18-1:
You have
various
ways to
block a
garment.

The final use of your design helps determine which method of blocking is the right one to use. Another consideration is your yarn type. Different types of yarn respond differently to water, steam, and heat, and using the wrong method can have disastrous results. But don't be alarmed; this section helps you avoid these pitfalls by giving you the scoop on the various blocking methods and when you use each one. Of course, before you begin any project, you need to make sure you have the right tools on hand, so the first section gives you a quick list.

If your design has pieces that you join together, such as the sleeves and body of a sweater or the different motifs for an Afghan, block each piece separately before joining. This makes joining them easier because each piece is the correct size and shape, and it gives you a more accurate finished size.

If the design that you're blocking is a garment, and it doesn't fit correctly before blocking (too small or too large), don't try to stretch it (or squash it) to fit when blocking. Blocking only shapes the garment; it doesn't change its size. If the garment doesn't fit, chalk it up to experience and pass it along to someone who can use it. Don't despair if this happens though, it's part of the learning experience, and we all make mistakes.

Gathering essential tools

You probably already have most of the tools you need to correctly block your designs. First, make sure you have the finished design dimensions from the pattern so that you know what you're shooting for. Second, find a flat, padded surface large enough to accommodate your design when you stretch it to its finished measurements. (You need a padded surface so that you can pin your piece down.) A bed, the floor, a large piece of sturdy cardboard covered in plastic wrap, an ironing board, or a mesh drying rack all work fine. Here are some other tools you may need, depending on which blocking method you're using:

- ✔ Rustproof straight pins
- ✔ Several large, absorbent towels
- ✔ Thin cotton towels (2 or 3 should suffice)
- ✔ Spray starch, liquid starch, or stiffening agent, available at most craft stores
- ✔ Steam iron
- ✔ Tape measure or ruler

Always pin out your crochet design with rustproof straight pins to prevent nasty rust stains.

Wet blocking

To *wet block* an item, you submerge the whole thing in water. This method works for just about any yarn, but read the yarn label just to be sure that it's not a dry clean only fiber. You can also gently wash your crocheted item at this time to rid it of the dirt and oils that the yarn is sure to have picked up from your hands. Use a mild soap (not detergent) made for delicate fabrics and rinse well in cool water before blocking. This method is useful for many items, including garments, Afghans, and home decor.

If you're not sure whether your yarn is colorfast, be sure to test a swatch before dunking your whole design into a tubful of water. Bleeding colors, especially in a striped design, can ruin your work. If you use a solid color, the effect of bleeding isn't as bad, although you may encounter some fading if you continue to wash it over time.

To wet block your work, follow these steps:

1. **Fill a clean, large tub or the sink with cool water and immerse your crochet design completely, allowing it to become thoroughly wet.**

   If you want to wash your design, now's the time to do it. Add some soap to the water and swish your garment around. Rinse well with cool clean water, taking care not to twist or ring the fabric.

2. **Drain the water from the tub or sink without removing your crochet project.**

3. **Press down on your work in the tub to remove some excess water. Pick it up and gently squeeze to remove more water, being careful not to let any part of it hang down and stretch.**

   Never wring your wet crochet item.

4. **Lay your design flat on top of a large towel and then roll the towel and crocheted design together like a jellyroll to absorb more of the water.**

   You don't want to remove too much of the water. Just enough so that the material isn't soaking wet.

5. **Place another towel on your blocking surface and lay your work flat on it.**

   Your blocking surface needs to be a place where you can leave your design undisturbed for a day or two because it may take that long to dry completely.

6. **Following the schematic (for garments) or measurements (Afghans or other nonwearables) for the design, use a ruler or tape measure to gently shape and stretch the item to the correct size.**

   If the design has three-dimensional elements to it, such as bobble stitches or popcorn stitches, gently puff them into shape. If the design is lacy, make sure to open up the loops so that the design is evident.

7. **Allow your design to dry thoroughly.**

If you need to dry your work in a hurry, place a large fan in front of the damp design to speed up the drying process. Don't place it so close that the fan can blow your masterpiece around, though.

Don't ever use a blow dryer to dry your design. The heat could shrink your piece or melt the fibers in a synthetic yarn.

Spray blocking

Spray blocking is similar to wet blocking, but instead of immersing the piece completely in water, you spray it with water to dampen the fabric. You use this method if your piece needs only a little bit of help to shape up or when you don't want to take the time to wet block. Kind of like spritzing your hair to spruce up your 'do when you don't have time to wash it. To spray block, follow these steps:

1. **Prepare a blocking surface suitable for pinning down your design, such as a plastic-wrapped piece of cardboard or foam board.**

2. **Lay out your design on the blocking surface, stretching it to the correct measurements. With rustproof pins, pin it in place along the edges every few inches to make sure it stays put.**

3. **With a clean spray bottle filled with lukewarm water, spray the design evenly to a uniform dampness.**

4. **Gently smooth the fabric with your hands to even it out, shaping any three-dimensional stitches as needed.**

5. **Allow the design to dry completely before removing it from the blocking surface.**

Heat blocking

You can *heat block* your design by either ironing or steaming it. Faster than wet blocking and spray blocking, steaming and ironing work best on natural fibers, such as wool and cotton, but you must take extra care not to burn the fibers. This method is not recommended for synthetic fibers, as they can melt, thereby ruining your design.

Ironing it out

This method works well for flat items, like doilies, that have no three-dimensional stitches. To block your design with the ironing method:

1. **Set your iron to the correct temperature as indicated on the yarn label.**

   If the label doesn't recommend a temperature, be cautious and set the iron on a medium-low setting, with the steam function off. You can always make it warmer, but burns are irreversible.

2. **Lay out your design on a heat-resistant blocking surface and pin it out to the proper dimensions.**

3. **Cover your crocheted design with a clean cotton towel or a pressing cloth. Then spray it with water to slightly dampen the cloth.**

   If you prefer to dry press, cover the crocheted design with the cloth and omit the spraying step.

4. **Iron the item through the cloth by gently pressing and then lifting the iron and moving to a new section. (See Figure 18-2.)**

   Running the iron over the design while pressing down flattens your stitches and may harm the yarn fibers.

5. **Allow your design to cool, then remove it from the blocking surface. If necessary, repeat the process on the other side.**

Figure 18-2:
Blocking by
ironing.

Steaming your fabric's pores

Steaming works especially well for correcting curling edges. It's also quite useful when you have to shape only a small section, such as a cuff or collar that won't behave. All you need to steam press your work is a normal steam iron, which you probably have in your laundry room.

To steam block your design:

1. **Set your iron to the correct temperature indicated on the yarn label.**

   If the label doesn't recommend a temperature, be cautious and set the iron on a medium-low setting.

2. **Lay out your design on a heat-resistant blocking surface and pin it out to the proper dimensions.**

3. **Holding your steam iron about an inch above the fabric, steam separate sections of the design, being careful not to allow the iron to touch the fabric.**

4. **Allow your design to cool and dry before removing it from the blocking surface.**

Gettin' tough: Blocking with starch

Doilies, collars, ornaments, edgings, and three-dimensional designs often require a little extra help when blocking in order to show off the stitches and, in some cases, to create the proper shape. When your design calls for a stiffer finish, it's time to call in the starch. *Note:* You use starch and stiffening agents almost exclusively with cotton thread.

For designs such as pillowcase or towel edgings, you want a lightly starched finish, or your piece may be too scratchy to use. Doilies and filet crochet designs require a heavier finish, so use heavy spray starch or liquid starch in order to show off the stitch detail and maintain the proper shape. To permanently stiffen your works of art, such as ornamental snowflakes and other three-dimensional designs, a commercial fabric stiffener, which you can find at most craft stores, is in order.

Blocking with spray starch

Spray starch is your ticket for a light- to medium-crisp finish. To block a crocheted item with spray starch:

1. **Hand wash the crocheted design with a mild soap (as described in the "Wet blocking" section earlier in this chapter) and cool water, rinsing several times to remove all soap residue.**

2. **With a clean towel (or several, if you need them), blot out excess moisture until the design is just damp.**

3. **Prepare a blocking surface suitable for pinning down your design, such as a plastic-wrapped piece of cardboard or foam board.**

4. **Spray one side of your design with starch and place the starched side down on your blocking surface.**

5. **With rustproof pins, pin out your design to the required dimensions, taking extra care to shape stitch patterns.**

    Work quickly so that you get the design pinned down before the starch dries.

6. **Spray the other side of the design, making sure that the fabric is lightly saturated.**

7. **Blot excess starch from the design with a clean, dry towel and allow it to dry completely.**

Immersing in liquid starch or fabric stiffener

Blocking a crocheted design with liquid starch allows you a bit more range when determining the desired crispness. Follow the manufacturer's advice on the bottle of starch for the amount of starch you need and whether you need to dilute or not.

If your final design has a permanent shape, such as snowflake ornaments, baskets, or other three-dimensional designs, use a commercial fabric stiffener in place of the liquid starch in the following steps.

To block with liquid starch, check out the steps that follow:

1. **Hand wash your design gently in cool water with a mild soap (as described in the "Wet blocking" section, earlier in this chapter), rinsing several times to remove all soap residue.**

2. **In a clean tub or sink, prepare the liquid starch solution.**

3. **Immerse your crocheted item in the starch solution and allow the solution to penetrate the fabric, which usually only takes a couple of minutes.**

4. **Prepare a blocking surface suitable for pinning down your design, such as a plastic-wrapped piece of cardboard or foam board.**

5. **Remove the item from the solution and, with a clean, dry towel, blot your crocheted item to remove any extra solution.**

6. **With rustproof pins, pin out the design on your blocking board to the required dimensions, taking extra care to shape stitch patterns.**

7. **After pinning, blot the design again to remove excess solution.**

   If you're using commercial fabric stiffener, be extra careful to remove as much excess solution from the stitches and between the stitches as possible. When dry, the solution can leave a hard residue, obscuring the design.

8. **Allow your masterpiece to dry completely before removing the pins.**

Going 3-D: Shaping Nontraditional Designs

Not all crochet is designed to be flat. One of the beauties of this craft is the ability to create three-dimensional designs, whether your creation is as simple as a hat or as complex as a decorative three-dimensional Lilliputian village that you work in many pieces.

Many of these three-dimensional designs need to be coaxed and shaped after you finish the actual crocheting, however. Most patterns include detailed instructions on how to finish and shape your work, or you can follow the wet blocking instructions earlier in this chapter. But instead of pinning your design out flat, you mold it over the appropriate shape and pin down the edges to allow it to dry.

Some of the supplies to have on hand when you're shaping a three-dimensional design are

- **A kitchen bowl:** Pick one in an appropriate size (comparable to the finished design measurements) for wet blocking a hat or shaping a doily into a decorative bowl.
- **Paper cups:** Shape cotton-thread Christmas ornaments, such as bells, with paper cups.
- **Plastic wrap:** Probably the most useful tool, plastic wrap can stuff, prop up, and shape many designs.
- **Preformed foam shapes:** Available in most craft stores, foam shapes, such as cones, can shape the bodies for crocheted Christmas tree toppers.

As you can see, you don't need anything fancy. Look around your house and you'll find that you already have many items on hand.

From This Day Forward: Caring for Your Work

Most of us take great pride in our creations, but when all is said and done, caring for the finished design is often an afterthought. Considering the many hours that you invest in making a crocheted design, taking the time to find out how best to care for your piece is worth your while. This section outlines different methods for washing your finished work and the best way to store it afterwards to avoid stretching and discoloring.

Scrub-a-dub-dub: Washing your work

As with all types of fabrics, you want to follow certain guidelines when caring for your work. Different yarns have different needs, so be sure to check the yarn label for specific care instructions. You don't want to throw a wool sweater into the washer and dryer, for example, unless you want to end up with a sweater for a doll. Hand washing, dry cleaning, and machine washing all work well to get your clothes clean, but beware the fiber content of your yarn. As with tags on store-bought items, the yarn label tells you how to take care of your piece.

Most yarn labels use the International Fabric Care Symbols shown in Figure 18-3 to tell you how to care for the yarn.

Figure 18-3: International Fabric Care Symbols for yarn care.

Normal wash   Hand wash   Do not wash

Dry clean   Do not dry clean   Machine washable

Cool iron   Warm iron   Hot iron   Do not iron

Hand washing

If the yarn is washable, hand washing the item with gentle soap made for delicates (not detergent) is by far the best way to go.

Depending on the size of the item you're washing, fill a clean sink or tub with cool to lukewarm water and add a small amount of soap. Wash gently and then rinse thoroughly. If practical, place your item in a colander when rinsing to avoid stretching the fibers. Squeeze gently to remove excess water; blot with soft, absorbent towels; and then lay flat to dry, blocking the item into shape using the original method used to block your work when it was first completed. Any time your piece gets wet, it has to be reshaped.

Dry cleaning only

If the yarn label says *dry clean only,* then dry clean it. You can be sure that the manufacturers have a good reason, the most likely one being that water damages the fibers. Take the item to your favorite cleaner along with the yarn label, if possible. Most of them will take extra special care if they know that the garment has been handmade.

Machine washing and drying

Some yarns, especially acrylics, are suitable for machine washing and drying, although hand washing is always the safer route. Before dumping your piece in the wash, though, read the label for the correct temperature for both washing and drying and be sure to set the speed to the gentle cycle. The agitation in washing machines doesn't make for happy yarn and can cause irreparable damage if too rough.

Drying your item by laying it flat is always preferable, but not always practical. If you must put your design in the dryer, make sure you dry it on the lowest heat setting.

Storing your work

The most important rule to remember when putting your work away is never, never, never hang a crocheted design. Hanging it stretches the stitches all out of shape, and the design may become unusable if left hanging for any length of time.

Garments should be neatly folded in a drawer or on your closet shelf — likewise with tablecloths and bedspreads. Smaller items that don't need to be folded should be stored flat.

If your crocheted designs (such as holiday items) are going into storage for any length of time, invest in some acid-free tissue paper. Placing the paper between the folds and around items keeps the dust and dirt off and preserves the fibers. And always put your work away clean. Time allows stains to set in, and they may not come out a year later.

Keep all your work in a cool, dry place, away from direct light. Ultraviolet light, excessive humidity, and extreme temperature changes all have adverse effects on yarn. Find a nice quiet place and let your work rest in peace.

Part V
The Part of Tens

"I honestly think that yarn is going to be strong enough."

In this part . . .

This part leads you to more adventures in the art of crochet and offers advice on how to make the most of your crocheting experience. We include a list of the best crochet resources for you to use to advance your knowledge of the craft, and we reiterate some of the best tips we have to offer to crocheters of all skill levels. Our list of interesting crochet variations may inspire you, too.

Chapter 19

Top Ten (Plus One) Crochet Resources

- -

In This Chapter

▶ Finding must-have reading material

▶ Surfing crochet Web sites

- -

*W*arning: Once you're hooked into crocheting, you can never get enough. You'll soon be browsing around for new patterns and more challenging techniques. In this chapter, we give you the best of the best crochet information that's available.

The books and magazines listed in this chapter are a wonderful source of stitch patterns and designs, and any of them would make a great addition to your crochet library. No matter how experienced you become, reference materials never go to waste. The Internet is also a wonderful way to search for new materials and ideas. We list a few of our favorite sites, but look around; you can find many more.

Crochet Fantasy

Crochet Fantasy is a full-color pattern magazine, published seven times per year by All American Crafts Publishing, Inc. Designs range from beginner to advanced levels in both adult and children's fashion, with an occasional home decor item. Special features include articles about various yarn companies, as well as new ideas and innovations. Stitch diagrams are included where applicable.

To contact: Call 800-877-5527 or go online at www.crochetfantasy.com.

Crochet!

Crochet! is a magazine published six times a year by The Needlework Shop and features innovative patterns for both fashion and home decor items. The skill level of the patterns ranges from beginner to advanced. Regular features include book reviews, what's new in crochet, and caring and sharing among crocheters.

To contact: Call 800-449-0440 or go online at `www.crochetmagazine.com`.

Knit and Crochet with Beads

This book is a complete study of the use of beads in knitting and crocheting and provides beautiful color photographs, detailed instructions, and clear illustrations to guide you through all the techniques presented. It boasts great projects from sweaters to jewelry and shawls to wristbands — each project is unique and inspiring.

Written by Lily M. Chin. Loveland, CO: Interweave Press (2004).

Encyclopedia of Crochet

This book contains comprehensive information ranging from the history of crochet to yarns and fibers, the basic stitches, and beyond. For lefties, it includes illustrations all the way through showing you how to work in reverse. Instructions for more advanced techniques, such as working with beads and wire, are included, as well as a stitch gallery and many pattern instructions.

Written by Donna Kooler. Little Rock, AR: A Leisure Arts Publication (2002).

Crochet with Style: Fun-to-Make Sweaters for All Seasons

This book is a compilation of 24 beautiful crocheted sweaters in a variety of yarns and styles. It shows how elegant, comfortable, and stylish crocheted fashions can be. Beautiful color photography and excellent instructions accompany each pattern.

Written by Melissa Leapman. Newtown, CT: Taunton Press (2000).

A Living Mystery: The International Art & History of Crochet

This book offers a complete and comprehensive history of the art of crochet. From its origins as the "poor man's lace" in Ireland to its development and use throughout the world today, a wealth of information is presented here. Vintage photographs and a world view of the craft make this a fascinating and thorough reference every crocheter will enjoy.

Written by Annie Louise Potter. A.J. Publishing International (1990).

The Harmony Guides: 300 Crochet Stitches, Volume 6

This book and *Volume 7: 220 More Crochet Stitches* contain almost every stitch and pattern you'll ever need. Besides the basics, they also include a large variety of patterns, filet crochet charts, motifs, edgings and borders, textured stitch patterns, Irish crochet instructions, and Afghan stitch in all its many variations. A must-have for any crochet library.

Published by Collins & Brown Limited (London: 1998).

The Reader's Digest Complete Guide to Needlework

Even though this book isn't strictly about crochet, the crochet section is comprehensive with clear, well-defined illustrations. It includes the basic stitches as well as a variety of stitch patterns and motifs. Other sections of this book include chapters about sewing and embroidery, both of which can be used in crochet.

Published by Reader's Digest Association, Inc. (Pleasantville: 1979).

How to Crochet

A well-laid-out book with clear, concise instructions and illustrations, the full page, colorful photography shows how your finished project will look. It takes you from the basics through more advanced techniques, all the while providing projects for you to practice.

Written by Pauline Turner. London: Collins & Brown Limited (2001).

Crochet Guild of America

www.crochet.org

This is the home site of the largest organization dedicated to crochet. Its members span the country and are continually striving to attract people to the craft of crochet. In addition to sponsoring crochet events in various cities around the country, their Web site has up-to-date information about new projects and gadgets, and there's a chat room where you can always find someone to help with a question.

Crochet Partners

www.crochetpartners.org

This is a very active Web site with a chat room full of avid crocheters from across the country. Many designers use this site to exchange ideas and get help with sticky problems. It's full of hints, tips, and ideas.

Chapter 20

Ten Do's and Don'ts of Crochet

*Y*ou weren't born knowing how to crochet, and you may stumble a few times while you figure out the craft (or even when you're a seasoned pro). Whether you're beginning a new project or in the midst of a work in progress, a few reminders can always make the process easier. This chapter gathers into one spot many of the crucial points we make throughout the book — tips and tricks to make your progress as smooth as possible. Turn to it whenever you're stuck or need a little push to get yourself back on the crochet track.

Check Your Gauge

Do remember to check your gauge before beginning any project and recheck it as you progress so that you don't have any surprises when you get to the end. Checking your gauge is particularly important when crocheting garments because the size of the finished item is crucial to your success.

Practice Makes Perfect

Do practice any new stitches listed at the beginning of a pattern. If you have trouble understanding a stitch, try to get help from a more experienced crocheter or contact the publisher of the pattern for clarification. If you find that the stitch is more trouble than it's worth, you may want to choose a different pattern for now and try tackling the more difficult pattern at a later date.

Reading Is Fundamental

Do read the pattern thoroughly before beginning any project. You should become familiar with any new stitches you may encounter, as well as potentially complicated construction techniques. If you know where you're going with a pattern, you're less likely to get lost en route.

Planning Ahead

Do purchase enough yarn of the same dye lot before beginning any project. Running out of a color in the middle of a project can lead to mismatched sections and disappointing results.

Give Green Eggs and Ham a Try

Do try new things. New stitches, new techniques, and new materials can renew your interest in the craft. Half the fun of any endeavor is discovering something new about it and mastering a new skill. If you don't crochet much anymore, maybe you need a new angle on the craft to inspire you.

Never Assume . . .

Don't assume that you know the definition of a stitch until you've read the pattern. Just because a stitch has the same name as one that you've encountered before, that doesn't mean it's made the same way. Also, remember that different publications can use different names for the same stitch.

Variety Is the Spice of Life

Don't hesitate to experiment with color and materials. Even though a pattern may call for a specific material or color scheme, you're not locked into someone else's choices. ***Note:*** If you want to get the same size item as the pattern details (for example, when you're crocheting a garment), you must make sure you use a yarn and hook combination that allows for the same gauge as the pattern describes.

Splurge a Little

Don't skimp on the cost of materials. After working long and hard on a project, you want the results to be something worth wearing, sharing, or displaying. Your choice of materials can mean the difference between a so-so project and a masterpiece of crochet.

If at First You Don't Succeed, Try, Try Again

Don't give up when you run into a snag or discover a major error in your work. Put the project down for a while and come back to it refreshed. You may be too close to the trees to see the forest. And if you find an error in workmanship that may affect the overall look of the piece, don't hesitate to rework the area, even if it means unraveling half your work. You'll be much happier in the end if you know your piece isn't flawed by an error that you could have corrected.

Relax and Enjoy

Don't look at crocheting as a chore. It should be a relaxing pastime, not just another item on your to-do list. Crocheting can reduce tension, provide an outlet for your creativity, and boost your ego when you receive all those rave reviews for your efforts.

Chapter 21

Ten Variations on Crochet

In This Chapter

▶ Composing variations on a technique

▶ Tooling around with something special

▶ Making rag rugs and other oddities

*O*ver the years, people have experimented quite a bit with the art of crochet. They've taken the basic stitches and found unique ways to manipulate them to create variations on the original art form. They've combined the use of the crochet hook with other tools to produce totally new techniques and experimented with a variety of materials to broaden the scope of the craft.

This chapter shows you the many possibilities of crochet. Some you may be familiar with, others will be new to you, and some may surprise you. But each demonstrates the versatility of a craft that's been evolving for centuries and will surely continue to grow and change as long as people have the drive to create. You may not want to tackle any of these variations now, but hey, it's always good to have something to shoot for, right? If you do want to try your hand, check out the resources in Chapter 19 to find instructions.

Special Stitch Techniques

Each technique in this section uses the typical hooks and materials found throughout this book, but they each vary in the way the stitches are manipulated.

Irish crochet

Developed in the mid-19th century, Irish crochet was inspired by the popular Venetian laces of the time. It's usually worked in fine cottons to produce the traditional delicate look. The technique is composed of a combination of floral and leaf motifs arranged on a board and then joined together with a network of crocheted mesh. Often the pieces are padded by working over a cotton strand called a *foundation cord.*

You can use Irish crochet to produce beautiful home decor items, such as pillow toppers, bedspreads, curtains, and tablecloths — anything you'd normally crochet with cotton (see Figure 21-1). Though not often worked anymore, you can still find examples of gorgeous blouses, dresses, collars, and even evening gowns worked in Irish crochet.

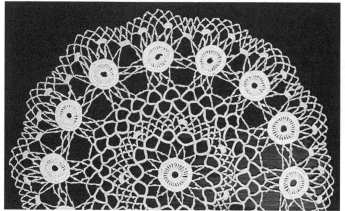

Figure 21-1:
Sample of
Irish
crochet.

Free-form crochet (or scrumbling)

Free-form crocheting, also known as *scrumbling,* is kind of like coloring outside the lines. Whereas most crochet patterns have you work a regular, symmetrical pattern in rows of uniform stitches or in neat concentric circles, free-form crochet opens the door to a more random and artistic approach to the craft. Although patterns can be written for such pieces, the beauty of this technique is that you can use your own imagination and instincts to produce your own unique creations.

This technique supports irregular stitch heights, curves, and zigzags; a mixture of highly textured areas with light texture; a combination of rounds with rows; and randomly shaped areas to create a patchwork look (see Figure 21-2). Combining different colors and textures of yarns also helps to enhance the effect of this technique.

Free-form crochet lends itself to unique fashions and accessories, abstract and pictorial wallhangings, as well as three-dimensional sculptures. Anything goes with free-form crochet.

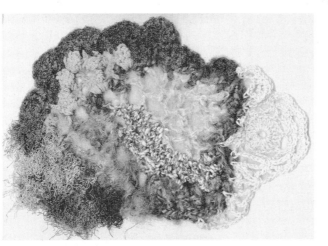

Figure 21-2:
Free-form
crochet
sample.

Surface crochet

Surface crochet is crocheting (generally with yarn) onto a crocheted fabric
background (see Figure 21-3), and it resembles embroidery. It's worked just
like a slip stitch over the surface of the background. You can surface crochet
in a straight line to add stripes to an otherwise solid piece or create pictures
on your background. It's frequently used to turn a horizontally striped piece
into a plaid by adding the vertical lines afterwards.

Figure 21-3:
Surface
crochet
sample.

Tapestry crochet

Tapestry crochet is a technique popular in Africa and South America that is gaining momentum throughout the crochet community. It's generally worked in single crochet in charted, repetitive patterns that resemble woven tapestries (see Figure 21-4). You can work tapestry crochet in rows to produce flat pieces or in rounds to produce three-dimensional objects.

What makes tapestry crochet different from standard single crochet techniques is the practice of working in more than one color at a time, carrying the unused color under the current color and working your stitches very tightly. You usually work it with a stiffer material, such as a sport-weight cotton, to produce the characteristic of a stiff tapestry, ideal for producing baskets, handbags, wallhangings, place mats, and hats. Working your stitches more loosely with a soft yarn produces beautiful fashions, such as scarves, shawls, and even sweaters.

Figure 21-4: Sample of tapestry crochet.

Techniques Using Special Tools

The following techniques, although related to crochet, require special tools to create their unique variations on the craft. Some inventive crocheters must have gotten bored and come up with these devices to make crocheting more interesting. Two forms of crocheted lace that use these special tools are *broomstick lace,* which uses a special needle, and *hairpin* lace, which has its own loom. The double-ended hook allows you to make a reversible fabric, with hooks on both ends (see Figure 21-5).

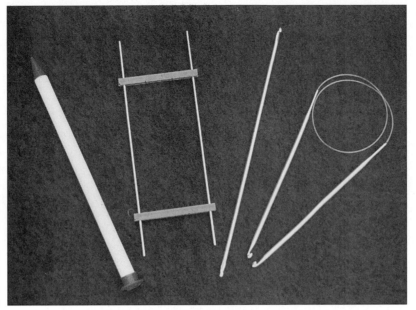

Broomstick lace

Broomstick lace is a crochet technique using a large dowel or needle to form clusters of loops within the fabric. The loops form circles of yarn that produce a unique texture (see Figure 21-6) suitable for Afghans, shawls, and sweaters. This technique can also work with fine cotton to produce unusual lacy home decor items.

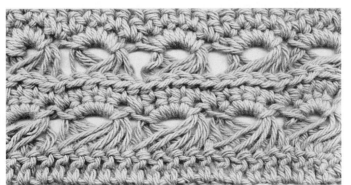

Figure 21-6:
Broomstick
lace.

Hairpin lace

Hairpin lace is worked on a hairpin lace loom (refer to Figure 21-5) to produce long strips of lacy loops. The technique was originally worked on actual hairpins, which are much smaller, but has since evolved into a larger version that's particularly suitable for making lacy shawls and Afghans (see Figure 21-7).

You can adjust the looms to different widths, so you can vary the laciness of the strips. How the loops are joined together can vary as well, allowing for myriad designs.

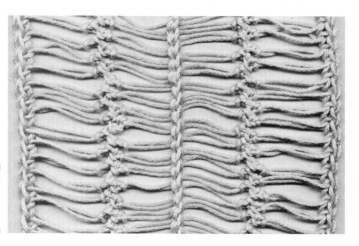

Figure 21-7
Hairpin lace
sample.

Double-ended crochet (Or cro-hooking)

Double-ended crochet (also known as *cro-hooking*) is similar to working in Afghan stitch (see Chapter 13). The difference between the two techniques is the hook. Double-ended crochet uses a long, double-ended hook (refer to Figure 21-5) that allows you to work stitches on or off from either end. The technique is usually used with two alternating colors, working loops onto the hook with one color, and then turning the work around and working the stitches off with the second color. It produces a fabric that's reversible with a different color pattern on each side (see Figure 21-8). The fabric is softer and more elastic than the basic Afghan stitch, making it ideal for Afghans, scarves, and stoles.

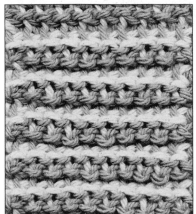
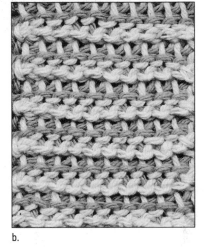

Figure 21-8:
Double-
ended
crochet
sample
showing
both sides
of work.

a.　　　　　　　　　　　　　　　b.

Unique Materials

Crocheters can be a pretty crazy bunch. Never satisfied with the methods of the past, they're always trying new techniques and new materials to work with. Check out the following ideas that people have come up with to broaden the scope of crochet.

Crocheting on fabric

If you have a fabric whose edges won't unravel, you can actually crochet an edging on to it with cotton thread. You can crochet edgings on pillowcases, tablecloths, or on a piece of linen to create a simple table mat. Working with heavier cotton or sport-weight yarn, you can produce fashions and accessories with suede pieces, felt, or fleece.

With lightweight fabrics, you can usually just poke through using a tiny hook. You may find linen pieces hemmed and equipped with small holes around the edges for the purpose of crocheting onto the fabric. With suede or heavier fabrics, you poke or punch holes into the fabric at evenly spaced intervals and work the stitches into them. You can also use crochet to join pieces of fabric together to create jackets and bathrobes, totes and purses, vests, and even skirts.

Crocheting with fabric strips

This technique may have evolved from hooking rag rugs, or maybe it came from an avid crocheter who ran out of yarn and had to resort to whatever material she had on hand. Wherever its origins, the technique can produce an interesting texture for crocheting. The fabric you choose can make for uniquely colored home decor and fashion items. You can use any fabric, although lightweight cotton works best. You cut the fabric into strips approximately 1 inch wide and then fold them lengthwise to hide the raw edges, or you can purchase precut fabric strips. Using a large crochet hook and usually working in single crochet, you can crochet useful rugs, unique baskets, and attractive totes. You can even use this method to produce unusual jackets and vests.

Crocheting with wire

Ready to try something really different? Try crocheting with wire. This technique goes hand-in-hand with free-form crochet to produce unique crocheted art. Using soft wire and a relatively large hook, you can produce beautiful crocheted sculptures. Soft, colored wire is now readily available in most craft stores. With the addition of some fun and funky beads, you can crochet yourself a choker and matching bracelet. Any of the basic stitches of crochet will work, but you shouldn't try this technique with the Afghan stitch. Keep it simple, as the materials produce enough of a challenge.

Appendix

Yarn Supply Sources

· ·

You can find most of the yarns used for the projects in this book at your local craft or yarn shop. If you're unable to find them or they're unavailable in your area, you can contact the following manufacturers directly.

Berroco, Inc.
14 Elmdale Road
P.O. Box 367
Uxbridge, MA 01569
508-278-2527
www.berroco.com

Coats & Clark, Inc.
Customer Service Dept.
P.O. Box 12229
Greenville, SC 26912-0229
800-648-1479
www.coatsandclark.com

The DMC Corporation
South Kearny Avenue
Port Kearny Bldg #10-A
South Kearny, NJ 07032
973-589-0606
www.dmc-usa.com

Fiesta Yarns
4583 Corrales Road
Corrales, NM 87048
505-892-5008
www.fiestayarns.com

Lion Brand Yarn Company
34 West 15th Street
New York, NY 10011
212-243-8995
www.lionbrand.com

Muench Yarns
285 Bel Marin Keys Blvd., Unit J
Novato, CA 94949-5763
415-883-6735
www.muenchyarns.com

Patons Yarns
2700 Dufferin St., Unit #1
Toronto, ON M6B 4J3
Canada
www.patonsyarns.com

Schachenmayr Yarns
Coats American Industrial and Crafts
Two Lakepointe Plaza,
4135 South Stream Boulevard
Charlotte, NC 28217
704-329-5800
www.coatscna.com

Schaefer Yarns
3514 Kelly's Corners Road
Interlaken, NY 14847
607-532-9452
www.schaeferyarn.com

Tahki/Stacy Charles
8000 Cooper Avenue
Building #1
Glendale, NY 11385
718-326-4433
www.tahkistacycharles.com

Index

• T •

Notes

Notes

Notes

Notes

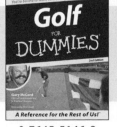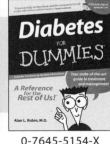

FOR DUMMIES®

A world of resources to help you grow

HOME, GARDEN & HOBBIES

0-7645-5295-3   0-7645-5130-2   0-7645-5106-X

Also available:

Auto Repair For Dummies
(0-7645-5089-6)

Chess For Dummies
(0-7645-5003-9)

Home Maintenance For Dummies
(0-7645-5215-5)

Organizing For Dummies
(0-7645-5300-3)

Piano For Dummies
(0-7645-5105-1)

Poker For Dummies
(0-7645-5232-5)

Quilting For Dummies
(0-7645-5118-3)

Rock Guitar For Dummies
(0-7645-5356-9)

Roses For Dummies
(0-7645-5202-3)

Sewing For Dummies
(0-7645-5137-X)

FOOD & WINE

0-7645-5250-3   0-7645-5390-9   0-7645-5114-0

Also available:

Bartending For Dummies
(0-7645-5051-9)

Chinese Cooking For Dummies
(0-7645-5247-3)

Christmas Cooking For Dummies
(0-7645-5407-7)

Diabetes Cookbook For Dummies
(0-7645-5230-9)

Grilling For Dummies
(0-7645-5076-4)

Low-Fat Cooking For Dummies
(0-7645-5035-7)

Slow Cookers For Dummies
(0-7645-5240-6)

TRAVEL

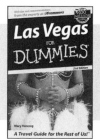

0-7645-5453-0   0-7645-5438-7   0-7645-5448-4

Also available:

America's National Parks For Dummies
(0-7645-6204-5)

Caribbean For Dummies
(0-7645-5445-X)

Cruise Vacations For Dummies 2003
(0-7645-5459-X)

Europe For Dummies
(0-7645-5456-5)

Ireland For Dummies
(0-7645-6199-5)

France For Dummies
(0-7645-6292-4)

London For Dummies
(0-7645-5416-6)

Mexico's Beach Resorts For Dummies
(0-7645-6262-2)

Paris For Dummies
(0-7645-5494-8)

RV Vacations For Dummies
(0-7645-5443-3)

Walt Disney World & Orlando For Dummies
(0-7645-5444-1)

Available wherever books are sold. Go to www.dummies.com or call 1-877-762-2974 to order direct.

FOR DUMMIES®

Plain-English solutions for everyday challenges

COMPUTER BASICS

0-7645-0838-5

0-7645-1663-9

0-7645-1548-9

Also available:

PCs All-in-One Desk Reference For Dummies (0-7645-0791-5)

Pocket PC For Dummies (0-7645-1640-X)

Treo and Visor For Dummies (0-7645-1673-6)

Troubleshooting Your PC For Dummies (0-7645-1669-8)

Upgrading & Fixing PCs For Dummies (0-7645-1665-5)

Windows XP For Dummies (0-7645-0893-8)

Windows XP For Dummies Quick Reference (0-7645-0897-0)

BUSINESS SOFTWARE

0-7645-0822-9

0-7645-0839-3

0-7645-0819-9

Also available:

Excel Data Analysis For Dummies (0-7645-1661-2)

Excel 2002 All-in-One Desk Reference For Dummies (0-7645-1794-5)

Excel 2002 For Dummies Quick Reference (0-7645-0829-6)

GoldMine "X" For Dummies (0-7645-0845-8)

Microsoft CRM For Dummies (0-7645-1698-1)

Microsoft Project 2002 For Dummies (0-7645-1628-0)

Office XP For Dummies (0-7645-0830-X)

Outlook 2002 For Dummies (0-7645-0828-8)

Get smart! Visit www.dummies.com

- Find listings of even more *For Dummies* titles
- Browse online articles
- Sign up for Dummies eTips™
- Check out *For Dummies* fitness videos and other products
- Order from our online bookstore

Available wherever books are sold. Go to www.dummies.com or call 1-877-762-2974 to order direct.

FOR DUMMIES®

Helping you expand your horizons and realize your potential

INTERNET

The Internet FOR DUMMIES

0-7645-0894-6

The Internet ALL-IN-ONE DESK REFERENCE FOR DUMMIES

0-7645-1659-0

eBay FOR DUMMIES

0-7645-1642-6

Also available:

America Online 7.0 For Dummies
(0-7645-1624-8)

Genealogy Online For Dummies
(0-7645-0807-5)

The Internet All-in-One Desk Reference For Dummies
(0-7645-1659-0)

Internet Explorer 6 For Dummies
(0-7645-1344-3)

The Internet For Dummies Quick Reference
(0-7645-1645-0)

Internet Privacy For Dummies
(0-7645-0846-6)

Researching Online For Dummies
(0-7645-0546-7)

Starting an Online Business For Dummies
(0-7645-1655-8)

DIGITAL MEDIA

Digital Photography FOR DUMMIES

0-7645-1664-7

Photoshop Elements 2 FOR DUMMIES

0-7645-1675-2

Digital Video FOR DUMMIES

0-7645-0806-7

Also available:

CD and DVD Recording For Dummies
(0-7645-1627-2)

Digital Photography All-in-One Desk Reference For Dummies
(0-7645-1800-3)

Digital Photography For Dummies Quick Reference
(0-7645-0750-8)

Home Recording for Musicians For Dummies
(0-7645-1634-5)

MP3 For Dummies
(0-7645-0858-X)

Paint Shop Pro "X" For Dummies
(0-7645-2440-2)

Photo Retouching & Restoration For Dummies
(0-7645-1662-0)

Scanners For Dummies
(0-7645-0783-4)

GRAPHICS

PowerPoint 2002 FOR DUMMIES

0-7645-0817-2

Photoshop 7 FOR DUMMIES

0-7645-1651-5

Macromedia Flash MX FOR DUMMIES

0-7645-0895-4

Also available:

Adobe Acrobat 5 PDF For Dummies
(0-7645-1652-3)

Fireworks 4 For Dummies
(0-7645-0804-0)

Illustrator 10 For Dummies
(0-7645-3636-2)

QuarkXPress 5 For Dummies
(0-7645-0643-9)

Visio 2000 For Dummies
(0-7645-0635-8)

Available wherever books are sold. Go to www.dummies.com or call 1-877-762-2974 to order direct.

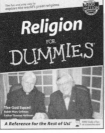